AND COYOTES HOWLED
Non-Fiction

DEDICATION

This is a tribute to my parents, Bill and Audrey Riley. By teaching self-reliance, they gave their seven children unique adventures, which left me this inheritance of memories.

With special thoughts of my deceased husband, Henry Helmstetter, who trustingly bankrolled publication of "And the Coyotes Howled" in 1997. For my children, Douglas, Janet Eileen and Curtis and other descendants of Bill and Audrey Riley.

With heartfelt thanks to my brother Lester Riley, Ernie McKinney and Everett (Toar) Lickfold, all who fought the Japanese invaders in the Philippine jungles during World War II. Lester drove a bulldozer clearing the jungles to make airplane landing strips, and later fought in the hell hole of Pelilieu where the Japanese were entrenched in caves along the Umurbrogol ridges. Ernie was captured in the Philippines and survived the Bataan Death March and three years of imprisonment in Camp Tarlac and Japan. When the U. S. dropped the atom bomb, he was a slave laborer in a Japanese coal mile not many miles from Hiroshima. All three returned to Pleasant Valley, but for awhile, seemed to be changed men.

ACKNOWLEDGEMENTS

In the 1990s Jeaninne Helmstetter and daughter Eileen pestered me into writing these "pioneer" tales which my writing group in Oak Ridge, TN helped me bring to life. Wheat rancher Ray Hunt gave me harvesting terminology and Tony Riley did the same with the logging. Ernie & Pat McKinney provided Philippine data. Dave Kyle early on transferred my writing to a computer disk. And in 2017, using her photography skills, daughter Eileen helped design the cover, and Grandson Preston solved my computer problems. Author Carmen Peone, Inchelium, WA, gave invaluable proofreading. Cover is Effie Riley Taylor's oil painting of house on the Curry Place, the farm house we lived in when she was born. My deep appreciation to all; I couldn't have done it alone.

INTRODUCTION

This book portrays every-day country life in Eastern Washington during the Great Depression of the 1930s. Because of the Curry farm's isolation, lack of electricity, telephone and plumbing, the time could easily have been in the pioneer days of the 1800s.

PROLOGUE

Ajijic, Jalisco, Mexico

Bouncing around in the Mexican saddle, I'm wishing I could trade this bony horse for Betty, our smooth-riding sorrel mare that years ago took Dora and me to the Pleasant Valley Grade School. Earlier while walking down Ajijic's cobblestone street, I had eyed the rental horses tied near trees. Although they were skinny and looked well used, I had the forlorn hope that one of them would have a smooth gait and could trot without jarring me to pieces.

It's December of 1990. For the eleventh winter, Henry and I are spending the winter in Mexico. Tennessee winters are mild, but they aren't as pleasant as those south of the border. Recalling the pleasant hours spent on horseback while growing up near Kettle Falls in northeastern Washington, I had decided to go for a ride on Lake Chapala's shore line.

Now my horse has slowed from his jarring trot to an easy walk. And no longer bouncing in the saddle, my thoughts wander. Sauntering along, I find myself taking a ride into the past. My eyes aren't seeing the hills on either side of this Mexican lake, but Monumental Mountain, miles way in the Huckleberry Mountain Range in Washington. That mountain dominated my view for several years of my childhood. Remembering it makes me think of the Andes Mountains of South America pictured in my seventh grade geography book. Then I see the picture that intrigued me the most. Its caption read, "Lake Titicaca, the highest navigable lake in the world." I had studied the pictures avidly, wishing I could see the people there and how they dressed, what they were like and what kind of houses they lived in. The only person I'd ever seen from another country was Chinaman Tai, the little man who sold fire- crackers at our Fourth-of-July celebrations at the Quillisascut Grange Hall. His English was limited, and naturally I couldn't speak Chinese. But back then, I had been too young and shy to say more than "Two packages of fire-crackers, please."

The few magazines we had at home didn't tell much about people in faraway lands, either. Every spare moment between chores, I read any magazine or book that got passed on to us. Whenever Mom needed me to help her, she knew she'd find me with my nose stuck in a book.

Stories about bullfighting in Spain and western tales in magazines entranced me with their Spanish words. My tongue formed unfamiliar words like "adios amigo", "senor", "senora" and "hasta luego". These stories fascinated me, but didn't satisfy my curiosity. During the Depression – and my barefoot childhood – I never imagined I'd get to see any faraway places. But years later, my husband, Henry, took me to many foreign places where we had exciting and unique experiences. In Linares, Spain, we parked beside the high wall of a bullring. When I read the tile plaque on its wall, I was thrilled to find that I was seeing the bullring dedicated to their native son, Manolete, the famous bullfighter of my stories.

In Morocco, sitting beside the driver of a horse-driven carriage I took the reins from the driver and drove down the main avenue of Marrakesh. In Peru, I wasn't "studying geography" in a book when I rode in a reed boat on Lake Titicaca, gazed at the Inca stronghold of Machu Piccu, or dickered in Spanish with a woman with a baby on her back and wearing the area's full skirt and brown bowler hat. In Japan after reclaiming my lost passport, I got thrown out of a police station. At a craft fair in Yugoslavia when a seller didn't speak English, my ears perked up when he said something in Spanish. Hearing familiar words was like finding a friend. In Egypt Henry and I arrived at our hotel after dark, thinking we were in the middle of Cairo. When I opened the window shade the next morning, I was surprised and delighted to see the pyramids not very far away.

And in Turkey, our dolma bus driver pointed to the "Turkish Insurance," the blue glass Evil Eye Protector over the windshield as he drove the wrong way down a busy street.   It's little wonder that faraway places and their people fascinate me.

*   *   *   *

After our winter in Mexico, Henry and I are driving across the high desert plains between Zacatecas and Saltillo heading home to Tennessee. For the past hundred miles we've seen nothing more interesting than sparse forests of Joshua trees and the distant granite peaks of the Sierra Madre Oriental Mountains. Then on rusty tracks of a railroad siding, we see some boxcar homes standing motionless. Flowers bloom in tin cans nailed to their wooden sides, and newly washed clothes lie spread over nearby bushes to dry.

My glimpse of these crude homes takes me back many years to a logging camp – and to the railroad boxcar that was once home to me. My mind wanders, just as it had when I was riding Old Bones along the lake shore and my thoughts go back to my mother's stories of her early life and into memories of my childhood on the farm.

BEGINNINGS   1920 - 1929

A bucket of water at the sheepherders' picnic helped Bill Riley get acquainted with Audrey Steeley. If the annual picnic hadn't been held that summer of 1920 in Meadows, Idaho, my parents probably would never have gotten married. They had lived in the same general area for about a year, but had seen each other only a few times.

The picnic drew a big crowd. It was a major event for this small town and its surrounding rural area. Children played games and grown-ups socialized before sitting down to eat at the picnic tables. Audrey and Bill – both very shy – had been sneaking peeks at each other ever since their initial greeting that day. Bill wanted to talk to Audrey, but felt tongue-tied, not knowing what to say. He had worked with her brother, Lester, and had visited his family a few times. But Lester wasn't at the picnic and Bill didn't know how to strike up a conversation. He kept eying Audrey trying to figure out what he could say to her. Finally, while she was eating lunch with her mother and younger brothers, he crept up behind her and dumped a bucket of water over her head. Bill had finally found a way to start a conversation, permitting them to have a good time together.   And before the afternoon was over, Audrey got back at him by pushing him into the creek.

Born on July 21, 1901 in Drain, Oregon, Bill (William Lorenzo Riley) was the second son born to Peter and Dora Wheeler Riley. An older brother, Frank, had been born two years earlier while the parents lived in the Colorado mountains. During this time Peter, a half-blood Cherokee, knew the area and guided a few wagons through the mountains to Oregon, where he decided to stay. After marrying Dora Wheeler, they lived in Oregon for a time while Peter searched for a steady job before moving away. In 1913 the family – now consisting of eight children – had moved to Cambridge, Idaho. Not having a farm of his own, Peter worked for other farmers at whatever jobs he could get, finally returning to Oregon. There was never enough money for a stable home life. At the time of his death in 1921, he was renting a farm near Redmond, Oregon. He was buried in the Madras cemetery.

In 1914 when Bill was thirteen, he had left home to work with his brother Frank, who had a job herding sheep. But a year or two later he struck out on his own and found a job working for Mr. Gilmore on his sheep ranch not far from New Meadows. It wasn't long before he had enough of herding sheep and rode his Harley Davidson motorcycle to Edward Osborne's cattle ranch in Meadows Valley to work for him. One of the other ranch hands was Lester Steeley, about the same age as Bill. The two young men hit it off pretty good and liked working together. One night Lester took Bill home with him to have supper and to meet his family.

One thing about his new friends surprised him. He couldn't figure out how Lester could be so tall and Audrey so short. Lester was a six-footer, but his sister Audrey was only five, feet, one inch tall. Standing beside her made Bill feel taller than his five feet, ten-inch height.

Audrey's parents were Mary Margaret Denney Steeley and George Steeley. Audrey was born July 30, 1903 in Cambridge, Idaho, two years after her brother Lester. She never knew her father, as he had deserted his family shortly before her birth. Soon thereafter, her mother married a Mr. Dryden and the family moved to New Meadows where Audrey went through the eighth grade in the town's two-story brick school house.

This husband gave Audrey's mother four sons – and a life of grief, often beating her. Many years later Lester said of his step-father, "He was a mean sonofabitch. He tied Mother up and beat her with a leather driving rein."

The summer Audrey was seventeen, she spent a few weeks with Mrs. Gilmore at their lonely sheep camp, helping with the cooking. When Audrey came home wearing her old worn-out coat, Lester felt sorry for her and bought her a new one from money he had made while fighting fires for the U.S. Forest Service. Although Audrey was at the sheep camp at the same time Bill worked for Mr. Gilmore, the two young people didn't meet until Lester took Bill home with him for supper.

Soon after meeting Lester's family, Bill saw a poster telling about the annual sheep herders' picnic to be held later that summer. Upon learning Audrey would be at the picnic with her family, Bill decided to go, too. After discovering his unique way of getting Audrey's attention, Bill lost his bashfulness and found lots to talk about. And a few months later when Bill asked Audrey to marry him, she said, "Yes." They were married the next year on September 12, 1921 in Council, Idaho.

Having only his motorcycle, Bill had to borrow a team and wagon for the twenty-five mile trip. Audrey wouldn't go without her mother, who said, "We'll have to take Frank along with little Bobbie, as he's sick today and can't go to school."

During the long ride to Council in the wagon, they ate the sandwiches they had brought. And after the brief wedding ceremony, they went to supper in a restaurant. Then Bill turned the team around and headed back toward New Meadows.   The fifty-mile round trip was too far to go in one day, so at day's end, Bill found a good spot beside the road and made camp for the night. He and Audrey's "bed" was a pile of quilts under the wagon. Her mother and the little boys slept in the wagon bed above them. In later years, Audrey remarked that it wasn't a very romantic way to spend their wedding night. Soon after this, Bill got rid of the motorcycle and bought a second-hand Dodge. Lester thought that was a good idea. He had borrowed the motorcycle a few times and found it wasn't reliable in rainy weather because it had a leather belt drive instead of a chain drive. He said, "Every time it rained, the leather belt got wet and stretched, and I had to push the darned motorcycle."

Bill and Lester farmed for one year, renting on a share-crop basis. That summer they had about 60 or 70 tons of good wild hay just right for sheep. As Lester told about it later, he said, "This old crooked farmer wanted to buy it and we set a fair price. Then he turned right around and sold it to a sheep man for a higher price, making a big profit from our hay."

For the next couple of years Bill worked in various places. Together with Lester, he rented a farm in South Meadows Valley. That farm house was Bill and Audrey's first home. During this time Bill and his brother, Frank Riley, worked with Lester in the sawmill in Meadows.

(More than 60 years after the sheepherders' picnic, my son-in-law, Dave Kyle, delighted me with the story Mom had told him about Dad dumping the bucket of water over her head. He said Mom got a sparkle in her brown eyes when she told about pushing Dad into the creek.)

On June 27, 1922, Audrey gave birth to her first baby, a son, in South Meadows Valley. She didn't have

the services of either a doctor or a midwife. When her pains had started, Bill ran all the way across the valley, wading a creek, to tell Audrey's mother, Mary, it was time. He was panting so hard from running he could hardly give her the message. But as soon as he got it out, he turned around and ran back to Audrey by his shortcut to be with her as soon as possible. Mary harnessed her horse, hitched it to the buggy and drove around by the road, arriving in plenty of time to deliver her first grandchild. Audrey had known all along she wanted to name the baby after her brother, Lester, if it turned out to be a boy. She admired him – and since Bill did, too, they named the baby "Lester Wilfred Riley."

Soon afterward, Bill, Audrey and baby Lester moved a short distance to McCall, where Bill worked in a sawmill for a few months. Then, leaving the South Meadows Valley, they moved about eighty miles south to a farm near Weiser, Idaho. They were still living there on March 14, 1924 when I was born. Dr. Ernest Finney drove out from town with a horse and buggy to take care of Mom. When she told the doctor she hadn't thought of a name for her new baby, he said, "Well, I think 'Ines' is a pretty name."

Taking the doctor's suggestion and adding her own middle name, Mom named me "Ines Lillian Riley." For the first three months, I was fretful most of the time. Mom said it seemed like the only time I wasn't crying was when I was nursing – and as soon as I finished, I'd start crying again. She couldn't figure out what was wrong with me, so took me to Dr. Finney in Weiser. Startled when he weighed me, he exclaimed, "Why, she hasn't gained much at all; she must not be getting enough to eat."

Dr. Finney told her to put me on the bottle and feed me a diluted mixture of Eagle Brand Condensed Milk. After Mom did as the doctor ordered, I started gaining weight and stopped crying all the time. Not making much money share-cropping, Dad decided a few months later to head to Oregon so he could look for a better-paying job. He'd heard the sawmills and lumber camps in Bend needed workers. Since he'd had some sawmill experience and was young and strong, he knew he could handle a job as either a mill hand or a lumberjack. He also knew it was impossible to earn enough money sharecropping to care for his growing family even by taking on any odd jobs that became available. Mom wondered what Oregon would be like. She'd never been out of Idaho, although Weiser wasn't far from the state line.

Thirty years after Mom first put me on the bottle, I was cooking with Eagle Brand Condensed Milk. Upon licking the spoon, I recognized a familiar taste, yet couldn't remember having used it before. Puzzled, I told Mom about it. She said. "I fed you condensed milk when you were a baby and it probably saved your life. You were nothing but skin and bones when Dr. Finney told me to give it to you."

It may have been that same milk that started me off to my eventual height of five feet, eight inches. By the time I was ten, I'd outgrown Mom. At fourteen, I was nearly as tall as Lester and only a couple inches shorter than Dad. Since Mom was so short and Dad wasn't tall for a man, I wondered what made me so tall and skinny. Upon asking Mom, she said, "Your grandmother told me that my father, Mr. Steeley, was over six feet tall, so you probably got it from him."

OUR FIRST HOMES

Lifting the pistol with a trembling hand, Mom pointed it in the direction where she'd last heard the footsteps. Her finger squeezed the trigger and the pistol blazed in the darkness. The shuffling noises circling the tent for the past few minutes had scared her. It was after dark and Mom was alone in the tent with Lester and me, only three and one. Dad hadn't yet returned from town where he'd gone to buy groceries. Our new home south of Bend, Oregon was a tent in the middle of the woods, some distance from where other loggers stayed. Mom felt alone and unprotected out in the wilds with only a tent around her and her two children, so had gotten in the habit of keeping Dad's loaded pistol close by.

That night she was glad she had it. She had put Lester and me to bed on our small pallets on the grass, blown out the kerosene lantern and crawled into her blankets nearby. She was almost asleep when she had heard the heavy footsteps outside. The unexpected noise in the forest's silence scared her. When the noises continued circling the tent, she was afraid someone was going to come into the tent and attack us. In a trembling voice, she yelled, "Who's out there?"

The footsteps halted, but there was no reply. The abrupt silence scared Mom almost as much as the noise had. She waited a moment; there was still no answer. And that's when she had fired the pistol. After the loud bang, there weren't any more strange noises outside the tent and Mom thought she might have killed someone. When Dad returned, she told him all about her scare. After daylight he went all around the tent checking for tracks and signs of blood. He also looked through the nearby brush and trees. The only thing he found on his search was a bullet hole in the wall of the canvas tent.

After arriving in Bend, Dad worked in a sawmill by the Deschutes River for a few months until that job ended, then got on with a logging company that was hiring sawyers to cut timber down south of town. He and his working partner sawed down giant Ponderosa pines. It was back-breaking work pulling the long cross-cut saw through such big trees.

Soon after Mom shot a hole in the tent, we moved to the main camp of the logging operations and lived in one of the cabins that the logging company had brought in on flatbed railroad cars. Close to other families, Mom stopped feeling frightened. We were no longer alone in the woods. While living in that cabin, Mom took a picture of Lester and me. That now-yellowed picture shows a little boy and girl standing barefoot in front of the small unpainted cabins in the midst of tall trees.

After we moved to the logging camp Mom enjoyed being near other women. One of her new friends was Mary Zamarripa, whose husband, Pete, was Dad's partner on the other end of his crosscut saw. While the men were working, Mary spent a lot of time visiting with Mom. She spoke Spanish as well as English and taught me to say, "agua," when I wanted a drink of water. And her little boy about my age taught me to say "caca" instead of "poop".

All our homes in the various logging camps were temporary and makeshift. But that tent in the woods was the flimsiest one we had. The rough cabin was better; it kept us dry in rainstorms. Soon Dad moved to a new logging area near Chiloquin, north of Klamath Falls.

Our new home was a railroad boxcar which the lumber company had outfitted as living quarters for the loggers' families. Our cots were at one end of the boxcar; the kitchen and eating area were at the other. It was better equipped for cooking than the cabin had been, but Dad still had to carry water inside in buckets. The boxcars stood on a siding of the railroad track, out of the way of logging activities. While standing on our top step one day looking at the shiny railroad track stretching behind us, I fell off. That shiny track came rushing up at me and hit me on the forehead! I vaguely felt Mom's arms as she carried me back up the boxcar steps and laid me on my cot.   It must have made quite a gash. Now, many years later, I still have a faint scar on my forehead where it hit the track.

From our boxcar home in the logging camp, we moved to an area between Sprague River and Klamath Falls. Dad worked for both the Algoma Lumber Company and the Pelican Bay Lumber Company. It was here that our new baby sister was born on May 27, 1927.   Mom and Dad named her "Mary Dora Riley" after their mothers, but somehow always called her "Dora". A few months later we received a note from Pete and Mary Zamarripa who had moved to an area near Sprague River. It was a birth announcement addressed to "Mr. & Mrs. Wm. L. Riley, Kirk, Ore. C/o P.B.L. Co. Camp #1" telling that Louis Neal Zamarripa had been born Sept. 14, 1927.

The addition of another baby to our family made Dad realize we needed a more permanent home than logging camps. That reminded him of the letter Mom had recently received from her mother. Grandma Mary and her new husband, Charley Adams, had recently moved to a farm near Rice, Washington, about thirty-five miles south of British Columbia, Canada. Her letter had said, "There are farms for rent here, cheap, and it's a pretty country. Colville is about 25 miles away and that's the county seat. You might like living in Stevens County."

Dad and Mom talked it over. Mom thought living on a farm where she could have a garden would be better for a family than having to buy all their food. Dad agreed, saying that farming would be a more dependable way of making a living than logging. And it might even be a little easier than sawing down trees all day with a cross-cut saw. After talking about it for several days, they decided to take a chance and drive up to Washington.

Dad finished out the logging season, got his pay and traded in our old Dodge for a second-hand Star touring car. It had four doors with isinglass snap-on side curtains that he could take off when summer me. The whole car was black; the metal body, the metal braces holding up the black folding canvas top and the skinny tires. Dad told us maybe next summer he would unhook the canvas top from its fasteners above the windshield, pull it back and fold it away near the top of the back seat.

In December 1927 he loaded our few belongings into the car, and the five of us headed north. Lester was five years old, I was three, and Dora was only seven months. Rice, Washington was over eight hundred miles away. It would take more than two weeks to get there because of a couple detours Dad intended to make. He was going to stop in Cottage Grove, Oregon to visit friends, then go on to the ocean. He and Mom, curious about how big it would look, thought it was worth driving out of our way to see it.

We arrived in Cottage Grove after dark. At breakfast the next morning Dad's friend swung me up into a high chair. I felt very tall sitting up so high! Then his wife set a bowl of corn flakes and sugar-coated banana slices on the tray in front. Eating corn flakes was another first. We had always had hot oatmeal or cream of wheat for breakfast.

Going on to the Oregon coast, we stopped at the town of Agate Beach and found a tourist cabin near the ocean. As soon as they had put our black suitcase into the cabin, we went down where the waves were running back and forth to shore. Looking out over the heaving water, all we could see was more ocean until it touched the sky. Dad wonderingly exclaimed, "It's big. If you could see far enough, you could see all the way to China."

We walked along the rocky beach picking up agates. When we held them up to the sun, we saw light through them. Some agates were almost clear while others were shining black. We found red ones and a few with two and three colors. Taking the prettiest ones to a rock shop, Dad asked the man if he could polish them. He told him it would take over a week to get a good polish, but he had some for sale already polished. He said, "You'll enjoy them; they'll stay shiny forever."

Mom liked them so well that Dad bought as many as he could hold in both hands. So we had agates we found as well as the polished ones from the rock shop that "would stay shiny forever." Despite the fun of finding beautiful agates and watching the ocean's waves, the next morning we continued our trip.

The polished agates always remained special to Mom. She kept them in her big trunk with other treasures. For years we took them out to admire their shine and could always smell the ocean on them.

Two days later when we finally got to Rice, we found it was a very small community straddling State Highway 22 (later re-numbered State Highway 25). It consisted only of a post office, a general store with a gas pump in front, an IOOF Hall and four or five houses. We learned later that a dirt road led east up past the school house and over the summit of the Huckleberry Mountain Range to Colville. Rice was named for William and Mary Rice, the first white settlers in the area. They had moved from Michigan and in 1883 bought 120 acres from an Indian named Nicolo. William, a farmer and also a carpenter, built several houses in the area besides the two on his property. The first school, Columbia District, was one-half mile south of the village. This was abandoned around 1900 when a new school house was built about a quarter of a mile east of Rice on the road leading up the hill.

Mom pulled Grandma's letter from her purse and read it again for the directions on how to find their house. Grandma had said she and Charley and their sons lived in Pleasant Valley on the Aldredge Place. It was up in the hills out of Rice on the Heidegger Road. About a mile and a half north on the graveled highway from Rice, we came to a dirt road with a sign pointing to Pleasant Valley. We turned right and soon passed a brown and white church and continued in a gradual climb up the Pleasant Valley Road. When we came to a two-story log house at a crossroad, we turned left onto the narrow dirt Heidegger Road and started climbing a steep rocky grade.

Lester helped Mom and Dad watch for mailboxes alongside the road, with the car slowing down at each one so they could read the names on the boxes. Three miles up the hill they found the one with Grandma's name on it. Dad pulled up by the wire fence in front of the house and stopped. Grandma had seen us drive up and came running out to the gate, calling excitedly, "Sis and Bill are here!"

Frank and Bob, Grandma's teen-aged sons, were right on her heels to greet us. Soon all the grown-ups were laughing, talking, hugging and shaking hands. I felt strong arms grab me as Uncle Frank lifted me out of the car. He told Bob, "I'll carry Ines and you can take Lester." That was the moment I knew our long drive from Oregon was over; I felt at home already.

GETTING SETTLED

We lived with Grandma and Charley Adams on the Aldredge Place for over a month while Dad looked for a farm to rent. Their house was full with our family of five added to their six. Grandma and Charley had Clifford and Dick, not yet school age, in addition to Grandma's older sons Frank and Bob. It was crowded, but we stayed with them until Dad found a farm to rent, called the Brady Place. It was about three miles north of Rice on Highway 22. The west side of the land ran down to the Columbia River. Dad moved us in late January of 1929.

To get farm equipment and household furnishings, Dad scouted the local auction sales. He didn't have enough money to buy new equipment, so stretched what he had by buying everything second hand. A few farmers were losing their farms because they didn't have enough cash to keep up payments. Buying used equipment was the cheapest way to outfit a farm, but several years later Mom said she got a little tired of using other peoples' worn-out junk.

Dad bought almost everything we needed at the auctions. He brought home everything from wood stoves, pots, pans and dishes for the house to plows, a harrow and rake, grain drill, manure spreader and mowing machine to work the land. He also bought work horses to pull the machinery, and cows for milking. Mom didn't want to drag us kids around all day, so stayed home and let Dad do the buying. She never knew what he would show up with from the auctions. One day when he'd gone to a sale looking for farm equipment, he came home with something for the house. When he carried in the pretty kerosene lamp, I "claimed" it, saying it was mine. With red peonies painted on the pale green sides of its squat glass base, it was the prettiest thing I'd ever seen. (Over 85 years later I still admire it sitting on my shelf in the kitchen, but somehow its light no longer seems as bright as it once did.)

We stayed on the Brady Place only long enough for Dad to plant and harvest one crop of grain. That fall he found another place to rent a couple of miles away. To get to the Meriwether Place, we drove toward Rice, then turned left onto the Pleasant Valley Road and up past the now familiar brown and white church. When we topped the little rise a short distance farther, we could see Monumental Mountain looming ahead, covered with pine, fir, cedar and tamarack trees. The whole mountain range was a beautiful sight, rearing up into the clear blue sky. Later on I would find the mountain even more beautiful all covered with snow. We came to a two-story white house that had a gate in front. Painted on the wooden sign over the gate was "New Caledonian Ranch." The owners, Gavin and Mary Jamieson, were of Scottish descent and had two children, Donald and Elsie. When we drove by this gate, we didn't know that years later Lester would buy that farm and live there. Opposite the New Caledonian Ranch was the small house where Sam and Effie Curry lived with their two little girls. And not far away we could see a two-story brown house where Bob and Betty Rose lived. Dad stopped the car at the next house on the right, the Meriwether Place, where we would live for a year.

The farm land along Pleasant Valley Road was hilly, with light, rocky soil. In the foothills of Monumental Mountain, a farm of one hundred fifty acres might have less than a hundred acres level enough to plow.

The two-room Pleasant Valley School, School District 32, was about three miles on up the road. Although Lester had been six in June, Mom and Dad didn't let him start school that fall. They felt six miles a day was too far for him to walk all by himself.

Only three public buildings were in the school district: the brown and white community church, the Quillisascut Grange Hall a mile and a half farther up the road, then the two-room Pleasant Valley Grade School about a mile farther. The grange hall, the largest building in Pleasant Valley, was the gathering spot for most social functions. In addition to its regular meetings, it sponsored Saturday-night dances, the annual Fourth-of-July celebrations, and other community events.

The Arzina Grade School was six or seven miles on up the winding Pleasant Valley Road from our school, and about the same distance from the Rice Grade School. While there were three grade schools within ten miles of us, the closest high school was in Kettle Falls, about seventeen miles away. All the high school kids from Arzina, Pleasant Valley, Rice and Daisy rode a bus to Kettle Falls.

After moving to the Meriwether Place, I received two very different presents. On Christmas morning Santa had left a very pretty doll for me, as well as one for Dora. She cuddled and played with hers, but I abandoned my present that couldn't do anything, preferring to play with our soft little black and white kitty that purred and snuggled close – and our dog that jumped up and down wagging his tail and licking my face. Mom must have noticed my lack of interest in the doll, as Santa never brought me another one.

My second present came that next summer after my fifth birthday when Dad gave me my first riding lesson. He didn't spend much time with us kids, as he was too busy plowing the fields and planting crops. So I was surprised one day when he took me out to the corral and led me to Brownie, our gentle work horse. Boosting me up to her back, he handed me the bridle reins, then showed me how to clench my knees to keep my balance. He said, "If you start to slip off, just grab hold of Brownie's mane."

Since I was riding bareback, there wasn't a saddle horn to hang on to -- and the ground seemed a long way down. I was going to hang onto that mane real tight!

I enjoyed my first riding lesson so much that I rode every chance I got after that. I pestered Dad or Mom to bridle Brownie for me. They didn't have to boost me up many times, as I soon learned how to make her stand close to the barn. I'd climb up the boards nailed to the barn and jump on her back then ride her around the barnyard and out into the pasture. I loved being on horseback and didn't care that I couldn't go very far. Although I felt like I was a long way from the ground on Brownie, I wasn't afraid. She never shied or jumped around. Lester and I could ride her any time Dad wasn't working her in the field. He knew we'd be safe; she wouldn't buck us off or run away.

The shortest ride I ever took came a few months later and lasted only about five minutes. It ended up with me hopping through the thistles to get back to the house. I'd ridden out through the barn yard, across the little bridge over the creek, and on out into the middle of the pasture. Brownie was ambling along slowly when she spotted a good patch of grass. Stopping, she abruptly reach down for a bite, her lowering head jerking on the reins. I didn't let go, so the sharp tug on the reins made me go sailing off over her head. I landed on the soft ground in front of her, still clutching the reins. The fall hadn't hurt me, but I realized that I had a different problem: I couldn't get back up on Brownie – and there were many young bull thistles covering most of the ground around me. They had sharp stickers and I was barefooted!

Picking my way through them, I tried to find bare ground, but the thistles were so thick I couldn't avoid stepping on several and got stickers in my tender feet. Tears ran down my cheeks before I reached the safety of the pasture grass. I cried again as Mom picked the stickers out with a needle. Giving me a hug, she said, "I guess you've learned to steer clear of thistles now."

After living on the Meriwether Place for a year, Dad heard of a farm for rent that was closer to the Pleasant Valley School. We moved to the Hays Place in September 1929 just in time for Lester to start school.

The Aldredge house where Grandma lived has long since been torn down. That land is now part of Terry and Tronlie Bolt's farm. Goldie Entwistle furnished some history about Pleasant Valley: Early settlers and trappers had named the area "Rat Creek Valley – perhaps because of the abundance of muskrats and its creek, "Quillisascut Creek after Indian Chief Quillisascut. Later residents changed the valley's name to "Peaceful Valley." That name remained until the day a citizen knocked a neighbor down with a monkey wrench and he retaliated with a two-by-four. Residents then changed the name to "Pleasant Valley."

1929 - 1931
Move to the Hays Place

The farms in the lower end of Pleasant Valley had fairly level fields for farming. But going to our new home, we would be climbing into the foothills. The ground sloped up gradually from the valley, permitting some farming on hillsides that weren't too steep to plow.

On moving day we piled into our Star and headed up the Pleasant Valley Road. Sometimes it was close to the creek, but often it veered away from it. This creek came down from Monumental Mountain near Loven's farm. Other small creeks fed into it on its way down to the Columbia River.

The first place we passed was Lou Schenegge's house on the right side of the road. His red painted apple packing shed was on the left side. He hired workers to pick the Delicious apples from the trees in his orchard. Next was the log house at the crossroad of the Heidegger Road. Up that road a short distance was the Walt Lickfold farm. Dad kept to the main road, which headed up toward the mountain. It seemed we were going to climb to the top; the farther up the road we drove, the hillier the land became. The Hays Place was not much over a mile from the Meriwether Place, but the terrain changed a good bit in that distance.

Shortly after the log house, we passed Hyatt's house on the right, two hundred yards or so off the road. Just as we started up the Hays Hill, we could see the Abernathy house on the left side past his orchard. After chugging up the hill in low gear, we arrived at our new home on the left side of the road, sitting at the top of the steep hill. Lawrence Hays, who later became one of our grade school teachers, owned the farm. Since at that time his house was the closest one to the top, people naturally started calling it the "Hays Hill".

 A few years later a small house was built on the other side of the road right at the top of the hill. First, the Raymond Heideggers lived there, and then Lawrence and Ruby Hays and their two children.

The outside of our new home on the Hays Place didn't look like it had ever been painted. The boards had weathered to a dark brown. It was both a one-story and a two-story house. The kitchen/dining room section was only one story and had a small porch running across the length of it. The parlor and three bedrooms were in the two-story part.

Hanging on the wall of the parlor was something that Mom called a "telephone." She said we could talk to someone far away with it. One day we heard it ring three times. Mom lifted the long receiver from its hook on the side. Her mouth was almost touching the black metal mouthpiece sticking out from the middle as she said, "Hello". She heard a neighbor's voice and talked to her for a few minutes. But soon Dad said we couldn't afford to pay the monthly charges, so had the telephone company take it out. He said we could go see a neighbor if we needed to talk – and not many had telephones anyway.

Living alongside the road with several neighbors nearby made Mom happier than when we lived in our tent in the woods. She liked to visit with our closest neighbors, Mrs. Abernathy and Mrs. Hyatt. Carl and Dell Rose and their children, Hazel and Harold, were only half a mile away, just across the road from the grange hall. Hazel, just my age, soon became my best friend. Her cousin, Ethel Rose, also became a good friend a few years later when her parents moved to a house near Hazel. Mom enjoyed visiting with all her neighbor ladies, but Opal Heidegger, who lived just beyond the grange hall became her closest friend. She lived in the first house up the hill from the grange hall. Opal and her husband, Howard, had three little girls, all younger than I. The Bovee and Harris families lived on up the road.

When Lester started first grade that fall, he found he had plenty of company walking to school. There was Buell Hyatt, about his age, and his brothers. Everett Lickfold, who was in the seventh grade, watched over the younger boys on their way up the road. When Lester saw them coming up the road, he ran out to meet them. I followed him to the gate, but Mom wouldn't let me go any farther. I stood there lonely at the gate, wishing I could go to school, too.

Since Lester was less than two years older than I, we spent a lot of time together. Dora, three years younger, was too small to join us swinging, wading in the creek or riding horseback. The first month after school started, I was lonesome. Then I remembered that Hazel Rose lived close enough that I could walk all by myself to see her. After Mom said I could go, I set out walking along the edge of the graveled road. The September sun had been shining hot all day. By afternoon it had heated the hot gravel in the road, making my bare feet feel like they were in a frying pan. I tried to step on the few bits of grass on the edge of the road. Then I came to some flattened-out horse manure. Cars had run over it, flattening it out until it was old, the color of straw. I stood on it until my feet cooled off. Noticing another flat pile farther on, I made a dash for it and stood on it for awhile, before going on.

Hazel must have been lonesome, too, as she was glad to see me. With my feet still burning, the first thing I suggested we do was go wade in the creek behind the grange hall. The cold water felt healing on my still-hot feet. When we went inside her house, she showed me her book of paper dolls and let me cut out some dresses for them. We put them on the dolls, folding the little paper tabs over the shoulders to make them stay on. While we were busy, her mother, Dell, had put raspberry jam on two pieces of bread for us. After eating the treats, I asked Dell if I'd been there an hour. My time was up, so I set out for home, dreading the walk on the hot gravel road. To my surprise, it had cooled in the late
afternoon and I didn't have to look for those flattened out piles of dried horse manure to walk on.

After that day Hazel and I spent a lot of time together. Once Mom left me at Hazel's while she and little Dora walked to the next house to see her friend, Opal Heidegger. On her return trip, she enjoyed visiting with Dell.

Even though I couldn't go to school with Lester, I started learning school work. After he learned the ABC's, he taught them to me. He also taught me how to spell a few words. I was so happy when I could spell "c-a-t". Then after Mom taught me to count to one hundred, I felt ready to go to school, But I had to wait until the next fall. It was about this time Dad and Mom started calling Lester by his name rather than "Son," because I had been calling him that too, thinking he had been named after the shining, golden sun.

Something very important that Mom taught us didn't have anything to do with school. She taught us to be careful with matches by showing us what happened when she scratched the match head. A flame burst out as she lit paper in the cook stove to start a fire. We saw how quickly the flames flared up and burned the paper and kindling. She told us never to strike a match unless we were lighting a fire or our kerosene lamps.

None of us kids ever started a fire in the house, but once Dad did when he accidentally knocked over a lamp. The glass lamp globe broke and the metal part holding the wick got unscrewed, letting kerosene spill on the wood floor. The lighted wick set the kerosene on fire, and Dad grabbed a small throw rug and covered the blaze, putting it out. That was an even better lesson for us than Mom's warnings. I was glad only the globe got broken, and not the lamp itself. It was "my" lamp, the one with red peonies on it that Dad had bought at the auction sale.

As young as Lester and I were, we had regular chores, such as keeping the kitchen wood box full and carrying water from the creek down below the house. Since these jobs took us outdoors, we didn't think of them as work. We spent our free time playing marbles, climbing trees, riding horses, wading in the creek, hunting wild flowers and swinging to the sky in our long rope swing tied to a limb of a tree in the front yard. Lester soon discovered that he could "walk" up the ropes to that high limb by hooking his bare toes around the ropes and pulling with his hands at the same time. He made it look so easy that I had to try it, too, and soon I was sitting up on that high limb about twenty feet off the ground, gazing all around.

That new "game" got me into trouble later on when friends came to visit Dad and Mom. While they were visiting outside, Dad asked me to show them how a five-year old girl could climb the ropes by just using her hands and bare feet. He said, "I'll sit on the swing seat and keep the ropes tight."

Being eager to show off, I got to that high limb as fast as I could. By their gasps of surprise, I knew that had impressed them. So I decided to show them how fast I could come back down. Instead of climbing down slowly, I loosened the grip of my hands and toes and slid all the way down to Dad's lap.

No one had told me about rope burns, but I learned all I wanted to know in that one quick slide. My fingers and toes were on fire, but I was too sheepish to admit in front of visitors how dumb I'd been, so didn't tell Mom about it until after they left. Only then did I show Mom where the ropes had burned me. She gasped and ran to get the bag balm, a salve Dad used on the cows' teats when they became cracked. After she daubed the soothing ointment on my burns, they immediately stopped hurting.

The closest we came to really hurting ourselves was when Lester took a drink of Black Leaf Forty. He and I had gone with Dad when he went to see our neighbor, Arthur Hyatt. Getting to their house, we found several other kids already there playing with Buell and his brothers. Dad went into the house and we joined the other kids outside. Soon the boys go to bragging about how tough they were. One of the older boys thought of a good way to prove which one was toughest. He led us up the hill to the hay shed and we went inside. Standing on his tip toes, he reached up high to get a bottle. Showing it to us, he said, "Lester, I'll drink some of this if you will."

On the bottle was a picture of a skull and crossbones plus some printing in big letters. Lester didn't want to admit he was afraid to drink it; the other boys would call him a coward. So he tipped the bottle up and took a swallow. When he gave it back to the older boy, he backed out and wouldn't drink any.

We left the hay shed and returned to where we had been playing near the road, fifty yards or so from the house. Soon after our return I noticed Lester lying curled up on the ground, looking sick. Buell ran up to the house and told his mother what had happened. Mrs. Hyatt came hurrying down carrying a big bowl full of beaten egg whites. She knelt beside Lester and propped him up against her knee. Then she forced him to drink all the egg whites, even though he didn't want to. In a few minutes, he threw up, getting rid of the poisoned Black Leaf Forty.

The worst thing that befell us on the Hays Place happened the first cold winter. One morning, I saw Dad come in from the barn and whisper to Mom. Then he went back outside, carrying his rifle. I knew something was wrong when Mom kept Lester and me from following him – and we soon heard a shot. Mom finally told us that Pansy, one of our milk cows, had broken her leg. In trying to get a drink out of the frozen creek, she had slipped on the ice. There was no way anyone could set a cow's broken leg, so Dad had to shoot her. I was heartbroken. Pansy had been the cow I liked best because she was so pretty and wouldn't kick me when I petted her. The other cows tried to kick us or hook us with their horns.

Since we couldn't afford to waste any meat, Dad butchered the cow. I told Mom not to tell me when she cooked the meat; I didn't want to know when we were eating Pansy.

Although Dad no longer had a job cutting down trees for a logging company, he still had to saw a tree down from time to time. In the winter our heating stove in the parlor burned a lot of wood, as he kept a low fire going in it all night as well as all day. And in cooking three meals a day, Mom used a lot of wood in the cook stove, too.

The first tree Dad cut down was a tall old fir growing on the hillside near our trail to the creek. Lester would have liked seeing the excitement, but it was a school day. Mom took Dora and me with her and we stood in the trail close enough to see Dad as he sawed and sawed all alone with his two-man cross-cut saw. Looking up, I saw the top of the fir tree start to sway. Scared that the tree would fall on us, I tried to jerk loose from Mom's hand and run back to the house. But she held on tight to our hands and wouldn't let us move. She said, "We're safe here. Dad knows exactly where the tree will fall because he has undercut it on one side. It will fall in that direction."

And sure enough, it did. It fell to the ground with a loud booming crash right where he had told her it would. I knew Dad was very strong, but now I learned that he was also very smart to make a big tree fall exactly where he wanted it to.

And he knew a lot about farming, too. That fall when Howard Heidegger was threshing his grain, Dad, Ernie Keck and other neighbors helped him. The farmers traded work because no one had enough money to pay anyone to help with the harvest. At noon, the six-man threshing crew came in for dinner. They were having a lot of fun talking while they ate. Howard's wife, Opal, had put steaming platters and bowls of food on the table and had just make a second pot of coffee. In telling a long story, Ernie Keck hadn't seen Opal re-fill his coffee cup. Without noticing it was now full of boiling-hot coffee, he took a big gulp, burning his mouth. Turning away from the table, he spit the coffee out on the wooden kitchen floor saying, "THERE now, damn you, blaze!

In telling us about it later, Dad said that Ernie had apologized to Opal for spitting on her floor as well as swearing. Ernie went to church regularly and didn't do much swearing, especially in front of women. For years we heard Dad tell this story so many time that we felt we'd been at Opal's table, too.

It didn't taken us long to get accustomed to living in a different place. Mom liked having so many neighbor women to visit. Lester was glad we lived closer to school, and I was, too. I'd be starting to school next year – and then I'd be joining the "big" kids going up the road instead of standing lonesome by the gate watching them leave.

CABLE FERRY CROSSING

"Tomorrow we're all going to the rodeo at Inchelium!" was Dad's surprise announcement one summer day when he came back home from the store at Rice loaded with groceries. Someone there had told him about the rodeo. Dad had been to the Colville Indian Reservation in Inchelium, but none of the rest of us had. The prospect of seeing a new place seemed exciting to us kids. We knew only that it was a small town on the other side of the Columbia River.

The next day while Dad was milking and doing the rest of the morning chores, Mom cooked breakfast and made some sandwiches to take along. After eating, it didn't take us long to get ready to go. To cross the Columbia, we could go upriver and cross the bridge near Kettle Falls or drive downriver past Rice and take the cable ferry at Daisy.

(The site of the ferry landing is now a bit downriver from the original landing. It was re-located after Coulee Dam was built and the rising impoundment of the Columbia River backed up from it.)

Dad said if we crossed the river on the bridge, it wouldn't cost anything, but might take about two hours longer than taking the ferry, which cost a dollar. The bridge crossing was about fifteen miles upriver past Kettle Falls, then we'd have another fifteen miles back south to Inchelium. He liked the ferry route best and was willing to part with a dollar to save the long drive on dusty graveled roads.

The thought of riding a cable ferry across the wide river scared me, as I had heard of a cable ferry at Kettle Falls whose cable had broken. It had drifted helplessly downstream and gone over the falls, and all the people on it had drowned. Knowing the schedule, Dad hurried us out into the car in time to be at the Daisy landing when the ferry would be on our side of the river. Just as we turned off the highway to the landing, we saw the ferry heading back our way. Other cars were already waiting in line; Dad pulled up behind the last car and turned off the engine.

We watched as the loaded ferry slowed down and docked. A worker in overalls jumped off and tied ropes to posts at the river edge, securing it to the landing. Dragging two long heavy wooden planks, he began making a ramp for the cars to get off the ferry. Leaving one end of the planks on the ferry, he dropped the other ends on the ground the width of the space between the cars' tires so that they could drive off. After unhooking the long chain in front of the cars, the worker motioned for them to start. The cars slowly rolled down the planks, then picked up speed as they passed us, climbing the slope to the highway behind us.

After the last car had driven off the ferry, the worker waved toward our line for the cars to start loading. By that time, Dad had gotten out of the car and cranked it, starting the engine. When the car ahead of us moved out, we followed. Just barely creeping along, we reached the planks. Our front wheels were aimed directly at the middle of each one so we wouldn't run off them and tip over into the water.

As cars drove onto the ferry, the wide planks bounced and shifted, making heavy thumping noises. The worker had to re-position them for each car. After cars had filled all the spaces, the worker fastened the chain across the back end and the ferry started moving slowly out into the river. A worker came by and collected the dollar toll from each driver. A few men got out of their cars while we crossed, but Dad stayed in our car and told all of us that we had to stay inside, too. Feeling safer in the car, I hadn't wanted to get out anyway.

The ferry didn't have a propeller nor an engine.   It pulled itself across the wide river on a cable strung overhead from one bank of the river to the other. That was where I got scared. We were sitting in the middle of a dangerous river on a oversized raft, with no motor to get us to shore if the cable broke. It bent in a big arc as the ferry's weight and the current swung us downriver. The safety of the far bank seemed far away. I was afraid the cable would break before we reached it and we'd go floating down the river and over dangerous falls like that other ferry had done.

The current along this flat stretch of river didn't seem very strong, but little eddies swirled around the back of the ferry. Since everyone said the Columbia was powerful and dangerous, I visualized it being hundreds of feet deep, and Dad was the only one who could swim. Despite my fears, I couldn't help from noticing the beautiful setting. Pine trees covered the hills on both sides of the clear blue river, and snow-capped mountains rose up in the north.

I was relieved when we finally drew close to the river's edge and the ferry nosed up to the landing. The worker repeated his performance of tying the ferry to the landing, unhooking the chain in front of the cars and positioning the wide planks for the cars' wheels. When it was our turn, we drove off the ferry onto solid ground once again.

The Star chugged uphill on the dusty road the short distance to the edge of Inchelium where we turned onto the road leading to the rodeo grounds. A lot of people were already sitting in the wooden bleachers surrounding the arena. We found a bench with enough empty space for all five of us and sat down to see what was going to happen.

In the corral cowboys rode bucking broncos, trying to stay on until the timer's whistle blew. Only a few of them succeeded. It was hard to ride a bucking, kicking, twisting horse without hanging onto anything but the hackamore rope. They weren't allowed to grab their saddle horns, and would be disqualified if they didn't rake their spurs along the horses' sides during the timed ride. Puffs of dust spurted up when the horses' hooves pounded into the loose dirt. And when the cowboys lost their balance and sailed off, more dust spurted up when they hit the ground!

After the bronc riding was over, the calf roping began. The announcer called a contestant, who rode into the corral and waited expectantly. As soon as a calf broke through the opened gate, the rider twirled his lasso and threw it around the calf's head, somersaulting it to a stop in a swirl of dust. With the other end of the rope secured to the saddle horn, the calf couldn't run off. The rider jumped to the ground, pigging string clenched in his teeth.   His horse backed up, taking the slack out of the rope. The cowboy tied the calf's front foot to a back foot. Whipping the string around, his hand made a blurred circle as he worked as fast as he could. The rider making the best time would win the contest. Other contestants, while waiting their turns to compete, practiced roping by throwing twirling loops over their heads and catching fence posts.

About this time, we got hungry. Mom found some shade behind the bleachers where we could eat. We waited while Dad went to the refreshment stand and brought back some cold bottles of orange pop. After eating, we returned to the bleacher seats. The day wore on and the sun became hotter. The corral dust got thicker, swirling around and settling on us. Before the rodeo was over, Lester, Dora and I were tired. And I noticed Mom breathed a sigh of relief when Dad finally said, "Let's go home."

We had been happy to see a new place. Our first rodeo in Inchelium had been exciting, but we had seen enough. Now we were ready to go. I felt too much relief in escaping the heat and dust to worry about the river crossing. Thinking about the return ride didn't fill me with dread as it had that morning. I just wanted to get back to the coolness of home as fast as we could – even if it meant crossing that deep river on a cable ferry.

The last time Mom and I rode across the Columbia River was in 1983 when the Columbian Princess, a modern ferry with a powerful engine, took us across to the Colville Indian Reservation to visit Pat and Ernie McKinney in their home beside the San Poil River.

Starting School

It was September 1930, my first day of school, and I was glad I didn't have to stand at our little gate and watch while Lester, Everett Lickfold and Buell Hyatt walked up the road, leaving me behind. I'd had my sixth birthday in March, so I could go with them! About a half hour later when we came into sight of white painted Pleasant Valley School, I knew I was finally going to learn to read. When Mom read stories to us, it always seemed like magic when she could tell what the funny "chicken-track" markings meant.

Nearing the grange hall, we saw Hazel Rose leave her house and come out for her first day of school, too. The next half mile to school, we passed a few other houses, but no other kids joined us. When we reached the school house, we waited outside with others who were standing there. Hazel and I had been watching the door and saw Miss Dean come out into the hallway and pull the rope hanging down from the bell that hung in its little white cupola atop the roof. Then we eagerly scurried inside.

In the past years when there had been enough pupils to fill both rooms of the school, there had been two teachers. But now with only about twenty-five, all eight grades shared the same room. I loved Miss Dean from the first day. With her slim figure, dark wavy hair and gentle manner, she was a beautiful lady. She taught us not to speak unless she asked us something and not to interrupt when she was hearing a class on the bench in front of the room. Lester and I knew better than to cause any trouble. Dad had told us if we got a spanking in school, he'd give us a harder one when we got home.

The teacher's desk sat at the front of the room. For every subject each class went up to the recitation bench facing her desk. While one class was reciting, the other classes studied at their desks, getting ready for their turn. As Miss Dean's white chalk wrote words on the blackboard, she told the first grade class what they said. After writing C A T, she told us what it was. And that's when I knew I'd soon be able to read just like Mom did! At the end of the school year, May 1931, I received a Certificate of Award "for being neither tardy nor absent" all year, which was signed "Arlean T. Dean." I was as proud of it as was of having learned to read.

Miss Dean taught two more years. When she got married in May 1933, the school board didn't renew her contract, as they had a rule against hiring a young married woman. If she became pregnant in mid-year, they might have difficulty in finding another teacher. I was sorry she wouldn't be with us any more. She had shown me that reading those "chicken tracks" was just as exciting as I'd thought it would be.

Thunder in the River
Kettle Falls – 1931

I reached the rocky edge of the Columbia River and stood looking down at the rushing water, unable to take my eyes from the pounding torrents as they went over the falls. Their roar filled my ears, shutting out all other sounds. The racing current and dangerous whirlpools frightened me. Upstream I saw several Indian men along the high, rocky riverbank. Standing on rickety wooden platforms jutting out over the swirling water, a few were spearing salmon while others tended large handmade basket-like nets suspended near the cascades. Some of the salmon fell into the nets while trying to leap up the cascades on their swim upstream. Farther away, a precarious-looking foot bridge connected the rocky riverbank to a small island. Six or seven men fished from there, perched on its jagged rocks.

It was right after lunch that day when our family had left the farm for the drive to the falls in the Columbia River. While telling us about the proposed trip, Dad had said, "I think you'll like seeing the Indians catch salmon."

After Lester, Dora and I had climbed into the back seat of our old Star and Mom was seated in front, Dad cranked the car to get it started. Once the engine was running, he put the long-handled crank back under the front seat, got behind the wheel and off we went, rattling down the dirt road of the Hays Hill at about twenty miles an hour. The wind whipping through the open car felt good on our faces. When we reached Highway 22 (later re-numbered Highway 25), we turned right and drove north. Several miles later we crossed the rusty looking iron-trussed bridge over the Colville River and saw, off to the left, where that river flowed into the mighty Columbia. Soon we entered the small town of Kettle Falls. Three or four miles past its northern edge, the highway headed downhill and we came into sight of the auto bridge spanning the Columbia.

We kids followed Dad and Mom up the sandy hill, walking in old wagon ruts that climbed up through pine trees to a bluff overlooking the falls. Mom, her stomach swollen with a baby, held Dad's arm for balance. Lester, Dora and I were barefoot and the fluffy dust felt warm on our feet. Topping the hill, we caught sight of about a dozen teepees, white against the dark green of scattered pines. They clustered together on a flat knoll above the river, not far from St. Paul's Mission. At seven I thought all new things were exciting, but these tepees were the most fascinating things I'd ever seen.

Dad had been hungry for smoked salmon for the past month and knew his Indian friend camped here was just as hungry for some of our pork. They were going to make a swap. Usually, Dad went alone on his trading trips, so this was a rare adventure for the rest of us. As we neared the encampment, we smelled smoke from the cook fires, and heard children laughing. Our first glimpse of the area showed a confusion of sight and sound. Little kids whooped and dogs barked as they raced between the tepees, making the day seem like a holiday. Men and women criss-crossed the area going about their work. The men, wearing overalls and shirts like Dad's, were carrying huge salmon up from the river. They were dressed like Dad, but some had hair that was different. They had long black braids that hung down their backs. Near the tepees, several women talked together while tending their cooking fires and the salmon drying on poles above the fires.

Here on the banks of the Columbia River in northeastern Washington, the tribes set up their tepees each summer, camping alongside the falls. They came to spear and catch the salmon going upstream to spawn, and would stay until they had enough dried salmon to last through the coming winter. Many lived nearby on the Colville Indian Reservation, but others came from as far away as northern Idaho and Montana. Getting a good supply of fish was important to all of them.

Arriving at the encampment, Dad saw a woman he knew and took Mom over to meet her. After a few minutes, he spotted his "trading" friend on the far side of the camp, and set off in that direction. Nine-year-old Lester never liked to sit still, so tagged along after Dad. Dora and I sat on the ground in the shade with Mom while she visited with her new friend. We all watched the action going on around us. Little kids were still playing their games, which looked like fun to me, but I was too bashful to join them. And women in long, loose dresses tended the fires. As they bent down to take care of the drying salmon, their long black braids – shining in the sunlight – swung down to their knees. Into the ground on both sides of each fire they had stuck an upright pronged stick, on top of which they placed a pole. On this pole they hung whole salmon, as well as thin strips, to smoke and dry over the fire. Dad told Mom to look at the length of the salmon, saying that some of them were as long as Lester.

Ever since we had arrived at the encampment, I had been eager to see the booming falls, which I could hear over the clamor of the camp. From where we sat, we couldn't see any part of the river or the men fishing from its banks. Dad wasn't there to take me, and Mom, tired from her heaviness and the long uphill walk, seemed content to sit in the shade and visit. When I asked when we would go look at the river, she said, "Maybe later."

More time went by. I decided no one was going to take me to see the river; I would have to go by myself. Mom didn't see me when I walked away. The thunder of the falls increased as I reached the rocky riverbank high above the water. I stood there looking at the swirling, foamy turbulence thirty or forty feet below. In fascination I watched the men fish, entranced by the sight before me. The cascades' pounding and splashing filled my ears – and kept me from hearing Mom's approach. Her arms wrapped around my waist and jerked me back, away from the river's perilous edge. She was right to be frightened for me, but I was irritated at being hauled away from such a good place to see everything. I hadn't finished looking. From my vantage point on solid ground, I had felt safer than those men fishing from their flimsy platforms over the roiling waters.

Later on, Dad led me back to the river's edge. He held my hand in a tight grip while I looked at the falls and the men fishing. There was so much to see, it took a long time to get enough of looking. I'd never before seen such a wondrous sight as those daring men netting and spearing the leaping salmon. With the water low in summer, I could also see large round holes – like kettles – in the rock ledges on the riverbank. Dad had told us that these falls and the town of Kettle Falls were named after these deep holes, big enough to hold two or three people. Each spring brought high water during the runoff from melting snows in the Canadian Rockies. Over the years, the strong current had banged logs and trees onto the rocks, swirling them around to gouge out the deep "kettles".

In late afternoon the men stopped fishing and came up from the river. The women had cooked something to eat. Dad's friend gave us some steaming salmon that his wife had cooked over the fire. When Mom handed a piece to me, she said, "Be careful and don't swallow any bones; they're so big you could choke on them."

I held the warm chunk in my hand and ate slowly, feeling for bones with my tongue. The juicy salmon tasted smoky, like some of the fire was still in it. Now I knew why Dad had been hungry for it. By evening I was accustomed to the pounding of the falls. As darkness fell, fires were built up again, and a different sound filled our ears. Finished with the day's work, the people gathered for some fun. Our family sat close together on the ground in the midst of the crowd, Dad's arms cradling me, while we watched an unusual and noisy game. About ten men and women sat on the ground behind a small log facing a similar group across an open space of about ten feet. Each person held two sticks and hit the logs, making a clackety-clack-clack sound. I asked Dad what they were doing. He said, "they're gambling by playing the 'Stick Game.' A player on one side hides a small bone in one hand and the other side tries to guess who has it."

I wondered what the clackety-clack-clack of sticks had to do with this game that reminded me of "Button, Button, Who's Got the Button?" The clacking went on and on. I couldn't see who held the bone and didn't know how much the players bet, but was no longer as curious as I'd been earlier. At seven years old, I was tired out from the long day and all the new things I had seen. I lay in Dad's strong arms, contentedly watching sparks from the big fires shoot up into the black night sky. With the muffled roar of the falls in my ears, I was lulled to sleep by the rhythm of the sticks.

Now in 2017, its been over eighty five years since I saw the Indians gathered at the falls spearing salmon and playing their Stick Game. Why is it, I wonder, that I can still see the tepee encampment and hear the clackety-clack-clack of the Stick Game, but can no longer smell the smoke?

Another Sister, Leola

August 17, 1931, marked the most important event that happened while we lived on the Hays Place. That was the day our new baby sister arrived. When Mom's pains had started, Dad drove her to Mrs. Julia Aldredge's Maternity Home in Kettle Falls where most of the area women had their babies. It was closer than the hospital in Colville, and didn't cost as much. Mrs. Aldredge called Dr. Gray in Colville, who got there in time to deliver the baby.

Dad came home and told us we had a new baby sister and that they had named her "Leola Evelyn." Those were the fanciest names I'd ever heard. Mom told us later that after having read the names in a book, she had decided to use them if she had a baby girl. The house seemed empty the ten days Mom was gone. When Dad brought her and the baby home, Lester, Dora and I were glad to see her. With Mom back home, the house came to life again. Seeing the tiny baby reminded me of the doll Santa had brought me three years ago. But watching Leola made me think that this "doll" would be different. Mom turned to me saying, "You can hold your little sister if you sit down."

Hurrying to a chair, I sat down and held out my arms. As Mom put her in my lap, she warned, "Be sure and keep your arm under her head so it doesn't flop over, and don't touch the soft spot on top of her head."

I felt the softness of her arms and legs. Her tiny face make different expressions as she squinted her eyes and opened and closed her mouth. Waving her tiny fists and kicking her legs, she was already a lot more interesting than that doll had been. Then when she opened her blue eyes and looked up at me, I knew she was going to be a lot more fun, too.

Hays Hill Adventures

On Christmas morning Lester and I found two new sleds leaning against the inside of the kitchen door. Their oak tops shone like a glare of ice in the sunlight and their runners glistened with red paint. Unlike Dad's second-hand equipment from auction sales, our presents were brand new.

Eager to go coasting, we started pulling on our coats, but Dad said, "You can't go until after breakfast, and besides, the sleds aren't ready to use yet. You have to sand the paint off the runners so they'll slip through the snow easily."

After breakfast Dad gave us pieces of sandpaper and helped us sand the red paint off. Lester and I put on our warm winter coats and hats then pulled on our five-buckled rubber overshoes, which kept our feet warm unless snow got down inside. As we were already wearing our long wool underwear, we knew we would be plenty warm coasting down the Hays Hill.

Zipping down the steep hill was just as exciting as we had imagined, the shiny runners taking us as fast down the hill as Dad drove our Star. That first day we coasted until we got tired of walking back uphill, pulling our sleds. And all through the winter we coasted, at times joining other kids in sleigh-riding parties on the Hays Hill. It didn't matter when we blocked the road off. If a car came along, the driver waited until word passed along for everyone to stop coasting and let the car go by.

Most of us had our own small sleds which held only one person, but one boy had a toboggan and another had a bobsled. Both had room to carry three or four kids at a time. We had to steer the bobsled with our feet instead of lying down on our small sleds and steering with our hands. Lester and I traded rides with them so we could have the excitement of riding with other kids; we shouted with excitement as we flew down the hill. But helping pull the heavy bobsled back up the steep hill was harder work than pulling our own light sleds, and we soon decided that we liked our sleds best.

On the coldest days, the older boys built a bonfire alongside the road that turned into the Abernathy house. After stopping to warm up a bit after each ride, we watched smoke curl up from their chimney which reminded us that our houses were warmer than the bonfire. When we got snow down inside our overshoes, it melted and our feet stayed cold until we went home. Our bonfire couldn't dry our feet, but sleigh riding was so much fun that we hated to stop until we got too cold to continue. All the kids living close to the Hays Hill loved it in the winter. It was perfect for sleigh riding: steep enough to give us a fast ride, but not too long.

But the hill meant something else to the grown-ups who had to drive up it when it snowed. Sometimes their cars got stuck and the men had to get out and put chains on the back wheels. The hill was at its worst when the snow on the road melted a bit during the day, then froze again at night. People living along the county road had to keep it plowed out during the winter. Dad's section of a mile or two extended above and below our house and included the Hays Hill. He kept it plowed out by pulling a home-made "vee" behind his team of horses. The vee was a triangular-shaped piece of equipment that he had made out of three long planks. A thin metal sheathing covered the front corner to reinforce it and to keep the snow from sticking on it. It was almost as wide as our narrow county road and cleared the snow off in two runs. Dad walked behind the vee holding the long, leather driving reins to guide the team.

At the beginning of winter Dad had fastened a double tree and two singletrees to the vee and left them attached to it all winter. After he hooked each horse's harness chains to a singletree, he was ready to start plowing the snow. The two horses dragged the vee along the ground, pushing the snow to the sides of the road. Despite his efforts, a few cars got stuck on the icy hill every winter. When Dad heard their wheels spinning, he went out and helped push the cars out of their snowy ruts. Sometimes he had to hitch our team of horses to the car and pull it up the hill. If cars had chains on, they seldom got stuck, but often drivers didn't know how soon they would need their chains. The road down near the highway would often be bare, while the Hays Hill still had snow. Driving on a bare highway with chains on broke the links, so drivers didn't put them on until they got to the snowy sections.

While the Hays Hill caused Dad a lot of trouble in winter, the steep pitch of the hill saved him the trouble of having to crank the Star to get it started. He parked it near our house on the edge of the road at the top of the hill. All he had to do was turn on the switch, take it out of gear, let the brake off and push in the clutch. The car would slowly start rolling, picking up speed when it got to the steep part of the grade. When he put it back into gear and let out the clutch, the engine started all by itself.

The next spring after our exciting sleigh-riding, we learned the Hays Hill could provide excitement without snow. Sam and Effie Curry came to visit and parked their open car off the road beside our little gate. They went on inside the house, but their two little girls, Arlene and Nadine, stayed outside to play with Lester and me. Sam had removed the car's snap-on curtains for the summer and folded the canvas top behind the back seat, making the car look like a roadster. Since it was newer than ours, Lester was very curious about it and soon he was standing on the running board, peering inside. The dashboard seemed to have different dials than ours did, and wanting to get a closer look, he opened the front door and climbed onto the driver's seat. Naturally, I climbed in, too. Dad had told us never to play in cars, but since we were only going to look, we thought it would be alright. Arlene and Nadine followed us and sat on the back seat.

In the front seat Lester could examine the odd looking dials and two long levers coming up from the floorboard. Soon he focused his attention on one of the levers. Wondering what it was for, he pushed it forward. When the car started moving slowly down hill, he found out. It was the emergency brake! And that's when the hill started giving us excitement in the summer time. In the front seat looking at the steep hill below us, I could feel my face turning white, and had visions of us smashed up into the trees beside the road. But Sam had seen the car moving and came racing out of the house, clearing the fence in one stride, and ran to overtake us. Jumping onto the running board, he reached in and yanked on the brake. The car jerked to a stop and we were rescued from our runaway ride. We were thankful Sam had caught up to us and pulled the emergency brake. If there had ever been as time to use it, this was it. It certainly HAD been an emergency!

Lester and expected to get spanked for getting into trouble, but we escaped that, too. We guessed the only reason Dad didn't spank us was because he was as relieved as we were that we hadn't been killed. Our investigation of Sam's car satisfied our curiosity to "learn something new". In addition to learning about the brake, we learned Dad always had a good reason when he told us not to do something.

A year later in 1931 when we moved to the isolated Curry Place, Mom missed her friends who lived close by. Lester and I didn't miss our friends, as we saw them every day in school. What we missed most was the winter excitement of coasting down the Hays Hill.

Many years ago the house on the Hays Place was torn down, leaving little to indicate where it once stood. The Hays Hill has been changed, too. The steepest part at the top was graded down, and fill added to the dip at the bottom. Tamed, it no longer provides the winter excitement of sleigh-riding.

1931 - 1936
Move to the Curry Place

On March 15, 1932 we moved to the Curry Place, an isolated farm about seven miles from the Hays Place. Sam and Effie Curry had decided to move back to Asotin, in the southern part of the state, and asked Dad and Mom to rent their farm. With less than half of its two hundred and forty acres level enough to plow, it was the biggest farm we had lived on.

Mom was heartbroken and cried when Sam and Effie left. Her other best friend, Opal Heidegger, had died just a few months before and the second loss to her was just too much to bear. It was the first time I'd ever seen her cry.

To get to the Curry Place, we drove down the Pleasant Valley Road and turned right at the log house on the corner of the Heidegger Road. We followed that narrow road up the rocky hill about three miles, passing the house where Grandma and Charley had lived. When we saw the mailbox with Abe Heidegger's name on it, we turned right, climbed a hill then drove past his two-story white house, following the half-mile road that ran through their alfalfa field uphill to the Curry house. The two-story house, once painted, was now faded to a mustard-yellow color. A small porch ran across the front. Downstairs was a small living room, kitchen and one bedroom. We climbed a bent stairway up to see two small bedrooms where Lester, Dora and I would sleep. Baby Leola would be sleeping downstairs with Dad and Mom.

Since it was March, the house was cold, so Dad's first job was to set up the wood heating stove in the living room, and the cook stove in the kitchen. He noticed the wood box in the kitchen was almost empty, so sent Lester and me out to the wood shed to get wood for both stoves. We also had to carry water from the well. Dad told us to grab some buckets and he'd help us find the well. Carrying our filled buckets into the kitchen, we set them on a small table near the stove where Mom had already put the wash pan. And that's where we washed our hands before supper. It would soon be getting dark, so Mom unpacked two lamps before she set about finding something simple to eat. Abe and Margaret Heidegger had a gas generator to make electricity, so had electric lights, but when it got dark, we still had to use our kerosene lamps.

The closest building to the house was the woodshed, next was the cellar, half buried in the ground, and the outdoor toilet was just beyond the cellar. The blacksmith shop had a lean-to shed tacked onto the side, which Dad said would be a fine place to park the Star. The barn was about a hundred yards away, far enough so the barnyard smells wouldn't reach the house.

Although many things in our new place were the same as at the Hays Place, Lester and I learned that our walk to school was much longer. Dad told us that it was probably three miles to school, but during the winter, we could ride our work horses to school, as there was a barn on the school grounds for kids who lived a long way away.

Our Neighbors, the Heideggers

Abe Heidegger handed me the big white seashell, saying, "Hold it up to your ear so you can hear the ocean roar."

I admired the shell's pinkish glow inside before putting up to my ear. Then, sure enough, I heard the sound of the distant ocean waves. Giving it to Lester, I watched his eyes widen at such a marvel. It was easy to imagine that we could hear an ocean that was miles away. We had gone to our mail box on the road below Heidegger's house and on the way home stopped to deliver a message for Mom. The next time we went to get the mail, four-year old Dora went with us, as she wanted to see the sea shell we'd told her about. Returning home on the uphill walk, her short legs tired out. Lester and I held her hands and half pulled her along with us. Upon reaching home, she dashed through the door ahead of us calling, "Mama, I heard the ocean roar!"

A few summers later Lester and I decided to go help Abe's hired hand, Marvin Tracy. In his spare time after the day's chores were done, Marvin was digging a hole above their barn. If he found water, Abe planned to pipe it down to the barn to water the cattle. The hole was dug into a hill about a mile from our house and Lester suggested that we go help Marvin. When we finally reached the diggings, we were tired from the long walk and the climb up the steep hill.

Marvin was outside his short tunnel, heaving big rocks into a heaping ore cart sitting on the tracks. Seeing us, he gave a welcoming grin and said, "I'll bet you walked all the way up here just to help me, didn't you?" With that greeting, he threw one last rock on. Then taking his water jug to the meager shade of the ore cart, he squatted down, tilted the jug and took a big swig. Glad to have reached our destination, we flopped tiredly down beside him. Still grinning broadly, Marvin said, "Digging rocks is hot work."

Hot and thirsty, we eagerly took the jug when he held it out to us. Swishing the cool water around in my dry mouth, I let it trickle down my throat, then said, "So is climbing steep hills in the summer," then got up and peered into the dusty-walled ten-foot long tunnel. I wondered how he was going to hit water in such a dry hillside. After Marvin had rested awhile, we asked what we could do to help. He said, "Well, if you want to, you can push the ore cart down the track for me."

The iron cart was piled high with rocks. With Lester on one side of the cart and me on the other, we put our shoulders against the back end and started pushing. It was so heavy we had to push with all our might to get it started. Then we kept pushing hard to keep it going. The ore cart suddenly ran off the end of the tracks and tipped over, spilling the rocks. Although Marvin hadn't warned us there was no stopper at the end, we felt sheepish for causing him extra work. He would have to find a way to haul the heavy cart back up the hill and get it mounted on the tracks again. At that point, figuring we had helped Marvin enough, we told him goodbye and took off for home.

Fifty-five years after Lester and I "helped" Marvin Tracy, Ruth Heidegger wrote about the well-digging efforts. "We didn't find enough water to make it worthwhile for all the work they did up there."

By Horseback and Shanks Ponies

Dad had told Lester and me that we could ride our work horses to school in winter, but we would have to walk the long trail to school in the spring and fall when he was using the horses to farm. We would be hiking the trail that the Heidegger kids had made when they had ridden past the Curry Place to school. So the next Monday morning we went to the barn, bridled two horses and set out on our new trail riding bareback. We had never had enough extra money to buy saddles.

So at nine and seven, we followed that trail to school, sometimes on horseback and sometimes on "shanks ponies," Mom's name for walking. Two years later when Dora was six, she joined us making the long trek. Being a spunky little kid, she kept up with us and never whined. We stayed on the trail in the mornings, but on the way home, we sometimes explored by taking different routes, ducking under the barbed wire fences. When we rode the horses, we had to stay on the trail where the gates were. No matter which route we took, Lester always obeyed Dad's strict rule to "stay together" so he could take care of us. Our main route to school took us through our neighbor's pasture where he kept his herd of cattle, including a bull. We knew all bulls could be dangerous, as a man near Rice had been killed by one. Frank's bull never chased us, but we always made a wide detour if we saw the cattle grazing near our trail.

Before falling asleep one night I kept thinking about how big and dangerous that Hereford bull looked. Then I saw him standing in the middle of the corral, not far from me. He snorted and pawed the ground, sending up clouds of dirt. Suddenly he charged, chasing me around and around inside the corral. Every time I got close enough to duck through the horizontal poles, I heard his thundering hooves bearing down on me and felt his hot breath on my bare heels. My heart raced and I gasped for air, but didn't dare stop running. Then the bull lunged forward, butting me, and I jerked upright in bed. My heart was still pounding so hard I could hear it. But I was safe at home, thankful it had only been a dream. Although the bull chased me only in my dreams, he was an ever-present threat to us kids when we walked through the pasture.

Going back and forth to school rewarded us with many adventures. When winter came, we rode the horses most of the time. But if we planned to ride our sleds during recesses at school, we took our sleds with us and walked, taking about an hour. Our trail was about a mile long before reaching the county road. By horseback, we got to school in less than an hour. Upon reaching the barn on the school grounds by horseback, we rode into it and removed the horses' bridles. Dad had long since taught us to use different kinds of knots. We tied their neck ropes with a slip knot to the stall, but always used a bowline knot around the horses' necks, as a slip knot could choke a horse. Before leaving the barn to walk to the school house, we tossed some hay into the manger for the horses.

Our trail shortcut was the shortest route possible. We always took that route on our way to school because we didn't want to be late. Going home was a different matter; we didn't have to get there by a specific time. If we felt adventuresome when on foot, we could detour from our route. Coming to a barbed-wire fence, we crawled under it. But on horseback, we had to stick to the trails leading to gates. Getting home, we rode to the barn and curried the horses. Both our curry combs had short handles, but were otherwise different. One was square with short teeth, the other was round with a continuous metal strip wound in circles and had longer teeth. And that's the one I used if Lester hadn't beat me to it. When we tied their neck ropes and turned the horses loose, they shook themselves and ran around the barnyard kicking up their heels like they'd just been let out of school, too.

We had our choice of work horses to ride. Lester's favorite was Pet, a blue roan that was pretty frisky. Dora and I rode double on Betty, a gentle sorrel mare. Since we didn't have saddles, it didn't take us long to get ready to go, as we just had to put their bridles on. I pushed the metal bit against Betty's clenched teeth until she opened her mouth, then pushed the bit in, pulled the bridle strap up over her ears and buckled her neck strap. I led her out the barn door, climbed on, then helped Dora get on. I held my foot stiff for her to step on while grabbing her hand, then hoisted her up behind me. She wrapped her arms around me and hung on all the way.

Hanging on was a good idea, as we rode fast to keep up with Lester. When it wasn't too hilly, he liked to gallop Pet and jump across ditches. So we galloped and jumped, too, clenching our knees to Betty's sides. When she trotted hard, I grabbed a handful of her mane to keep from falling off; Dora just hung on to me a little tighter. The day Betty bucked us off, Dora and I learned that hanging on tighter wasn't enough to keep us from falling off. A friend had climbed on behind Dora, but gentle Betty laid back her ears, put her head down, arched her back and bucked all of us off. Her "lesson" to us that day was that she didn't like three people on her back.

The worst part about riding bareback was getting back on the horse when we fell off. I still wasn't tall enough to jump on from level ground. I'd have to find something to stand on or lead Betty to a side hill and climb on from the uphill side.

Dora and I relied on Lester to keep us safe – as well as for adventures. I took this for granted until one cold winter day when he was sick and didn't ride with us. And that left me, at nine years old, to take care of Dora, who was only six. When we came to a big snowdrift across the trail on that blizzardy day, I found out just how much I had depended on Lester. He wouldn't have tried to make the horse go through the snowdrift. On setting out for school that morning, I had chosen to ride Pepper, a big black mare with long legs. Going home from school, we had come out of the trees into the open where the icy wind bit into our faces There at the top of the hill, we were about a quarter of a mile from home. The snow swirled around us, stinging our faces and getting down our necks. Pepper had been plodding through the knee-high snow on the trail, but halted abruptly at the edge of a snowdrift, about belly high on her. It had completely covered the trail, the snow blowing in swirls off the tops of drifts all across the field. I kicked Pepper's sides with the heels of my heavy overshoes. She eyed the drift, but refused to go through it to the trail on the other side. I kicked her again and slapped her with the reins, but she still wouldn't move. Then I remembered that Lester had once said, "If you give a horse its head, it will know which way to go." Also, I thought if we got off Pepper's back, she would it make it through, then we could get back on her.

As soon as we slid off her back and let go of the reins, Pepper skirted the highest part of the drift, and I knew I'd made a mistake in getting off of her. She swung back into the trail on the other and high tailed it along our trail. She plowed through the deep snow so fast I couldn't catch her. In my plight I'd forgotten that I wouldn't be able to get back on her. Dora and I were already cold, our hands and faces stinging, but sitting on her warm back had at least kept our bottoms and legs from feeling frozen.

Soon our hands and faces became numb. Snow got inside our overshoes, making our ankles numb as well. Our overall pant legs got wet then froze stiff, rasping with each step. I was glad we were wearing our hated wool underwear, but even yet, felt half frozen. The snow continued blowing in our faces as we followed Pepper's hoof prints in the deep snow. Topping the rise, we were glad to see our house down below. The smoke from the chimney made us feel that we'd soon be inside our warm house.

As we were later than usual, Mom and Dad had been watching for us from the window. Seeing Pepper coming down the hill alone, Dad became alarmed and put on his winter coat and high boots and set off on foot to find us. Dora and I were glad to see him coming up the trail; maybe next time we would really need help. Reaching the house, Dora went straight inside, but I headed for the barn to let Pepper inside and to feed her some hay as usual. Dad astonished me by saying, "You go on inside the house and get warmed up."

In the house I felt guilty for shirking my duty, as taking care of our horses was our own responsibility. I took off my warm mittens and saw my hands were blue. Mom was afraid I might have frostbite, so wouldn't let me get too close to the heating stove. As my blue colored hands warmed up, they turned red, then started hurting. I'd been cold lots of times, but my hands and face had never tingled and stung like this. I hoped I'd never get that cold again.

We all knew that Mom and Dad expected us to learn something every day at school, but the lesson I learned that day didn't come out of a book. Pepper taught me to use a little horse sense. Her sidestepping the drift showed me I could solve some problems better by looking for an easier way around than plunging head first into the hard part.

When the snow had a crust on it and could support our weight, we took our sleds to school instead of riding the horses. We could coast a long way across Frank Rupert's open field, over his snow-covered barbed-wire fences to the road below his house. The crust was hard and we went flying down the hill so fast the wind made our eyes water and we could hardly see where we were going. That was the fastest day we ever got to school. Coasting on the crust was the most thrilling activity we had all winter. But we couldn't do it very often. The crust didn't form unless weather conditions were just right. We were always excited on mornings when Dad or Lester came inside from milking and announced, "there's a crust on the snow today!"

When we first started going to school from our new place, we carried our lunches in paper bags. But bags were scarce and didn't last long from our rough treatment. Finally Mom solved the problem by making shoulder bags out of the legs of worn-out overalls. Then she sewed straps on them so we could sling them over our shoulders, leaving our hands free to hold the reins –and the horses' manes. After having my eleventh birthday, it became my job to make our school sandwiches. For one, I mixed Karo syrup and peanut butter together. For the other, I used leftover venison steaks on Mom's homemade bread. Dad heard me complaining about having the same old things every day, and scolded me, saying, "You're lucky; when I was a boy, the only sandwich I had was made by spreading lard between two slices of bread."

That made me more appreciative, but a few weeks later I traded my venison sandwich to a friend for her strawberry jam sandwich. But getting hungry before school was out, I regretted my trade. The jam sandwich hadn't stuck to my ribs like the venison had – and somehow I never got around to telling Dad about my foolish trade.

With no thermometer, telephone or radio, we had no way of knowing exactly how cold it was. But Dad could tell it was much colder then usual one bitter-cold morning. When he had gone to the barn to milk the cows, the freezing air had puckered up the inside of his nose, and his boots had made sharp crunching sounds on the frozen snow. He told us that it was too cold for us to go to school on horseback and that he would take us in the bobsled. Even though it was freezing cold, Dad wanted us to get as much schooling as possible. He had been able to go only through the fourth grade.

The bobsled was the only way he could get us to school, as the road down to the Heidegger house was snowed in. After breakfast, Dad drove the team up the house. He and Lester had harnessed two horses and hitched them to the big bob sled, our low wagon bed mounted on a double set of metal runners. He had tossed in a lot of dry straw into the sled for us kids to sit on to help us keep warm. And while Mom was cooking our mush for breakfast, she had heated some flat irons on the kitchen stove. When we had our coats, hats and boots on and were ready to go, she handed us the irons wrapped in old pieces of rags so they wouldn't burn us. With hot irons beside us in the straw and quilts tucked around us, we snuggled down behind Dad who was sitting on the sled's seat. I felt sorry for him sitting on the cold seat exposed to the freezing wind.

Before getting to the top of the hill a couple of hundred yards away, the horses had white frost all over their muzzles and chests. The steam coming from their noses was freezing at every breath. Dad got off the sled and held his hands over their nostrils to thaw the frost. When he climbed back on, we saw his black three-day old stubble of beard had turned white, too!

Our route that morning was a bit longer than usual, as the sled was too wide for our horseback trail. Instead we followed a rough wagon track going through our field and pasture and connected to the road going past Frank Rupert's house. When we arrived at the school house, no one was there. But Raymond and Ruth Heidegger's house was just across the creek and Raymond had seen us pull up. Standing on his front porch, he waved at us and yelled, "Come on over."

Dad drove the bob sled over the bridge and stopped the team by their yard gate. We went into their cozy, warm house. After being in the freezing wind, the warmth felt good on our faces. After their greetings, Raymond asked, "Bill didn't you know it was thirty-six degrees below zero this morning? School has been canceled until this cold weather breaks."

So the only time Dad ever took us to school resulted in us having to turn around and going right back home again. But we were very thankful we hadn't gone by horseback that morning.

All winter we wore long-sleeved and long-legged wool underwear under our flannel shirts and bib overalls. Dora and I struggled every morning making the underwear legs stay down while pulling on our long cotton stockings. But once we got them up and our garters fastened to the tops, the legs stayed down. We hated the lumps the thick folds made under our stockings, but had to put up with it. We also hated having to wear itchy underwear after the temperature got above freezing. In late winter, after having a few days above freezing, we tried to convince Mom we didn't need it any more. But she told us, "Spring hasn't come yet. Until we get warm weather that stays, you can just keep on wearing your long underwear."

And she was right. A few days after that, we had another cold spell. Riding home in the snow and wind, we were glad Mom hadn't been fooled by our "warm weather" story.

Going to school by shanks' ponies wasn't as much fun as going by horseback. But we had more adventures when we were on foot, as we could take different routes. In late spring we liked to go the long way so we could see early blue flowers blooming in the rock slide, about a half-mile from the house, and the big patch of foot-high sunflowers covering the slope below the slide. By fall the leaves had become stiff and dry, and faded to a whitish-gray color. The wind rubbing the dry leaves together made them sound just like a rattlesnake rattling.

One fall day as we walked through the sunflowers on our way home from school, we heard a rattling-rasping and thought it was just from the leaves rubbing together. But Lester thought the sound was different and held his hand up for Dora and me to stop. Following the sound with our eyes, we finally spotted a rattlesnake coiled up. His rattle was held above his mottled body and his narrow head pointed straight at us. His beady black eyes stared piercingly at us and his rattle was vibrating so fast we could just see a blur. All of us grabbed some big rocks and threw at him and soon had him killed. With the toe of his shoe, Lester nudged the limp body. Seeing the rattler was dead, he cut off its rattle with his jackknife.

Leaving the snake's body there in the dry sunflower leaves, we took the rattle home to show Mom and Dad. We excitedly told them all about killing the rattler, feeling proud to having gotten rid of something dangerous to us. After counting the four segments and the button at the end of the rattle, Dad said, "This rattlesnake wasn't as old as some we've killed, but just as poisonous."

After all of us took turns shaking the rattle to hear the rasping noise, Lester dropped it in the saucer holding several other rattles we had collected.

And there was something else to hear every evening after moving to the Curry Place. We heard coyotes howling about as soon as darkness fell. Dad said there must be quite a pack of them to make that much noise, so that fall he decided to set out some traps to catch them. He had set a few in a grove of trees near that patch of sunflowers and told us to go check on them on our way home from school. He'd seen tracks of other animals, so was hoping to catch muskrats and mink as well and sell the pelts. He told us if the traps had caught anything, we were to get the animal out and take it home.

Upon reaching the first trap, we saw it was empty. Its steel jaws were closed. Dora and I watched as Lester pried the jaws apart and re-set the trap, putting the trigger on the catch so the jaws would stay open. Going on through the aspens, we heard a noise ahead. Looking up, we saw a coyote springing up and down and jumping sideways. Caught in a trap, he was trying to get out of it. The trap was chained to a heavy log so he couldn't run away with it.

We saw that we had a problem, as we couldn't take the coyote out of the trap while it was alive. But Dad had explained to Lester what he had to do if this ever happened. He had said, "Get it on its side and stand on its shoulder to compress the heart."

Lester managed to wrestle the coyote to the ground without getting bitten or scratched. We then took turns holding it by the chain and standing on it. Lester finally finished it off by hitting it on the head with a club. Now it was safe to take it out of the trap. We felt we had helped a lot by saving Dad a long walk out to check his traps.

Not all of our trips back home by shanks' ponies were that exciting. Most of the time it was just a lot of hard walking. On one trek home from school, remembering that Frank Rupert had said that one of his cows had lost her bell, we decided to hunt for it. Having seen his cattle grazing in the far corner of his pasture, we decided to go look for it there even though it would take us quite a ways from our trail. We crawled under his barbed-wire fence and walked up the hill. Frank's dog, Sport, tracked us down about this time to keep us company. After reaching the grazing area, we spread out and searched the ground, looking around bushes and through the tall grass. It wasn't long before Dora and I heard Lester yell, "I found it!"

We were fond of Frank and his wife, Julia. In calling them by their first names, we weren't being disrespectful; just showing we liked them. The only people we called "Mr." or "Mrs." were elderly, or someone we didn't know well – or didn't like. Although they were grandparents, we didn't look upon them as being old. And they seemed to know they were special people to us.

On our way to school, we didn't have time to stop and play with Sport. As we ran down their lane, Sport joined us, running with us until we got part way down the county road. But on our way home from school, he'd come down the lane in front of their house to meet us. Since we had time, we were always glad to stop and scratch his ears and belly and tell him what a good dog he was. Lying on his back, he wiggled his whole body, sweeping the ground with his tail. Every day, he followed us up through the barnyard and part way up our trail before turning and going back to his house. The few times we by-passed the house to follow the fence line up the hill through the pasture, he still tracked us down. Sport was really smart – and a big help to Frank by bringing the cows in all by himself. At milking time in the late afternoons, Frank called the dog to him. Waving his arm in the direction of the cows, he said, "Go get the cows, Sport."

The dog would streak out to where the cows were grazing, circle around behind them and get them started for the barn. He never chased them, just trailed them so they kept going. The cows must have been smart, too. They often headed for the barn as soon as they saw Sport coming their way. All Frank had to do was go out and open the gate so they could get into the corral.

A few years later, after we moved to another farm, Frank told Dad how much Sport missed us. "He still waits in the lane every day for those kids, acting puzzled because they don't come by. He even runs up and down the road looking for them."

Before this, Sport had always been able to track us down, but now for the first time, couldn't find us. Frank went on to tell Dad that he should take the dog; that "he was more yours than ours" and that he sure missed us kids. Dad didn't accept his offer because he knew Frank wasn't physically able to go out to get the cows. A few months later Frank told Dad that Sport had died without ever having been sick. He added, "I think he just died of a broken heart."

Then we were all sorry we hadn't taken Sport to live with us. We had missed him, too.

While living on the Hays Place, I won a Certificate of Award for not being tardy nor absent all year. But I was prouder of the one I got from Miss Dean in 1933 after we moved to the Curry Place. On our long trail, it hadn't been easy to get to school on time every day by horseback and shank's ponies.

Baby Sister Effie – 1933

Feeling nervous away from home, Lester, Dora, Leola and I tagged along behind Dad as he opened the gate in the yard fence in front of Mrs. Aldredge's Maternity Home in Kettle Falls. We hadn't been there for over two years, not since Leola was born. Now we had another baby sister, born on May 5, 1933, and again, Dr. Gray had driven from Colville for the delivery.

When Mom's labor pains started, Dad helped her into the car and headed out, leaving us kids home alone. On their way past Heidegger's, he stopped and hurried inside to tell them that they were on the way to the maternity home. Their seventeen year old daughter, Ruth, had promised to come up and stay with us until Dad returned.

Seeing Ruth walking up the road, we ran out to meet her. Since it was past time for supper, Ruth set about seeing what she could find to eat. Lester said, "I'll go out to the cellar and get a quart jar of canned venison."

While Ruth and I were peeling potatoes to boil, Lester asked Ruth if she'd like to have anything else from the cellar. She said, "Yes, some corn or green beans would be good with the meat, and I'll make some gravy to go with these potatoes."

So Ruth found plenty for supper and cooked a good meal. Then Dora and I washed the dishes and put them back in the cupboard. About that time we noticed Leola had started getting cranky. With our thoughts on Dad's return and news of the new baby, we had forgotten to put her to bed, so quickly got her undressed and into her small bed.

An hour or so later, twin beams of car lights cut through the darkness of the woods below and soon we saw the dark shadow of our Star stop in front. At last Dad was home. Coming through the door, he said, "Well, we have us another girl," and left to drive Ruth back down to her folks' house. We were excited about our new baby sister, so the next day we asked Dad if we could go and see Mom and the baby. But he said, "You can wait; I have to plant grain tomorrow and it can't wait."

Three days later, he finally took us to see Mom and baby Effie. Walking into the house, we spotted Mom immediately. She and two other women were lying in narrow beds in the large front room – but there weren't any babies in sight. We'd been lonesome for Mom, so quickly gathered around her. I wanted to hug her, but thinking she might not be strong yet, just stood near her bed. As soon as she pulled two-year old Leola into her arms, we knew she was ready for our hugs and all bent over and hugged her at the same time. When she asked what we had been doing, we guessed she'd been lonesome for us, too. While telling her everything, we kept craning our necks to find the babies.

Finally, Mom noticed our curiosity. Smiling, she pointed to three bassinets lined up in the next room and said, "Your little sister is the one on the left."

Leola stayed in the crook of Mom's arm while Lester, Dora and I went over to the babies. Looking at them, we decided ours was the prettiest – and just as pretty as her name, Effie Eileen Riley. Mom had long ago decided that if she had a girl, she would name her after her dear friend, Effie Curry. And she had added "Eileen" because that was the heroine's name in a story she had just read.

We hoped Mom could come with us that day, but Dr. Gray had said she must stay and rest for ten days, just as she had when Leola was born. He knew she wouldn't be able to get much rest at home with five children to care for. Mom must have told him she didn't have a washing machine and had to scrub clothes on the washboard. We were happy when the time was up and Dad brought her and Effie home. Once again, our house felt warm and complete.

For a few days, we eagerly took turns holding our new baby sister. We couldn't help feed her, as Mom was nursing. But a couple of months later, Mom had to put her on the bottle, then we could help. As I looked into her smoke-colored eyes, I wondered if they'd be brown like Mom's, or blue like Dad's and the rest of us. And we all wondered if her hair would stay black or turn blonde like Leola's had. Mom's glossy, dark brown hair was slightly wavy. Dad, mostly bald, had a fringe of straight, black hair. Lester's was also black, while Dora and I had dark brown hair, straight as horses' tails.

Mom showed Dora and me other ways we could help, although I was nine and Dora was only six. We burped Effie after she finished her bottle, and cuddled her when she was just fussy. When she needed her diaper changed, I took it off, cleaned her bottom and pinned the dry diaper on with large safety pins. And if the belly band covering her navel had gotten wet, I changed it, too, cleaning her navel with a piece of cotton dipped in boric acid solution, then put a clean belly band on her.

Dora helped by getting two-year old Leola dressed and taking her out to the toilet. She had been toilet trained at nine months, but still needed someone to take her outside. Dora kept an eye on her, as she could disappear quickly if she got outdoors.

The next summer, when Effie was a year old, she disappeared. She and Leola had been inside with Mom, but the rest of us kids were playing outside. All of a sudden, Mom came rushing out the door, looking upset. She sounded upset too, when her words all rushed together, "can't find Effie anywhere in here . . . must have slipped outside when I wasn't looking . . . you kids go see if you can find her."

Lester took off on a run for the granary, barn and blacksmith shop to see if Effie had wandered that way. Dora headed around the corner of the house to look in the woodshed, cellar and the garden. Always fearful of the wells, I made a beeline for the one near the road, terrified that Effie might have gone that way. Calling her name as I ran, I reached the well and looked all around it and even looked down into the dark water. Then I ran a hundred yard to the other well, not seeing her there either, so ran back to the house. Just as I got there, Lester returned from his search and Dora came around the corner of the house from the other direction. No one had seen Effie, so we went into the house to see if she had come back. Almost as soon as we got into the kitchen, someone spotted her little blonde head poking out from under a pile of clothes. She was sound asleep on top of the stack of ironing on a little square table against the wall. One of Dad's blue work shirts covered all but the top of her head. No wonder Mom hadn't been able to find her.

We were all relieved Effie had decided to take a nap instead of going for a walk. Most of all, we were happy she wasn't lost. Seeing her lying asleep with her blonde hair sticking out reminded me of our first glimpse of her black hair at Mrs. Aldredge's Maternity Home when we wondered if her hair would turn color. Now we knew. At a year old, she had shiny gold hair, just like Leola's.

43

Exploring the Hills

"Come see what I found," Lester called excitedly. Dora and I wheeled around to where he knelt on the rocky ground. "I told you we'd find that killdeer nest." We looked down at the four spotted eggs lying inside a circle of pebbles. A few minutes earlier we had laughed as the mother killdeer tried to lead us away from her nest by acting like she had a broken wing. When we saw her flopping around, half running and half flying, we knew her nest was close by, and soon spotted it. Lester had explained that killdeers laid their eggs on rocky ground instead of making nests in trees. At ten and eight, Lester and I had been exploring the hills for over a year, but hadn't taken five-year old Dora with us before.

The wild area of the farm, too steep or wooded to plow, furnished pasture grass for the cattle and horses and was perfect for exploring. It drew us like a magnet. As much as we liked finding birds' nests of all kinds, we didn't like finding nests that yellow jackets made. Looking like wrinkled gray balloons caught in the branches, we viewed them with dread instead of pleasure. Because the bees stung us, we felt it was our duty to destroy their nests, so threw rocks at them until the yellow jackets chased us away. Some times we knocked their nests down without getting stung.

We roamed the hills so much in the spring and summer that we knew when all the wildflowers bloomed. White spring beauties were first, then shiny yellow buttercups, fuchsia shooting stars, yellow bells, blue bells, columbines, sunflowers, lavenderish rock flowers and bushes of service berries and syringas. Indian paint brush and lavender-pink mariposa lilies came last, the circles on their petals making them look like butterflies tied to the ground.

Mom loved wild flowers, and made us feel we'd done something special if we only brought a fist full of dandelions. Tied down in the house taking care of Leola and Effie, she didn't have time to walk the half mile to see wild flowers growing in the hills. The first time we took branches of creamy white, syringas to her, she breathed in their fragrance and exclaimed with delight, "Oh, that's Idaho's state flower; some call it 'mock orange' because it smells like orange blossoms."

On one of our first explorations of our new farm, Lester and I had seen three animals. Smaller than our cows, they were bouncing along stiff legged, heading straight for the barbed wire fence. I yelled, "Look, Lester, billy goats!"

The lopsided grin on his face told me he knew they weren't billy goats. All of a sudden, they gave a bigger bounce and sailed over the fence. Their white tails were the last we saw of them as they disappeared over the hill. And that's when I finally realized they were deer. Lester had known all along, as Dad had often taken him hunting.

One afternoon as Lester, Dora and I were walking through an aspen thicket, Lester decided he'd try to "ride" one of the smaller trees. He climbed almost to its top, then still hanging on, threw his body away from the trunk. The tree bent over with his weight and swayed back and forth. When it went back to its upright position, he again gave a big lunge away from it. The tree swayed and he flew back and forth "riding" until it ran out of motion. "Boy, that was fun," he said, "why don't you try it?"

Dora shook her head, but it had looked like a lot of fun to me. I found a shorter tree than Lester's and climbed to the top. When it started bending, I hung on tight with my hands, but swung my legs out away from the trunk, making the aspen sway back and forth and giving me an exciting ride.

That first day of tree riding made us soon want to do it again, but Lester's tree swayed so strongly that he lost his grip and it flipped him off. He landed on the ground with a thud and just lay there. Worried about him, we knelt beside him and saw a trickle of blood coming out of his ear. After a couple of minutes, he staggered to his feet, looking dazed. That's when we decided the next time we wanted to go riding, we'd better grab a horse instead of a tree.

Exploring the farm so much, we learned to watch where we stepped with our bare feet to avoid thistles, sharp rocks, and most importantly – fresh cow piles. With our eyes focused on the ground so much, we found bugs and worms and small round doodle bug holes in the soft dirt. The dusty gray doodle bugs lurked at the bottom, waiting for tiny insects to fall down the smooth sides where they killed them with the pincers on top of their heads. Lester put his mouth close to a hole and mumbled, "doodle, doodle, doodle", and waited for a movement at the bottom. Finally, he saw the soil move, and used a splinter to lift the bug out to show us.

(Sixty years later when finding doodle bug holes in the dirt under my back porch, I had the strange urge to stoop down, and say "doodle, doodle, doodle".)

It was during these times of boredom that we tried forbidden things like smoking. Neither Dad nor Mom smoked, but a few of Dad's friends did, rolling their own cigarettes. Finding a pack of cigarette papers that one of them had left, we decided to see what smoking was like. Lester said, "We'll pick some Indian tobacco that's growing out by the pig pen. It's all dry and brown and looks just like tobacco."

We stripped a handful of seeds off the dock plant, our "Indian tobacco," and Lester showed us how he'd
seen the men make a cigarette. Pouring some seeds on the thin white tissue, he then spread it out, rolled the paper around the tobacco and licked it to seal his "cigarette." It was uneven and lumpy and almost looked like the real thing. After I made one, he dug a match out of his overalls pocket and lit his cigarette and then mine. Three big puffs were all it took to show me it wasn't much fun. My tongue felt like it was on fire – just like the blazing tip of the cigarette. Later that summer we found an old cigar that someone had left behind, and decided to find out what "real" tobacco tasted like. After taking a few puffs, I handed it to Lester. He looked at me and told me had my face was turning green. That didn't surprise me, as I felt green – and a minute later I threw up. That day I swore I'd never smoke another cigar. We lost all interest in gathering Indian tobacco and rolling our own. Feeling green and throwing up cured me for life of any interest in smoking.

But we never lost interest in our home-made sling shots. When I had seen that Lester could hit targets better with his sling shot than with a rock, I asked him to help me make one for myself. We carried them with us everywhere, even to school. With little rocks lying all around, we never ran out of ammunition. We couldn't shoot at our chickens, cows or horses, but there were lots of other targets. We shot at snakes, ground squirrels, yellow-jacket nests, fence post, knot holes, or just circles we drew in the dirt. We kept our sling shots in our pockets where they'd be handy when we needed them.

When winter came, we could no longer roam the hills. Spending more time at the house, we taught Leola how to make snow angels. She laughed, thinking it funny to see us lying in the snow making "wings" with our flailing arms. Dad didn't want us to ride the horses just for fun, even though he wasn't working them. When bad weather kept us cooped up in the house, we couldn't do much except play checkers or dominoes. And that's why Lester, Dora and I felt so exhilarated when spring finally came and the snow melted. We could go exploring again!

Pleasant Valley Grade School

The fall Dora started first grade and Lester and I were in the fourth grade there weren't enough pupils in the school district to need two teachers, so Mrs. Ethel Graham became the teacher for all eight grades. We hadn't heard much about her, only that her husband's name was Billy and that they were renting a cabin above John Byrds's farm. One of the boys jokingly said he would greet her by saying, "Good morning, Teacher, how is your old GRAY HAM?"

When Miss Dean had married Thurman Rose, the school board had to hire a new teacher because of the policy against hiring married women young enough to have babies. Although not having a gray ham, Mrs. Graham did have gray hair.

That first day, all of us kids stayed out in the school yard to play until the bell rang, then hurried inside, eager to satisfy our curiosity about our new teacher. As soon as I saw her dark piercing eyes in her stern-looking face, I knew no one would have the nerve to ask Mrs. Graham about her "gray ham" or make any other smart-alecky remarks. Her manner indicated she wouldn't stand for any nonsense.

"Good morning, children, take your seats," were her first words to us. We saw a slim older woman standing stiff as a poker in her dark skirt and white blouse. Tight marcelled waves of gray hair went all around her head. Behind steel-rimmed spectacles, her sharp eyes seemed to be sorting us all out. She stood beside her desk at the front of the room and gave us some instructions. "The first graders will sit in the row next to the heating stove, and the eighth graders in the row next to the windows. Pupils in other grades will sit at the desks in between for now. Next week I'll assign specific desks."

She sat down at her desk, her back stiff and straight, and called the roll. As each of us answered, "Here," her eyes tracked down the voice and studied us, as if putting a face to the name in her roll book. After seeing her standing tall, it came as no surprise to learn she expected us to have good posture, too. Often I'd be slumped over a book, when she appeared before me saying, "Sit up straight, Ines. Don't slouch in your seat."

Since Mrs. Graham was the only teacher for the thirty or more pupils in all eight grades, she kept an eye on all phases of our education. She pointed out every misspelled word on our papers, whether they were geography, history, or spelling. It didn't make any difference which subject it was, all the words had to be spelled correctly. The same was true of punctuation and grammar. If we made a mistake of any kind in any subject, she corrected us.

We diagrammed many sentences in our English class. That enlightened us by showing some words were nouns - or subjects – when we hadn't thought of them that way. A sentence in our exercise book was, "Some of the girls wrote stories every day." At that time in our subject-learning, it was a tricky sentence to diagram. After much thought, I chose "some" as the subject, and "wrote" as the predicate. One of the girls asked what I had put down as the subject. When I told her, she scoffed, saying, "That's wrong; "some" can't do anything, 'girls' is the subject."

I was sure of myself, still it was a relief later when Mrs. Graham confirmed that my choice was correct. I felt so good that I didn't even rub it in to my friend that the word, "some", could do something!

That November Mrs. Graham announced we were going to put on a Christmas program at the grange hall, something that had never happened before. It would be in the evening, and we would have recitations, songs and plays, and invite all our families and friends to come. She would see if we could get a Christmas tree, too! She added that we'd start learning our pieces right away. There would be lots of memorization, and quite a bit of practice and rehearsing.

For the next month we spent our time memorizing our parts in the plays instead of studying from books. About a week before the Christmas program, we spent our afternoons at the grange hall to rehearse on the stage. At lunch time, we all walked the mile down the road from the schoolhouse, eating our sandwiches on the way. A few times Mrs. Graham's husband, Billy, came in his little Model A Ford pickup to drive her down to the grange hall so she wouldn't have to walk. And just like every day when school was out, he was there after practice to drive her home.

Ethel Rupert, whose daughter, Fay, was just Dora's age, volunteered to play the piano for our songs. Mrs. Graham was then free to direct the program and do the prompting in the plays. Both the one-act play and the three-act play had long lines for us to learn.

After a month of practice, the time came for our program. Mrs. Graham had told us to be at the grange hall about a half-hour before starting time, and to stay in the kitchen to get ready for our parts. We didn't even have time to admire the beautiful Christmas tree standing near the stage next to the built-in baby crib. Until I peeked through the stage curtains and saw the hall was full, I hadn't realized we had a big audience. All the benches lined up on the dance floor were filled and people were standing up in back. It seemed that not only our families, but everyone in Pleasant Valley, Arzina, Rice, Daisy and Gifford had come to see our Christmas program.

Mrs. Graham welcomed everyone, then announced the first song. When it ended, the curtain closed and the audience clapped loudly. At the end of the program – after the two plays and other songs, Mrs. Graham came from behind the curtains and called all the pupils stand with her. She announced the program was over; we bowed, and the audience clapped and clapped, even more than they had before.

Just then sleigh bells jingled outside and we looked over to see Santa Claus coming through the door! In his red suit and white cotton beard and carrying a bulging gunny sack over his shoulder, he strode past the audience, laughing, "Ho, ho, ho," and stopped by the tall Christmas tree. If I hadn't known better, I would have thought he was real.

Santa began calling the names of everyone in our school, giving each one a small paper sack of hard candy. He still had more sacks in his bag, so called the names of every child in the audience, no matter what school district they were in. Everyone under high school age got a sack of candy from Santa.

That was the best Christmas most of us had ever had. It was also the beginning of a tradition. Mrs. Graham earned a reputation as a fine program director. Every year the grange hall was packed with people who came to have a good time – and perhaps see that their children had candy for Christmas.

A few years later when Lester and I were in the seventh grade, the enrollment increased and the school board hired a second teacher, Lawrence Hays. Since Mrs. Graham had taught us several years, they gave her the title of Principal. She would teach the lower grades and Mr. Hays took over the upper grades. He wasn't a stranger in our valley; he owned the Hays Place which we had rented. And the Hays Hill we used to coast down in winter had been named after him. He was married to Walt and Frances Lickfold's, daughter, Ruby, who always had a smile on her face. Lawrence and Ruby had two children, Mervyn and Helen, and by hiring him, the school got two extra pupils.

For the first time since I started school, both rooms of the school house were now used as class rooms. The extra room that had once served as a living quarters for Mrs. Graham and Billy, was now put in use as a classroom, as the kids from the Arzina Grade School had come to our school on a trial basis. Their enrollment had dwindled to less than twenty pupils and their school board could no longer afford to hire a teacher. This addition swelled our enrollment to over forty pupils. Since those pupils lived too far to walk to school, the van that picked up high school students picked them up and brought them to Pleasant Valley School. The van took the high school kids as far as the Rice store and from there, a large bus took them on to the Kettle Falls High School.

Our best friends from Arzina were Gerry, Billy and Janice Entwistle. Our fathers had hunted together for years, so we knew them better than some of the kids we'd been going to school with. Toward the end of the trial year of consolidation, Dad had many discussions with Pearl Entwistle, a member of the Arzina School Board. Dad, on the Pleasant Valley School Board, tried to persuade Pearl to vote to consolidate with us. But at the end, the Arzina board members decided to consolidate with the Rice District. They thought since it had three full classrooms, it would offer more in the long run.

Our school work wasn't all study. We went to track meets usually twice during the school year. When we competed at Rice, only the few local schools were involved, but when competing in the district track meet at Colville, all the schools in the county were there. Before our first track meet, we practiced running, jumping and all events which we'd be entering. We had a fifty-yard and a hundred yard dash, relay races, high jumping, broad jumping, running broad jump and pole vaulting. To make our landing softer under the pole vault, a few boys dug a pit under it and filled it with sawdust. After trying to pole vault a few times, I gave it up because of the hard landings; the sawdust hadn't exactly made it a soft landing.

Everyone in school liked taking part in track meets. It was exciting to get ribbons for winning, and reminded me of the Fourth-of-July races at the grange hall. The district meet in Colville was more formal and orderly than the local track meets. When we country kids got there in our usual overalls, we saw town kids were wearing shorts outfits. Before every competition, an official called the names of those who had entered. For my first race several girls lined up with me. Accustomed to the starters saying, "On your mark, get set, go," I wasn't expecting a shot to be fired, so didn't start running when the others did. In the next race I was ready for the shot, got a good start and won a ribbon. Waiting for the next competition, the standing broad jump, we girls were standing together and one of the town girls noticed my bare feet. She exclaimed, "You're not going to jump without tennis shoes, are you?" I quickly replied, "I can jump farther without them."

I didn't tell her that I didn't have tennis shoes. Limited by shortage of cash in our family, we had only one pair of shoes at a time, and oxfords were more necessary than tennis shoes. And after I light-footedly won the blue ribbon, beating her and everyone else wearing tennis shoes, she no longer looked scornfully at my bare feet.

At the end of the track meet Mrs. Graham and Mr. Hays seemed pleased with their barefooted and overalled pupils. In spite of not having shorts outfits or tennis shoes, we won a lot of events. At the end of the competition, most of us proudly clutched blue, red and white ribbons on our way back to Pleasant Valley.

Five years after Mrs. Graham came to our school, Lester and I graduated from the eighth grade. Never once in those years did we hear anyone ask her about her "gray ham".

In 1967, after all the Riley kids got through grade school, Pleasant Valley School District No. 32 was dissolved. Like the Arzina School, its enrollment had dwindled too much, as people were giving up on farming and moving. Lawrence Hays bought the two-room school house and tore it down for its lumber. But the bell and its bell tower went to Paul Holter, who had served as a school board member for many years. It wasn't long before the Rice School also closed. The small farms could no longer support families, and people were leaving the area to find work elsewhere. Buses now take all the children in those areas to schools in Kettle Falls.

Coulee Dam Under Construction

Mrs. Graham, an innovative teacher, was full of surprises. After having begun our tradition of a Christmas program at the grange hall, she planned something else that we had never done: we were going to ride a bus more than a hundred miles to see the dam being built at Grand Coulee. Promising that it would be educational, she added, "It's something you will long remember."

In telling about the huge dam being built south of us in the Columbia River, Mrs. Graham said that in 1933 President Franklin D. Roosevelt had authorized funds for the dam to be built under his Public Works Administration program. She added that the dam would provide irrigation to hundreds of acres of desert land around Pasco and Moses Lake in the Columbia Basin. Besides turning useless land into productive farm land, the dam would furnish electric power for industries, which would make more jobs during the Depression.

After getting the school board's permission for the two-day trip, Mrs. Graham made plans for the first week in June, right after school was out. She rented a bus and lined up a volunteer bus driver and several parents to go along as helpers. Then she reserved some tourist cabins in Soap Lake where we would stop overnight. I was glad when Mom volunteered as a helper, after Dad had agreed to take care of Leola and Effie. Mrs. Graham thought the "unique quality" of the lake made the extra miles worthwhile. Not understanding what she meant, I had to wait until we got there to find out.

The bus started out in the cool of the morning, but before we had reached the wheat country around Davenport, we could tell it would be a hot day. All we could think of was getting to that cool lake so we could go swimming.

The week before, our family had gone to Colville, primarily to buy me a bathing suit. Lester and Dora could get into theirs, but I had grown out of mine. Mom and I went into the J.C. Penney store, but couldn't find a suit in my size. Then she astounded me by saying, "Let's go across the street to Barman's and see if we can find one that fits you."

Her statement shocked me, as Barman's clothes were always more expensive than Penney's, and we had never gone there before. Getting to that store, we found several suits in my size, but the bright orange, two-piece suit caught my eye. It felt good when I put it on, and saw in the mirror that it looked good, too. I hoped it didn't cost too much. When Mom said we could take it, I was overjoyed.

And now that we had arrived at Soap Lake, I'd soon be wearing it. The bus had taken us to the tourist cabins first. Eager to get cooled off from the day's hot ride, it didn't take long for us kids to change into our swim suits and get back onto the bus for the short drive to the lake. Arriving there, we made a screaming dash for the clear water and jumped in, splashing water over our heads and into our mouths. The soap lake was well named; it tasted terrible, and reminded me of the times Mom had made me wash my mouth out with soap when I'd said a cuss word. Now we knew what Mrs. Graham meant by the "unique quality" of the lake.

Because of the minerals in the water, we could float easier than we could in the little cove in the Kettle River where Dad had taken us to try to learn how to swim. Despite all its minerals, the water was just as clear as the Columbia. My orange bathing suit glistened as I flashed through the water doing the side stroke. When a couple of boys swam by doing the crawl, I tried to copy them, but splashed more of that soapy-tasting water into my mouth. I decided it would be more fun to flip over and float while watching the clouds overhead.

At the end of that wondrous day, we were all tired and went to bed early. Our group of over thirty people filled several cabins. I shared a sagging double bed with another girl, and during the night she wet the bed. The next morning, while the owner of the cabins and Mrs. Graham were having a serious talk, they kept looking in our direction. Having seen my bed-mate's wet nightgown, Mrs. Graham asked her if she had wet the bed. She denied it, putting the blame on me. But Mrs. Graham had already noticed that it wasn't _my_ nightgown that was wet. My respect for her increased when she hadn't even asked me about it.

That morning we loaded onto the bus and went to see the men working on Coulee Dam. We stopped when we were about a quarter of a mile from the face of a cliff where many men were working. It was hard to imagine what was being built among the rocks in all the noise and whirling dust. Jackhammer workers clung to rocky cliffs drilling holes for dynamite, and other men swarmed over a high framework of scaffolding. It looked like dangerous work. Soon all work stopped in one area so powder monkeys could set off dynamite to blast off the face of a rocky cliff. A huge section of it disappeared in a cloud of dust and flying rocks. It took several seconds before the noise of the blast reached us. Even so, it was the loudest noise I'd ever heard. After several minutes, the dust cleared and we saw a big scar on the rock face. We watched the activity for a couple of hours before turning around and heading back toward the quiet and peaceful life of Pleasant Valley.

Building the dam was very dangerous. Before it was finished in 1941, several construction men died in accidents. The men were so desperate for any kind of work during the Depression, they willingly risked their lives just to earn money.

Dad's Gunshot Wound

When Dad went after a deer, he usually got one. But one time he came home empty handed when he shot himself instead of a deer. The grazing land and thickets of brush on the wooded hills of our isolated farm enticed deer, which often grazed there along with the cattle. When Lester and I found their narrow, pointed prints, we traced their firm impressions with our fingers and visualized a deer standing there recently. But one day, instead of hunting on the mountain above our house, he drove about ten miles over to the Arzina area to hunt with his hunting partners, Pearl Entwistle and Bill Preston.

We raised a few calves and lambs, but couldn't kill them for our own use. Dad sold them to get a little cash money to buy things we couldn't raise – like sugar, clothes, gas and tires. We came as close to living off the land as anyone, relying almost totally on deer for our meat supply. Dad usually hunted with a thirty-thirty lever-action Winchester rifle, but also carried a pistol in a home-made shoulder holster for the killing shot of a deer that was downed but not dead.

On the day he came home empty handed, he drove over to the Arzina area and picked up Bill Preston and Pearl. They hunted on foot on the mountain in back of Pearl's farm and were separated by several yards, aiming to meet up on the other side of the hill. As Dad walked across a side hill, he noticed a dense thicket below him. Knowing deer like to lay in the shade during the hot part of the day, he suspected some might be in the thicket's coolness. He didn't want to walk down the hill, so decided to roll a big boulder into the brush, hoping the noise it made crashing through the brush would scare a deer out into the open so he could get a shot at it.

He bent over the boulder to pry it from the ground. As he strained to free it, his pistol fell out of the holster and dropped butt first onto the boulder. The impact made the pistol fire and the bullet tore through Dad's flesh below his left armpit. He felt under his arm, and when he saw his blood-coated hand, he passed out cold. Bill Preston and Pearl heard the pistol shot and came running, expecting to see Dad standing over a dead deer. Instead, they found him unconscious on the ground – and no deer in sight. Not knowing what was wrong, they bent over to look at him closely and saw blood soaking the front of his shirt, but noticed he was still breathing. About that time, he opened his eyes, relieving their minds. When they unfastened Dad's bib overall strap and unbuttoned his shirt, they saw blood seeping out of the left side of his chest near his armpit. Pearl felt his back, and found his shirt was wet with blood. They rolled him a little to one side and discovered blood oozing out of a hole where the bullet had gone out.

Bill Preston took off his own shirt off and folded it into a thick pad for a bandage, placing it directly over the bullet holes and pressing it to stop the bleeding. Then buttoning his shirt and fastening his overall strap, they tied a piece of binding twine around Dad's chest to keep the bandage in place. Anxious to get him to a doctor, Pearl asked him if he thought he could walk. Dad replied, I'm a little dizzy, but I think I'll be able to make it in a few minutes."

After waiting a short time, Pearl and Bill Preston helped him to his feet and led him down the mountain to the car. Pearl drove as fast as he could over to our place to pick Mom up so she could go to Colville with them. Both men had seen Dad cut the throats of many deer and the blood gushing out hadn't bothered him. What they didn't know was that Dad got sick when he saw <u>human</u> blood. They were surprised later when he told them that seeing his own blood had made him pass out.

When Lester, Dora and I got home from school that day, we were shocked to find Dad in bed in the afternoon. Standing in the open doorway, we could see he was pale. Mom said, "Your father has been shot, but he'll be all right."

Then we crowed through the door to see for ourselves. Even if we hadn't seen his ash-colored face, we'd have known something was wrong. It was the first time we'd ever seen him in bed during in the daytime. In shocked silence we stood beside the bed, feeling scared because of his close call with death. He looked so weak, we were afraid to say anything for fear it would tire him out and make him worse. After we were assured that Dad wasn't dying, Mom said, "We'd better let him rest now; you kids come back out to the kitchen and I'll tell you what happened."

Then she told us how Dad had been shot and how Pearl had driven him to the doctor, ending up with, "He's lucky the bullet didn't go in a couple more inches to the left and hit his heart. Now you see why we tell you to always be careful with guns."

The doctor had wrapped white cloth strips all around Dad's chest to hold a thick pad in place over the holes. We didn't get to see where the bullet had gone through until two days later when Mom let us watch her change the bandage. It was scary seeing how close the bullet had come to his heart. The bullet holes were ugly, shiny and blackish-red with dried blood. I didn't see how they could ever heal shut.

But it didn't take Dad long to recover from his wound. The bullet holes healed, leaving two round, shiny-white, smooth scars. For years afterward when we saw him with his shirt off, we stared in fascination at them, realizing each time how lucky he was not to have been killed. The scars were good reminders to us of what a bullet could do to a person, as well as to a deer.

Dad seemed to feel a little sheepish about shooting himself and passing out. And although he and his friends kidded each other almost every chance they got, I never heard Pearl or Bill Preston razz him about his bullet holes. Perhaps it was because it was too serious to joke about.

Years later my children were just as fascinated by the scars as I had been. All three of them asked time after time to hear the story about how "Papa Bill" got shot. And in a recent letter from Goldie Entwistle, she recalls this incident. "They took him over to your folks' place and Audrey went with them to the doctor. When they got back from town, they were still talking about Bill getting so sick when he saw his own blood.

Hunting Lessons

"By grab, I believe this deer is too big for us to carry home," Dad said to Lester and me. Dressed in our bib overalls and work shirts, we stood looking down at the large doe. Needing meat for the table when it wasn't hunting season, Dad had shot a doe rather than a tough old buck. Dad added, "I'll have to get a horse to pack it home."

He picked up his rifle and took off up the hill to the barn, about a half-mile away, leaving us to guard the deer in case a coyote came along. Dad had already cut the deer's throat to let it bleed out. Lester and I had helped him gut it by keeping the deer on its back, holding the legs out of the way of the knife while he cut down the full length of the stomach. I ran my fingers over the pointed hooves, black and shiny, wondering if they had made the tracks we'd seen earlier in the dirt around the spring.

After Dad got the entrails out, he cut the heart and liver loose. And Lester had cut a forked stick from a nearby bush, so was ready when Dad handed the slippery organs to him. He pushed one side of the stick through the heart and the other through the liver, making them easy to carry. While waiting for Dad's return with the horse, we had found some heavy sticks and pushed the guts down the hill, out of the way of loading the deer.

Betty, our sorrel horse that Dora and I rode to school, was the only horse gentle enough to pack a dead deer. Our other horses were too skittish at the smell of blood and couldn't be trusted. Dad returned, leading Betty, and Lester helped him heave the deer up onto her back. Then taking her neck rope, he led her up the hill while Dad walked alongside to steady the deer and keep it from falling off. I carried the stick holding the heart and liver, breathing in their familiar smell, and thought of how good they would taste for supper.

Reaching the barnyard, I veered off to the house, but Dad and Lester went on past the barn, leading Betty to the thicket behind the well. Going into the kitchen, I gave the heart and liver to Mom, who put them to soak in a pan of cold water. Upon seeing them, she had said, "Good, I see Dad got a deer."

I ran out to watch Dad and Lester. Reaching the thicket, they tied a rope around the deer's hind legs and hoisted it up to a tree limb, the one with the pulley wired to it. The deer needed to hang a couple of days before it was cut up. The shady thicket was cool – and before hunting season opened, it made a good hiding place, just in case a game warden happened to come looking around. Although the deer had to hang for awhile, the heart and liver were ready to eat for supper. Mom had washed them, cut them into thin slices to fry in her big cast-iron skillets.

Dad first started taking me hunting when I was only eight. He'd been taking Lester for a couple of years and I'd been eager to go, too. We were too young to carry rifles, he just needed us to do the "driving" for him. It didn't matter to him that I was a girl; he knew I could run through the brush, too, and chase the deer out so he could get a shot at them.

Before it was against the law to hunt with dogs, Dad had taken our dog, Tan, to chase the deer out of the brush so he could get a shot at them. Old Tan never attacked the deer; he only scared them so they'd run out of hiding. He was smart, and when he heard Dad mention his thirty-thirty rifle or "deer hunting", Tan's ears perked up and he'd go stand by the rifles, ready to go. But when he wasn't supposed to go with us, we had to tie him up so he couldn't follow.

Dad's method of hunting was to get on a stand – a spot where he knew deer would pass by – and send us through the thickets to chase deer out. He knew from past hunts which direction the deer ran and where the best spots for his "stands". That morning, after taking Lester and me into the timber below the house and telling us when we should start our drive, he had left us to get on his stand. For the specified time we waited, we talked only in whispers, but when we began the drive, we yelled and whacked the bushes and trees with sticks to make a lot of noise. Our sweep through the brush on separate routes covered a wide area. If any deer were around, they jumped up and ran, their flight taking them past Dad's stand.

We didn't know that we had "jumped" a deer until we heard the boom of Dad's rifle. We stopped and stood still. Another shot boomed. To be sure he was through shooting, we waited like he'd told us to; not wanting to get into his line of fire. We licked our lips, thinking how good the heart and liver were going to taste. Besides, we were tired and ready to go home. Tramping across the hills and through the brush was hard work.

No more shots came, so we set off to find Dad. Coming out of the thicket, we looked around and like so many times before, found him squatting beside a dead deer, sharpening his jack knife on a little whetstone. The round whitish outline of that whetstone marked the bib pocket of all his overalls. He must have thought it bad luck to sharpen his knife before a hunt, as he always waited until after he had killed his deer to do it. But it took more than luck; he was a good hunter and never missed if he had a clear shot. As his drivers, we learned there was a lot more to hunting than just shooting. He taught us about tracks. A deer made a different kind of track when running than walking. He'd see a big deer track where the two parts of the pointed hoof had spread apart, and say, "Now here's a big buck and he's running to beat hell!"

Lester and I became so curious about deer tracks that we watched for them on our way home from school and taught Dora to watch, too. On horseback one day while passing a boggy thicket, Lester's horse, Pet, shied suddenly, almost jumping out from under him. Wondering what had startled her, we scanned the ground for tracks. Instead of finding deer tracks in the soft dirt, we were surprised to find a big bear track, looking odd with the toes completely separated from the oblong pad. A scary feeling came over me as I realized that the bear might be just inside the thicket line. Lester exclaimed, "So that's what scared Pet – she smelled the bear, and he must still be in there!"

With that, he lit out fast, heading Pet across the plowed field toward home about a quarter of a mile away. I kicked Betty into a gallop and yelled, "Hang on, Dora," and we hightailed after Lester. Ten minutes later when he pulled Pet up at the barn, we weren't far behind.

Dad showed us more than just tracks. On another hunting trip, we came across a patch of flattened-out grass. Lester and I felt it with the palms of our hands, and were surprised to find the ground warm. Looking at the flat space, then at the dark brown, oval droppings that were still steaming, Dad said, "Some deer spent the night here, and they've just left; look for tracks to see which way they headed."

At the beginning of every hunting trip, he told us where to meet after getting through with the drive, describing the location where he'd be, so we could meet and walk home together, even though he wanted us to be able to find our way home alone if we got separated. On one of my first drives when I eight, I went a slight bit astray. When Lester and I had started the drive, we walked several yards apart. But mis-judging my route through thick brush, I veered too far right. Coming out onto the open, I couldn't see him anywhere. Scanning the country side for him, I could see the lower ridges and swales below me. I could see Split Rock far below and the Columbia River almost a mile beyond. But I couldn't spot either Dad or Lester, who should be on the stand together by this time. I looked long and hard, and finally spotted them sitting together on a hillside far below, looking very small. They were so far away, I didn't know if they could hear me, but cupping my hands around my mouth, I yelled as loud as I could, "Dad, wait for me."

Hearing me, he yelled back. "Come on down here."

With so much rough country separating us and no trail through the brush, I couldn't see an easy route. Feeling foolish, I yelled, "How am I going to get there?"

Dad yelled back, "Fly!"

Heading down the slope, I dropped into gullies and picked my through brush, losing sight of them. It took me at least twenty minutes to reach them. Relieved to be with them at last, I sank to the ground beside Dad, leaning against his knee. I felt safe again.

Long before we were old enough to shoot, Dad had us kids help him clean and oil the rifles. Fully loaded, they stood in a corner behind the kitchen door. Neither he nor Mom worried about us kids playing with the rifles. Early on, we had learned that if we didn't obey our parents, we got a slap on our behinds. Training us early, they said that guns weren't playthings, and we never touched them unless we were told to do so. Dad explained, "A rifle isn't any good unless it's loaded. If I have to shoot in a hurry, I don't have time to load it."

To clean the rifles, Dad, Lester and I went outside on the porch where there was less chance of hitting someone if the rifle accidentally fired when we were ejecting the shells. I carried "my" rifle and watched to see what Dad would do. Pointing his rifle at the ground, he worked the lever of the Winchester. The shells flipped out, landing in the dirt at our feet. After checking to see that the last shell in the barrel had come out, he carefully lowered the hammer. Then we picked up all the shells and put them in our overall pockets to later reload the rifle. After watching, I felt I could empty my rifle without any problem. He warned me, "You have to pull down hard on the lever or the shells won't come out."

Copying him, I pointed the barrel at the ground and pulled the lever down hard with my right hand. I had seen the effort it took Dad to lower the hammer, so when I had flipped out all the shells, I handed the rifle to him to let the hammer down. He'd told us we could hurt the firing pin by letting the hammer down hard, and I knew my thumb wasn't strong enough to hold the hammer and let it down easy.

We three sat on the porch, each with a rifle in our laps. Mom had given us a clean white cloth. Dad tore off a thin piece about four inches long. After putting it through the eye of the cleaning rod, he squirted a little oil on it. Ready to start, he pulled the rifle's lever down to open the breech. Standing the rifle on its butt, he pushed the cleaning rod into the muzzle until the white cloth appeared at the open breech. After running the cloth through the barrel a few times, he replaced the oily strip with a clean one and ran it down the barrel to remove any excess oil. He then took the cleaning rod out of the barrel. Holding the rifle up to the light, he looked down the barrel to see that it was clean.

Satisfied with the inside, Dad took the used oily strip and wiped the heavy wooden stock, the steel magazine, hammer and long barrel, being careful not to bump the sights. All through, he re-loaded, putting one cartridge in the firing chamber and six in the magazine, pushing them one by one through the little spring opening, like a trapdoor, on the outside of the rifle. Finished cleaning and oiling his rifle, Dad stood it behind the kitchen door, saying, "Now it's ready for the next time I need it."

Lester and I were now ready to clean two other rifles. Looking down the barrel of mine, I was surprised to see it wasn't smooth like the outside, but had lines looping all down the inside. "Dad, why does the inside of the barrel have all these lines in it?," I asked.

He replied, "Those are called 'riflings' and they help make the bullets go straight."

In unloading the rifle, I had been surprised to find working the lever-action so enjoyable. Its oiled metallic sound was nice to hear and, with my right hand gripping the lever, I could feel a silkiness in the smooth-working action. When we finished cleaning and oiling the rifles, we took them to Dad to reload, giving him the shells out of our pockets. By cleaning the rifles and carrying them home after a hunt, we became comfortable with them long before we were old enough to shoot.

A few years later he got us started shooting by saying, "I want you to do some target practicing today. Take the twenty-twos and go shoot those ground squirrels that are digging holes up in the alfalfa field."

Apparently Dad's hunting lessons sunk in. None of us ever got truly lost in the woods or had any hunting accidents. Having seen Dad's gunshot wound, we knew what a bullet could do to a person. One of the most important lessons he taught us was that a gun is a dangerous weapon; that we should never point it at anything unless we intend to shoot.

Although I was never much of a deer hunter, Dad's hunting lessons gave me a life-long love of the hills and mountains. And more than eighty years after he said never to point a gun at anyone, I cringe when a child points a toy pistol at me.

Going to Town in the Star

The wind blowing through the open car whipped at our faces, but summer's cool breeze felt good. Dad had unsnapped the clear isinglass curtains from the Star's door frames and would leave them off until fall when the weather turned cold. But he left the black canvas top up for protection from the sun. We were heading for Colville to stock up on food supplies that we couldn't grow and to buy new shoes for us kids before school started.

Even though we were going only fifteen or twenty miles an hour down the hill, the car bounced as we ran over loose rocks on the narrow dirt road of the Heidegger Hill. From my seat on the right side, I had a good view of the drop-off into the small canyon. I hoped we wouldn't meet a car coming uphill, as the solid rock wall on the left and drop-off on the right didn't leave much room for passing. Mom sat in the front seat holding baby Effie; Dora and Leola were squished between Lester and me in back.

Colville, about twenty-five miles away, was the main shopping area for many miles around. It was also the county seat. Dad drove to town several times a year, but today the whole family was going. Lester, Dora and I needed new shoes before school started and Mom had other things on her shopping list, too. We all felt we were going on a real outing. Our drive would take almost an hour. After reaching the Pleasant Valley Road, we could go faster, as it was almost level the rest of the way to the State Highway, which was paved and didn't have any sharp turns.   Soon we came into sight of the Columbia River, then crossed the Colville River and drove through the small town of Kettle Falls. Dad had to shift into low gear to climb the crooked uphill road leading to Meyers Falls. From there it was only a short distance to Colville.   It was our biggest town in the county with many buildings made of stone or brick. The cream-colored courthouse had a lawn and big shade trees, making it look cool even on hot days. There was also a hospital, post office, banks, library, two department stores, Greyhound bus depot, restaurants, a dime store and hardware store, a couple of taverns and a weekly newspaper, The Stateman's Index. The fair grounds, with a grandstand, horse racing track and exhibit barns, were down
a hill from the main part of town, near the flour mill.

Dad parked in front of the J. C. Penney store. He took Lester to Newland's Tavern to use their rest room; Mom took us girls inside Penney's and up to the second floor to its rest room before we began shopping. In addition to food supplies and our school shoes, Mom needed to buy other things: long cotton stockings for herself and us girls, long woolen underwear for all of us, and cotton material so she could make some dresses. Dad and Lester joined us in the shoe department and watched as Dora and I tried on sturdy oxfords; Lester tried on work shoes that came up above his ankles. Dad felt the toes to make sure they had room for growth, as they had to last until school was out next spring. Then he left us to return to the tavern to meet other farmers and play a little penny-ante poker. Mom took us kids with her to buy our groceries.

On our way to the store, we passed another tavern which had a large wooden sign over its door, "No Indians Allowed." Dad had several Indian friends and I wondered why they couldn't join him in the tavern. Mom explained that it was against the law to sell liquor to them. The law was passed a long time ago when settlers were coming west. The government didn't want traders to sell firewater to Indians, who might then get drunk and attack the settlers. Now, many years later, the law hadn't been changed.

After buying supplies at the grocery store that we couldn't raise on the farm – like oatmeal, farina, sugar, rice, macaroni, cheese, peanut butter, Karo syrup (in half-gallon cans with bails), raisins, soap and a few other items, Mom was finished with shopping.   We didn't have to buy flour. Once a year Dad took some of our wheat to the flour mill and traded for enough flour to last a year. Mom baked almost all of our bread, and we seldom bought meat. Dad butchered a pig and a small sheep every year. He couldn't kill our steers for our own use, as he needed the cash money he got from selling them. Besides, he could always get a deer when we ran out of other meat.

While we'd been at the grocery store, Dad had gone to the R.E. Lee Hardware Store to buy ammunition for his deer rifles and the twenty-two rifles. He'd also bought a paper bag of hoar hound drops, his favorite candy. It was sweet, didn't cost much and lasted a long time. And soon we were all in the Star again, heading home. When we reached the Colville River about a mile out of town, Dad pulled off the road for a picnic lunch. I helped Mom make sandwiches from salami and bakery bread. Lester, Dora and I ate ours quickly so we could wade in the river for a few minutes. Then we all piled into the car again for the long ride home, sucking our hoar hound candy.

Winter Driving

Because of our frequent snowstorms and freezing weather, Dad didn't go into town more than two or three times all winter. After each snowstorm, he had to hitch a team of horses to his home-made vee snowplow to clear the snow off the road the half mile or so down to the county road below Abe Heidegger's house. Getting the Star ready to go took a lot of time and work. He had to put chains on the back tires, fill the radiator with water and turn the crank until the engine started. The chains were needed, as both the Heidegger Road and the Pleasant Valley Road had snow left on them even after snowplows had gone over them. And when snow was on the highway clear to town, Dad left the chains on all the way. Since they got a lot of wear, a link often broke, then it clanked against the fender making a continuous whap-whap until he stopped and wired the link back to the main chain.

When Dad returned home after driving in winter, he drained the radiator so there wouldn't be any water to freeze and crack the engine block. So when he needed to go somewhere again, his first step was to fill the radiator with warm water. After that, he could work at starting the engine. If he hadn't driven for a month or so, the car was difficult to start. Putting the gear shift in neutral, he pulled out the choke, set the spark and gas levers which were on the steering column. Then he took the long handled crank from under the front seat, stuck the end into a hole just below the radiator and turned the handle as hard as he could. If it started, he removed the crank and ran back to the driver's seat to adjust the choke and slow down the racing engine. When the engine stopped spluttering and ran smoothly, he put the crank back under the seat -- the Star was ready to go. He had to be careful to set the spark lever just right. Some drivers had had their thumbs dislocated or an arm broken if the spark came too soon, as it caused the crank to kick backwards. If Mom had to go somewhere in the summer, she had a hard time cranking the car, despite the good muscles she had developed.

When we had very far to go in winter, we could expect a cold ride, as the engine provided almost no heat. Mom took along two or three flat irons that had got hot while she was cooking breakfast. About the only places we went by car in the winter was to town or to the grange hall. No heat got as far as the back seat, so we took warmed blankets along to cover us kids. As soon as cold weather came, Dad had put the isinglass snap-on side curtains back on the car, which kept out most of the wind. Getting to our destination, he covered the hood of the car with a heavy blanket to keep the water in the radiator from freezing. It helped retain some of the engine heat, giving protection until our return trip. When we got home again, he reversed the process and drained the water out of the radiator.

Because of all the effort involved in winter driving, we didn't go any place unless we had a special reason. That was fine with me. Going down the steep, slippery, snow-covered Heidegger Road didn't appeal to me. We hadn't heard of any cars that slid off the road into the canyon, but I didn't want ours to be the first one.

Trapping

"Are coyotes good to eat?", the boys watching Dad asked as they came upon him skinning out the two he'd just taken out of his traps.

Without hesitating, he replied, "Oh yes, we eat them all the time."

He had thought of a good joke he could pull on our neighbor and friend, Frank Rupert, the boys' grandfather whom they were visiting. Living in Colville and spending little time on the farm, they hadn't learned much about country life. The boys eyed the skinned coyotes hanging from a tree limb, and continued their questioning, "What parts are best?"

Dad held up a back leg and replied, "I like thin slices cut off of this; they fry up into good steaks."

Since Frank wanted his newborn calves to be safe from coyotes, but was too feeble to do any trapping himself, he was glad to have Dad's trap line extended into his farm. After finding the coyotes in the traps, Dad had tied their hind legs with a rope and hoisted them up to a tree limb. While he was skinning them out, the boys, who'd been exploring the range, had spotted him and gone to investigate. The boys eyed the hanging coyotes, one all skinned out down to the red flesh, the other still wearing its grayish-tan fur coat. Curious, they had started their questions. Pointing to the front leg, Dad continued his joke, "We use this part for mulligan stew; but the ribs don't have much meat on them, so we just feed them to the dogs."

Still thinking about Frank's reaction to getting coyote meat for supper, Dad cut off the hind quarter and said, "Frank would sure be glad to get some fresh meat. If you take this to him, he could cut off some steaks for your supper."

The boys thought that would be a good idea, so Dad 'generously' sent the whole hind quarter home with the boys, chuckling to himself when he thought of Frank's explosion at getting it. And he was still chuckling when he came home, bringing the coyote hides – but no meat for our supper! He told us what he'd done, knowing Frank would enjoy the joke, too. And sure enough, the next time he saw Frank, they laughed at the ridiculous idea of eating a coyote. For years they both got a kick out of telling people how Dad had furnished fresh meat for Frank's supper.

That first winter after we moved to the isolated Curry Place, we'd heard coyotes howling and yipping and saw their tracks. After finding muskrat traps and the small tracks of mink, too, Dad made up his mind to try to catch these fur-bearing animals, as he could sell their pelts to the fur buyers in Spokane. When no one in eastern Washington had a dime to spare during the Depression, he had just discovered how he could make some extra money. So during the winter when pelts were best, he had started his trap line. He located the best places to set his traps by finding animal trails. They weren't beaten-down trails, just numerous light prints in the dirt. After the first snow, they were a lot easier to spot. He spaced the traps out along these trails and in the openings through the brush.

As the oldest girl in our family of five children, I had chores to do in the house before helping Dad outside. Upon hearing him tell Lester that he could go with him that morning to check his traps, I told him I wanted to go, too. Now ten, I was still a tomboy at heart, wanting to be outside in the hills rather than cooped up in the house. I finished washing the breakfast dishes, then swept the kitchen floor, and was ready to go when they were. We watched Dad set a coyote trap. He scooped out a depression in the middle of an animal trail, pried open the jaws of a trap and set it, then placed it in the low spot. Picking up the chain attached to the trap, he fastened it to a log and said, "If there isn't a log or a tree near where I want to put my trap, I'll drive a strong stake into the ground and fasten the chain to it. If the trap's chain isn't fastened to something solid, the animal will just run off, dragging the trap with him, and we'll be out the trap and the pelt, too."

After fastening the chain to a log, he took a small bottle of dark liquid out of his pocket. Unscrewing its lid, he sprinkled a few drops on the trap, saying, "This scent covers up the man-smell."

The bottle held some store-bought scent that smelled like rotten eggs. After getting a whiff of the vile-smelling stuff, Lester and I knew why coyotes wouldn't be able to smell Dad's scent on it; we couldn't smell anything for awhile. Then he put a few small sticks over the trap to partially conceal it, being careful not to touch the round trigger of its gaping jaws, which would spring the trap.

After getting that first whiff of the scent, we always knew when Dad had been setting traps. If he spilled even one drop on his hands, the smell clung for a long time. Our strong lye soap didn't get it off the first time he washed. And the few times he got careless and spilled scent on his overalls were even worse. Mom's wash day was hard enough without having to smell rotten eggs while she scrubbed his clothes on the washboard. When we heard her say, "Bill, I wish you'd be more careful with that scent," we knew she was a trifle upset with him.

Most of the animals he caught were muskrats, but a few mink and coyotes got into his traps, too. The mink pelts brought the most money, coyotes the least. But some years the government paid a five dollar bounty money for each coyote, which helped make up for the smaller payment on their pelts. Dad checked his trap line about every other day. When he caught an animal, he stepped on the spring to release the trap's jaws, took the animal out, re-set the trap, put scent on it and then concealed it. When he found traps sprung, but empty, he set them again, hoping they'd catch something the next time.

Coyotes were heavy, so he skinned them out before going home. Since the smaller animals weren't too heavy to carry, he took them home and skinned them there. He put all the pelts on his home-made stretchers to dry. Watching Dad skin a muskrat reminded me of the way I pulled a sweater off over my head. Using his sharp jack knife, he started by cutting clear through the leg bone right above the paw, while leaving it attached to the hide. He hung the muskrat up by its hind legs so it was upside down and easier to work on. He continued by cutting the skin across the back end of the body, making a long cut from one hind leg over to the other. This let him pull the hide down all around the body while cutting the thin tissue between the hide and body. Making careful strokes with his knife, he said, "If I nick the hide, the fur buyer will call it a 'damaged' pelt and won't pay as much money."

When he had the hide pulled down to the head, he had to cut more slowly, making short strokes. The tight skin seemed to be glued to the head bones. It took almost as much time to skin the head as it had done to skin the whole body. When he finished, the hide was whole, but wrong side out. It looked like its owner had pulled it off over its head – just like a sweater, and walked off, leaving the body behind. And this is the way Dad pulled it over the top end of the stretcher, the shiny dark fur on the inside and the raw white hide on the outside so it could dry. He had made wooden stretchers in different sizes to fit the animals he caught. A mink was small and skinny, so its stretcher had to be long and narrow, five or six inches wide and sixteen to eighteen inches long. A muskrat was broader as well as longer, and its stretcher was about twice as wide as the mink's. It was the same with the coyote stretcher. Adjustable in width, it was longer and wider than the muskrat's. Dad tapered the top ends of the stretcher boards so they were smaller to fit the skin of the head. He also made the stretchers long enough so he could carry them without touching the pelts. It took two or three weeks for them to cure. One afternoon when we got home from school, Dad was taking some muskrat pelts off the stretchers. Running to him, I eagerly asked, "Can I help?"

"You can if your hands are clean," he said, so I hurried into the house and washed. I picked up a pelt which I knew was a muskrat by its size, I carried it over to a block of wood and sat down. Holding onto the white rawhide pelt with one hand, I pulled the wooden stretcher out with the other. Although the pelt was stiff enough to stand by itself, it was still pliable. I turned the pelt right side out, pulling the hind part down over the head. And once again, the whole glossy, dark brown fur was on the outside
where it belonged, looking almost like it had before Dad took the muskrat's body out of it.

I stroked the pelt in the direction the fur lay, from its head to its tail, admiring its softness and beauty. The next pelt I worked on was a mink, smaller than the muskrat. As I turned it right side out, the glossy fur appeared so dark it was almost black. Holding it on my lap after removing the stretcher, my fingers sank into the silky softness of the beautiful fur. I tried to picture the rich lady who'd be wearing a coat made from mink pelts, wondering how anyone could be rich enough to buy one. During these hard time, we kids went barefoot all summer because we'd worn out our old shoes and couldn't get new ones until just before school started. When Dad was telling Mom how much money he thought he could get from the pelts, he said that he didn't know, then added, "I sure hope our new president, Franklin D. Roosevelt, will be able to bring better times to farmers."

Of all the time Dad spent working his trap line, the day he pulled the joke on Frank by sending him the coyote meat for supper gave him the most enjoyment. A few years later Frank got even with him. We'd had a heavy rain that lasted for several days, and part of Frank's hillside slid down, crossed the county road and ended up in our oat field, the trees still standing upright. After the rain, both men had gone out to survey their land and met at the landslide. Lester and I had tagged along with Dad and we heard Frank's joking reply, "Bill, "I want you to bring my land back and put it up on my bank where it belongs. That will teach you to send coyote steaks to me!"

Wash Day

It was wash day, and with breakfast over, Mom gave Lester and me what she called her marching orders. "Get busy and start carrying water to fill the tubs and wash boiler. I want to get an early start and it will take quite awhile to heat the water for our washing."

We grabbed two 10-quart galvanized milk buckets by their bails and set out for the well, about a hundred yards from the house. Halfway there, we heard a clanking behind us and turned to see Dora swinging a bucket so she could help, too. At thirteen and eleven, Lester and I were strong enough to carry a full bucket of water in each hand, but eight-year old Dora could only carry one. Dad helped a time or two, but the main job of carrying water fell to us. This wasn't much work except for wash day and our Saturday-night baths, which for seven people meant many trips to the well.

Lester untied the well bucket's rope from the pulley and framework and let the bucket drop. The pulley made it easier pulling a full bucket up out of the well than if we'd had to lift it up hand over hand. Lester filled our buckets, then poured enough water in Dora's so it was half-full. Returning to the kitchen, we emptied the buckets it into the wash boiler on the stove and headed back to the well for more. It took several trips to fill the wash tubs and boiler. Mom had a good hot fire going. She wanted the water to heat up fast so she could finish scrubbing clothes before noon, as the summer sun would   make working outside too hot for comfort. The reservoir attached to the right side of the cook stove heated only a small amount of water, not near enough for the amount needed.

In summer, we set up the wash tubs on benches in the yard so we could scrub clothes on the washboard outside and not slop water all over the kitchen floor. Washing clothes in the winter, we always had to mop the floor because we couldn't keep from splashing water out of the tubs. It was also cooler outside away from the hot cook stove – if we could finish before the sun got too hot. The round-ended wash boiler and the two round zinc wash tubs took a lot of water, requiring many trips to the well. And later, when the rinse water got soapy, Mom dumped it out and we had to carry more water. So that Mom wouldn't run out of firewood for the cook stove while heating water, Lester and I also had to keep the wood box full. But with the woodshed close to the back door, that job was easy.

While we kids were busy with our jobs, Mom started sorting the dirty clothes into different piles. She threw all the white clothes into one pile, the colored clothes into another, and bib overalls into yet another pile. As Dora and I wore overalls most of the time, the same as Dad and Lester, they were enough to make a big stack by themselves. After Mom was finished sorting, she put some of the white clothes into the boiler and shaved some soap curls from a bar of yellow Fels Naptha soap into the boiler full of clothes. I thought the soap curls looked a lot like the shavings Dad made from a piece of stove wood when he started a fire.

After the first batch of clothes had boiled for a few minutes, Mom lifted them out piece by piece with her long clothes stick, which she had made by peeling the bark off of a green tree branch, and put them into the wash tub. Then she put a second batch of white clothes into the boiler. Now she could go to work on the first batch of white clothes that had boiled. She took the wash board off a nail on the wall, put it into the wash tub full of dirty clothes and started scrubbing. The wash tub sitting on a bench was at a good height for both Mom and me to work. We set the legs of the washboard in the bottom of the tub of hot water and rested its wooden top against our stomachs. Mom scrubbed until her arms got tired, then I took over. I had started helping her scrub on the board when I was about nine. Until then I had only helped by carrying water and wood, and hanging clothes on the line. At eleven, I felt like an old hand and could scrub on the washboard for ten or fifteen minutes before my arms gave out.

Washing one piece of clothing at a time, we scrunched it up in our hands while rubbing it up and down on the metal ridges of the washboard. This scrubbing, combined with the yellow soap we used, got most of the dirt out. Washing sheets and towels was the hardest to do. Mom washed those, leaving the smaller pieces for me. The soap was never hard to find, as it sat on the narrow "shelf" above the ridges of the washboard. After washing each piece, we ran it through the hand-operated wringer into two tubs of rinse water until that batch was finished. Since the washboard was propped against our stomachs, it was impossible to keep our fronts from getting wet. Putting the clothes through the wringer got more water out than squeezing them by hand. One person turned the handle of the wringer clamped onto the edge of the wash tub while another fed the clothes through the rollers of the wringer. Lester, Dora and I took turns doing this while Mom was busy taking more clothes out of the wash boiler on the stove. After rinsing and running them through the wringer a second time, they were ready to be hung on the clothesline to dry.

Because of their thick material and size, denim overalls were too heavy to scrub on the board. We put them into a tub of warm, soapy water and let them soak until we had washed everything else, then started on them. We pushed the plunger up and down several times into the pile of overalls in the tub. The plunger was a piece of cone-shaped tin with spiral chambers within, attached to a straight wooden handle like a broom stick. It got the overalls pretty clean, except for Dad's where he had spilled oil or scent from his trapping on them.

Mom starched all the dresses, blouses and even Dad's blue chambray work shirts. After making the starch by boiling corn starch and water, she thinned it out with more water before dipping the clothes in the starchy mixture and running them through the wringer. On a summer day, the clothes dried in an hour, but in winter, it was a different story. On a freezing day, the lighter pieces froze almost as soon as we pinned them to the line – and our fingers felt like they were freezing, too. Later, when we took the frozen pieces off the line, they were so stiff it was like carrying a stack of boards. But when they thawed out, they were dry! After washing and rinsing the last pile of dirty overalls and hanging them up, we still weren't through. We had to empty the water from the wash boiler and tubs, wash them and then mop the kitchen floor.

It's no wonder that the drudgery of wash day made all of us tired.   There wasn't an easier way to do it, as we didn't have electricity or the money to buy a gasoline-powered washing machine. Ironing the clothes wasn't any fun, either. After sprinkling our shirts and dresses, we set them aside until our flat irons got hot. To test the iron's heat, we clamped the wooden handle to it and lifted it off the stove. Slapping our wet fingers against the bottom of the iron, we knew by the sizzle if it was hot enough to use. When the iron lost its heat, we put it back on the stove, removed the handle and clamped it to one of the other irons that was hot.

Mom and I could finish the basket of ironing in about three hours. Only one of us could work at a time, as we just had one ironing board. Even taking turns, it seemed like we'd never get done. None of us enjoyed wash day or the ironing day that followed. But all the hard work we did made Lester, Dora and me enjoy our freedom, and that's when we went out and roamed the hills.

Doctor Mom

A bunch of mad yellow jackets swarmed out of the hole in the outside wall of the house and attacked me and two of our visitors. We ran back to the front of the house where Mom talked with the others. Knowing how to take care of bee stings, Mom quickly made up a baking soda paste to put on them. After putting globs of it on the visitors' stings, she turned to help me. I'd been stung so many times, I'd already broken out in red welts all over my body. Dabbing the white paste on my arm, she soon realized she needed to use a different cure. Dropping my arm, she said, "Ines, I'm going to give you a soda water bath; it's the fastest way of covering all your stings."

We set a zinc wash tub in the yard and filled it with water, then Mom dumped a whole box of Arm & Hammer baking soda in and stirred it up. Before the soda dissolved, I had my clothes off and was in the tub. I didn't care if the visitors saw me naked – I just wanted that healing water to stop the stinging. Her soda bath was the right medicine, as the welts soon disappeared and the stinging stopped. She had told us that Dad would find a way to deal with the yellow-jackets. And she was right about that, too; that night he sprayed poison into the hole in the side of the house. The next morning there were no more yellow jackets buzzing around, so he nailed a board over the hole to keep others from coming in.

The bee stings were a nuisance, but weren't as dangerous as the rusty nails we stepped on with our bare feet. At the spot where an old barn once stood, loose boards lay strewn around, some with nails still in them. While running across that area one day, I stepped on a short board with a nail sticking straight up. The nail went so far in that when I lifted my foot to walk, the board lifted off the ground, too. Being a bit squeamish about blood, I didn't want to take the board off. So with it nailed to my foot, I hopped fifty yards to the house to find Mom. Unlike me, she wasn't squeamish, but took hold of the board and pulled it off. Then she mixed boric acid in water and told me to put my foot in it. After about a half hour of soaking, she dried my foot, then poured turpentine over it making sure some of the turpentine went into the hole. It stung enough to make me cry, which I hadn't done when I stepped on the nail. The puncture wound healed and I didn't get lock-jaw or blood poisoning. It was a wonder, as none of us had ever had a tetanus shots.

Nails caused our worst injuries, but didn't keep Mom very busy. Picking slivers made her keep a sharp needle handy. Slivers came off the wood we packed into the house, and it seemed like we couldn't walk through brush without getting thorns stuck somewhere. We wouldn't tell her about them until they festered. Then she dug them out with a needle and poured turpentine on our sores.

Mom took good care of us, too when we had measles and chicken pox. Having heard sunlight could damage our eyes when we had the measles, she kept the window shades pulled down, and made us stay in bed long after we wanted to get up and roam around outside. None of us kids ever had a problem serious enough to go to a doctor. When we got bad colds in the winter and coughed a lot, she rubbed Vick's VapoRub on our chests before bedtime. And many times we awakened to find her bending over us, rubbing another application on. When we had whooping cough, and she thought we needed stronger medicine, she put mustard plasters on our chests.

She made the mustard plaster by mixing together flour and dry mustard and stirring in enough hot water to make a gooey paste. After putting the mixture between two pieces of cloth so they stuck together, she put the plaster on our chests for about fifteen minutes. Mom was careful not to use too much mustard in the mix or leave it too long, as it could otherwise burn our skin. We liked the treat of milk toast that she gave us when we were sick. After toasting a piece of home-made bread on top of the cook stove, she soaked it in warm milk, put it on a plate, poured cream on it, and then sprinkled sugar on top. It somehow tasted better when we were sick than when we were well.

We liked Mom's medicines better than Dad's. He had two remedies for colds and sore throats. One was kerosene, which he poured from the lantern. Holding it by its base, he tipped it just enough to dribble some of it into a spoon. After adding a small amount of sugar, he handed it to the sick one, saying, "Coal-oil is what I took for a cold when I was little. It will be good for your throat."

Not having much faith in Dad's doctoring, we suspected his cure might be more dangerous than the cold. We knew kerosene was burnable, but if he told us to do something, we obeyed. His other "cure" for a sore throat was a hot toddy. He gave it to us at bedtime, pouring a tablespoon of his own moonshine whiskey into a cup of hot water and adding a teaspoon of sugar. We would have drunk more than one cup if he had let us, as the hot toddy tasted a whole lot better than his dose of kerosene. His first doctoring of Leola made him re-think his dosage. She had sat in his lap, happily drinking the liquid as he spooned it into her mouth. Then she slid off his lap and walked toward two-year old Effie, sitting on a stool. Trying to hug her, Leola staggered, pulled Effie off the stool and they both fell to the floor in a pile. Leola burst out giggling and Effie joined in this new "game." Seeing the reaction to his "medicine," Dad decided it was too strong for a four-year old.

Since Mom never made use of either of Dad's "special medicines," we felt she never approved of them. But some time later, we kids were glad she didn't agree with him. When Effie had almost choked trying to swallow his spoonful of kerosene, she said, "That's enough. That's the last time we'll take kerosene for a cold."

We had the usual childhood diseases, stepped on nails, ran into barbed-wire fences on our sleds, got stung, fell off or got bucked off the horses and fell out of trees. Despite all these, none of us were ever hurt so badly that "Doctor" Mom couldn't cure us.

July 3, 1935

Tomorrow we'd be going to the grange hall for the annual Fourth-of-July celebration. Dad and Mom wouldn't think of missing the festivities on the most exciting day of summer when almost everyone in the area would be attending. Thinking about last year's celebration, I remembered how Paul Holter had started our foot races by calling, "On your mark, get set, go," and how my age group of girls had run as fast as we could to the finish line. Besides having a chance to win money in the various races, we would have fun playing with friends we hadn't seen since school was out in May. They all lived across the hills more than three miles away, and since Dad wouldn't let us ride the horses in summer when he was working them, we would have had to walk to visit them. Mom, who seldom left the farm, was looking forward to the outing even more than we were.

Dora and I were having our straight hair wound up in rag curlers so we could have curly hair for the big day. To get it, we were willing to put up with the tugs as Mom wrapped wet strands of our hair around rag curlers, which would stay in our hair all day.

The Quillisascut Grange sponsored the celebration. But it wasn't only for members; it was for everyone. More than a hundred people drove in from miles around to enjoy it. Some helped with the program or to work in the booths and help with the races. Others, like Mom who had to watch over Leola and Effie, came just to share in the holiday fun and visit with friends. Grown-ups probably considered the main events to be the big picnic under the shade trees and the short program inside the hall. The program last year had consisted of a couple of speeches, some patriotic songs and a special march by the grange's drill team.

Our heads were full of the fun we were going to have at the celebration. Since early June we had been counting the days off; now only one day was left. But that day offered no excitement, just hard work. We had to shock a late cutting of hay. Several days of rain in June had kept Dad from mowing earlier. Then after he mowed the hay, he had to rake it into windrows to let the hay dry. If not totally dry before we hauled it to the barn, it would mildew and make the cows and horses sick.

Dad had other work to do, so Mom, Lester, Dora and I had to do the shocking. But Lester, at thirteen, was strong and could shock almost as fast as Dad could. As soon as Mom finished winding my hair up, we were ready to start while the morning was still cool. Taking our pitch forks and a gallon jug of drinking water, we headed out past the barn to the hay field. Effie and Leola went along, as at two and four, they were too little to stay in the house by themselves. All five of us kids were bare footed as usual and wore bib overalls. Mom wore a faded old cotton house dress and heavy oxfords.

After an hour, the blazing sun had burned off the morning coolness. Sweat ran down our faces as our pitchforks pulled the loose green hay from the windrows and piled it in individual shocks. Dust and small bits of hay settled on us and got down our necks, making us feel itchy. We didn't enjoy working in the hot sun, but it was a perfect day for drying thick hair wound up in rag curlers.

After finishing the shocking that afternoon, we got ready for our baths. Lester and I made several trips to the well, carrying two buckets of water at a time. While it heated in the copper-bottomed wash boiler on top of the cook stove, Mom mixed up a cake to take to the picnic. By the time she it put together, the oven was just the right temperature and the cake baked while we bathed.   The warm water felt good after our hot, sticky work in the hay field and we felt refreshed, as well as clean. We'd been so dirty when we finished that we hadn't even minded the extra work of carrying water.

Fourth-of-July of July Celebration

The big day that we had been anticipating for the past month had finally arrived! It was a holiday that gave us more fun and excitement than Christmas. After having slept on the hard lumps of rag curlers, Dora and I were glad to unwind them – and equally glad to see our straight hair was now in springy ringlets. While we had shocked hay, the sun's heat had given us baked-in curls.

In the excitement of getting ready to go, we forgot the hot work of the day before. We girls put on dresses instead of bib overalls, and Lester wore his newest overalls and shirt. Mom looked nice in her best cotton house dress. Since Dad seldom wore anything but bib overalls and a blue chambray work shirt, he looked all dressed up in a pair of belted pants and long-sleeved white shirt with garters on the sleeves. After Dora and I had washed the breakfast dishes, we waited impatiently for Dad to say it was time to go. We asked him when we were going, and all he said was, "Not yet. We don't want to get there too early."

He and Lester had long been finished with the morning chores of milking the cows and feeding the pigs and chickens. And while getting breakfast, Mom had boiled potatoes and lots of eggs. After Dora and I chopped up the potatoes and took the shells off the hard-boiled eggs, Mom made deviled eggs and a potato salad. She also frosted the cake she had baked yesterday. But she decided that wasn't enough food to take, so sent Lester out to the cellar to get a quart jar of pickled beets. Finally, about ten o'clock, Dad said what we'd been waiting all morning to hear, "Well, I guess it's time to go."

With that, he pulled his billed cap on over his bald head and went out to the car shed. He backed the car out and drove up to the front of the house. Lester and I helped Mom carry the food out while Dora brought Leola and Effie to the car. Leola didn't need any help, but Effie still needed a boost up onto the running board. The rest of us climbed in, and off we started to the celebration.

The day was already warm, so the breeze blowing through the open car felt good. We drove down past Abe Heidegger's house and onto the county road, past Abe's cherry orchard and the Aldredge Place and Van Hoff's and on down the Heidegger Hill to the log house on the corner of the Pleasant Valley Road. Turning left, we climbed the Hays Hill and drove past the house where we used to live and soon reached the grange hall.

Many people had beaten us there and were busy setting up canvas game booths. Dad hustled over to help them, as he was going to be running the baseball throw. Lester, Dora and I helped Mom take the food out and set it on tables under the trees. When she told us she wouldn't need us any more, Lester went off to be with Dad while Dora and I took off to find our school friends. Relieved of any work to do, we felt a wild abandon at the utter freedom of the day.

With aprons covering their best cotton dresses, Ethel Holter, Blanche McKern and Dessie McCarroll were inside the small refreshment stand putting Cracker Jacks, candy bars and other goodies in place. Their husbands, Paul, Morse and Jack were setting up other booths. Early that morning, Paul and Ethel had driven to Colville to get ice cream and cones, candy bars, different kinds of soda pop – and ice to keep them cold. The Old Dominion Creamery had put the big round cartons of ice cream into padded cloth bags, which would keep the ice cream hard all day.

As I walked around the area with Arlene Conner, Ethel and Hazel Rose, we saw Paul Holter and Dee McKern marking distances on the side of the road for the foot races. They marked a starting line, then stepped off and marked fifteen and twenty five-yard finish lines for the races that would take place on the road that afternoon. A fast runner, I knew I'd soon be winning some prize money after crossing the finish line.

By the time the program inside the hall was ready to start most of the work outside was done. But sounds of hammering came through the windows as my friends and I found seats on one of the benches set up on one end of the dance floor. Dora was sitting with Bonnie Chinn, Lillian and Jean Heidegger; Mom sat on a nearby bench with Leola and Effie. Dad and Lester were still outside, doing some of that hammering.

The program began with the Pledge of Allegiance. Then twenty men and women of the grange's drill team marched out onto the floor. Women wore white dresses and men wore white shirts and pants. Each one wore a wide blue sash which crossed from one shoulder to the opposite hip. Following exact patterns, they crisscrossed the hall, going up its length and back and forth across the width. I wondered how they remembered to do everything at the right time to keep from running in to each other. When the drill team finished, we sang "America, the Beautiful" after which the Master of the grange introduced the speaker, an officer in the state's Pomona grange, who said he was glad to be with us, then began his formal speech.

The sounds of firecrackers, hammering and men's voices came through the windows, punctuating his speech. We kids, not understanding much, wished he'd hurry up and finish. Despite the open windows, the hall got stuffy and I got impatient, wanting to go outside. At last the speech was over. We sang The Star Spangled Banner, which ended the program, and we kids slid through the open door and raced to freedom of the outdoors.

By this time everyone was hungry. The women hurried to set the rest of the food out. Once the grange chaplain said grace, we all got in line and filled our plates. I kept in mind to save room for a piece of coconut cake, my favorite dessert.

After lunch, the carnival booths opened and people gathered around to try their skills to win a box of Cracker Jacks, a celluloid kewpie doll, jacks, or other prize. Some of the profits went toward prize money for the races, so I was glad to see several people trying their luck. One booth was a coin toss into a saucers, and another was a ring toss where a hoop had to circle objects about six feet away. The baseball throw consisted of a long iron rod with cloth dolls suspended on them. A wide fringe all around them made them appear bigger than they were. When a ball hit one at the top, it flipped over backward in a somersault, and if it hit at the bottom, it tipped over frontward. Dora and I headed for the baseball throw, as Lester had said he was going to try to win a prize there. His aim was pretty good after throwing rocks at snakes and other natural targets on our long hike from school. We got there just in time to see Lester throw a ball at the dolls suspended on the iron rods. He hit one and it spun round and round. But his next ball hit the fringe on the sides of a doll, and it missed, making a sharp thwack as it hit the canvas at the back of the booth.

Finally, it was time for the races. We Riley kids could run faster barefooted, so took our heavy oxfords off. The first race was for the youngest children, and Dora won first prize in the girls' eight-year old race. And soon the starter called out, "All girls eleven years old line up for the next race."

Heart pounding in anticipation, I put the toes of my left foot on the line scratched in the dirt road. Then all six of us leaned forward, waiting for the call of "On your mark, get set, go!," and at the word "go," I leaped forward and ran as fast as I could until my chest touched the binding twine marking the finish line. Pulling the twine out of the men's hands, I knew I had won first prize of a quarter.

Clutching the big coin, I could almost taste the ice cream cones and pop that it would buy. I watched the next races, waiting for the sack races and three-legged races. For the sack race, each "runner" would climb into a gunny sack and jump to the finish line. The three-legged race was more fun than the sack race, but harder. Each runner's leg was tied to a partner's leg and we had to keep in step as we ran. If we didn't keep in step, we fell down, tumbling in front of others who were still on their feet trying to run. At the end of the race, even the losers had so much fun that they didn't mind not winning.

With many events, almost every kid who entered won something. Lester, Dora and I won more than our share of prizes. Lester said it was because of the running we did on our way to school. Winning first made us almost giddy thinking of all we could buy, and then we had nickels and dimes for getting second and third. A few years later when my friends, Dorothea Heide, Betty-Jo Peters, Arlene Conner, Ellen McNutt, Ethel and Hazel Rose and I had won money, someone took a picture of us eating our ice cream cones together.

After all the races were over, I set off to the refreshment stand and bought a nickel strawberry ice cream cone. That tasted wonderful, but I was thirsty, so bought a grape soda, also for a nickel. Then I went to find Mom to show her my prize money. She was sitting at a picnic table holding Effie on her lap, with
Leola perched beside her. Lester had just brought her a bottle of orange pop that he had won with his prize money. Then I felt guilty for not thinking to take something to her, too. But not seeming to notice my thoughtlessness, she exclaimed about all the coins I had left.

Returning to the refreshment stand, I bought a roll of red paper ammunition for my old cap gun. After threading the loose end into the gun an snapping the hinged side shut, I pointed it at the sky, pulled the trigger and banged away. Then, wanting some firecrackers, I looked through the milling crowd until I spotted Chinaman Tai. Although about a foot shorter than most grown-ups, he was easy to find. I just listened for his shrill voice as he wandered through the crowd pulling his little red wagon, calling "Fi cackies, fi cents," in his sing-songy voice. I knew he was selling firecrackers for five cents a package. Catching up with him, I tugged at his loose sleeve to get his attention. He stopped his sing-songy calls and swiveling around, bringing his face close to mine. As I looked straight into his dark eyes, I was startled that we were the same height, and wondered why a grown man was so short. I handed him my dime and said, "I want two packages of small firecrackers, please."

He bent down to get them from his wagon, which also held other novelties from China – magic flowers that "bloomed" when dropped in water, tiny fans and umbrellas. His small hand picked up the red tissue-wrapped firecrackers and held them out to me. I felt his cool hand as I took them, and saw a hint of smile touch his face. Putting my dime in his pocket, he turned and continued pulling his wagon through the crowd, calling "Fi cackies, fi cents."

Chinaman Tai was the most unusual person at the celebration. This was due only partly to his size. The long, black pigtail hanging down the middle of his back would alone have set him apart. The only other men I'd seen with braided hair were those fishing at Kettle Falls in the Columbia River. And they had two braids instead of just one.

We had never heard him called anything but "Chinaman Tai," and never saw him except at the Fourth of July celebration. When Lester and I asked Mom about him, she said, "I've heard that he lives down near Daisy and pans for gold in the Columbia. He must not find much, as he looks like could stand a good meal."

No one wanted the day of fun to end, but almost everyone had cows to milk and other evening chores to do. So at about four o'clock the visiting ended and men took down the canvas booths and lifted up and closed the hinged sides of the refreshment stand. And taking over our jobs again, Lester, Dora and I took charge of Leola and Effie and helped Mom carry our dishes to the car. All day Mom had kept the little girls close to her so we older children could have our day of complete freedom.

As our old Star chugged up the hills toward home, we were content and tired and didn't have much to say. Under Mom's watchful eyes, Leola and Effie had waded in the creek and played around the tables with other little girls. Lester, Dora and I had won over a dollar apiece and bought everything we wanted. Even Dad and Mom had a good time. Between Dad's shifts at his stand, he'd visited with all his friends, catching up on everyone's news. Mom had gotten acquainted with newcomer Letha Peters, and had visited with Goldie Entwistle, Ruth Heidegger and Ethel Rupert as well as many other friends. She hadn't seen them much since we had moved from the Hays Place.

Dora and I still had pretty hair; the curls having lasted all day. The only sad note was knowing we had to wait a full year for the next Fourth-of-July celebration. Chinaman Tai died soon after that in 1937. From then on, it was never the same. We missed seeing him and hearing his shout, "Fi cackies, fi cents." Buying firecrackers at the refreshment stand wasn't as much fun as buying them from the small man who wore his hair in one long pig tail hanging down his back.

Later on we learned more about him. His full name was Wang Fok Tai. Born in 1860 in China, he was fourteen when he came to Stevens County with his brother, Ah Nim, and their uncle, Dock. They lived in a shack near Daisy, not far from the Columbia River, and began placer mining for gold. The three had lived together until 1918, when Uncle Dock died. Word had gotten around that the brothers had found and hidden a large amount of gold. On July 4, 1921, a small group of likkered-up men drove in to rob them. Finding Ah Nim home alone, they beat him, trying to force him to tell where he had hidden his gold, but he died without telling them. When Chinaman Tai died, he was buried next to his brother, Ah Nim, and his uncle, Dock, in the old cemetery across the road from the Rice school house.

Years later Ralph Byrd told me that Chinaman Tai often picked up and ate chickens that had been killed by cars on the highway. One day when Ralph's father asked Tai how he was feeling, he had replied, "No feel good, no feel good. Ate chicken dead too long."

In the summer of 1993 Lester took me to the cemetery to show me Tai's grave. On the small hill overlooking the highway and the Rice Mercantile Store, he led me to the right side of the road going through the cemetery. Bending down, he brushed aside the dry white grass to show me three small markers. Seeing "Wang Fok Tai," made me feel I had found a piece of my childhood. I wished for a package of firecrackers to set off in memory of this small man who had brought happiness into the lives of a bunch of country kids.

Wheat Harvest in the Big Bend

We five kids clustered around Mom in front of the house watching Dad drive away, seeing the empty space behind the car get longer and longer. He was heading south to get a job in the wheat harvest in the Big Bend country, about 150 miles away and would probably be gone a month. Already we felt an emptiness without him, but Mom would keep us from getting lonesome -- and keep us busy. Lester would be doing most of the barn chores by himself, but Dora and I would be helping him bring the cows in from their hundred-acre pasture. After locking them in their stanchions, he had to climb the ladder into the hay mow and toss hay down into the manger. In addition to milking four cows twice a day, he cleaned their gutter every morning after letting them out of the barn.

Leola, who was almost four, wanted to learn to milk. She went to the barn with Lester carrying a small lard pail with a bail. After Lester seated her on a milking stool at the cow's flank, he said, "All you have to do is squeeze a teat and milk will squirt out."

Her small hand could barely reach around the cow's fat teat. But she squeezed hard and pulled down at the same time and out came a dribble of milk. She kept at it until milk came a little faster. "Look, Lester," she called, "I got enough to cover the bottom of my bucket!"

After they brought the milk to the house and Lester had run it through the cream separator, Leola bottle-fed a lamb with some of the milk. She had gotten this job by accident when a little orphan lamb had chosen her to be its mother. Its own mother had died and Dad had brought the lamb into the house to show how cute it was. Since Leola had been the one to give it its first bottle of milk, the lamb followed her around when she went outside. At feeding time, Mom filled its bottle with warm milk and pulled a large nipple over the top. As soon as Leola stepped out the door with the bottle, the lamb butted its head against her in its eagerness to eat. She laughed and went to the edge of the porch to sit down before she got knocked down.

Since I was the oldest girl, Mom expected me to keep an eye on Leola and Effie when they went outside with us. So they "helped" as we carried water from the well, fed the chickens, gathered eggs from the chicken house, and carried wood. Effie was only two when she picked up a small stick of wood to carry to the wood box in the kitchen.   The job we three older kids liked best was getting our mail two or three times a week, as it gave us an excuse for a short visit with the Heideggers. During Dad's absence, they always asked how we were getting along and if there was anything Mom needed. So all in all, we had plenty of chores to keep us busy the summer of 1935 while Dad was gone.

He had heard of a wheat rancher in the Big Bend Country who needed extra hands. That central area of the state had miles and miles of wheat ranches, some with more than a thousand acres. Because of the more southerly location, that grain was ready to harvest before ours was. They summer-fallowed about half of their land, but since some still had hundreds of acres planted in wheat, they always needed extra hands during harvest.   It had to be cut as soon as it was ripe. If a delay occurred, the grain shattered out on the ground as it was being cut and went to waste.   It was a good time for Dad to work away from home. Before he left, he had finished planting our oats, barley and spring wheat, and cut our hay and put it in the barn. Our winter wheat, the first grain to ripen, wouldn't be ready to harvest until late summer.

The month turned out to be a long time, but finally we saw the Star coming up the road and it soon stopped in front of the house. Dad stepped out of the car with a big grin on his face and, looking at Mom, said, "Sis, I got a whole pocket full of money," and just kept on grinning. When I was younger, I thought "Sis" was Mom's name, as Dad never called her by her name of "Audrey".

He made good wages and brought it all home. It was plenty to get us through the summer until he sold some grain from our harvest. Still beaming at being glad to bring money home, he handed Mom the mail he collected on his way past our mail box. We were all happy to see him, but none more so than Lester and Mom. Lester was relieved that he wouldn't have to milk four cows twice a day by himself, as Leola's "help" apparently hadn't done much good. And Mom, even knowing she could count on the Heideggers for help in an emergency, had felt more isolated than usual without a car. In talking about it later, she said, "I don't know what we'd have done while Bill was gone if one of us had gotten hurt so far away from a doctor."

For the next week or more, Dad told us about the Big Bend wheat country and his job working on the combine sewing filled grain sacks. He didn't complain about the long hours. Accustomed to hard work, he was happy he'd been able to make extra money.

His job as a sack sewer included helping the teamsters care for the horses. He couldn't help take care of the machinery, as getting grease or oil on his hands would soften them. Handling the rough gunny sacks full of wheat, he needed tough, work-hardened hands. His day had started around daylight in helping the teamster feed, water and harness the horses that made up the team pulling the combine. Getting them ready was quite a job even before going out to combine the grain. The day ended with unharnessing and currying the horses, then giving them hay, grain and water.

Often the ranchers had to use more than twenty horses hitched together as a team to pull the heavy combine across the rolling wheat land. Three or four combines, depending on the size of the ranch, followed each other around the fields cutting wide swaths in the standing rain. Besides pulling a heavy machine, the horses furnished the power to turn the inner workings that threshed the grain.

Dad said that his job as sack sewer kept him sitting on the combine in the "dog house", sewing the tops of the filled grain sacks. This sacking area was on the left side of the combine. On the right side was the header, with its apron platform, reel and sickle. The straw and chaff blew out of an opening all along the back, sifting straw trails across the newly cut stubble ground. Tending the grain spout and sewing the filled sacks shut kept Dad busy.

He hung empty burlap sacks on hooks over the ends of the two spouts. As soon as one sack filled with grain, he shut off the valve in that spout and opened the other, directing the grain into the empty sack hanging from it. Hefting the full sack to one side, he quickly replaced it with an empty sack, hanging it on the spout before sewing the filled sack shut. Before starting to sew with his large sack needle, he gathered up a handful of the loose burlap at the top, making an ear on it. Throwing a double half-hitch around the ear with his twine, he made a secure knot, pulling it tight before whipping the needle through the top with three stitches. There he took a double stitch and again pulled it tight. Making nine to twelve more stitches, he made a second ear at the other end of the top with his double half-hitch before cutting the twine off with the edge of the steel sack needle. Sharp in the center, it slashed the twine without causing him to waste a second. He had sewn the sack shut. The spring steel needle enabled him to quickly put it on another thirty-inch doubled twine to sew the next sack.

Dad said, "I had to hurry so I'd be ready to tend the other sack when it got full, but still make sure the half-hitches wouldn't come undone. The knots had to hold while I dropped the hundred-pound sack of grain to the ground and while the men in the grain wagon picked it up."

He did this difficult job while sitting on a machine that bounced and swayed as it was pulled across the humps and hills of the wheat field. A side hill could cause one side to be a little lower than the other, making his work harder. When they got to a steep part, the teamster stopped and leveled the combine by cranking up a wheel on the downhill side to a higher position.

There was good money in harvest. The wheat farmer paid wages by the day, but a day's work was from daylight to dark, and it was hot, dusty work. Dad and the teamster riding on the combine were covered with dust kicked up. The big bull wheel of the combine dug into the field, making furrows where it slewed and slipped going around the side hills. A roiling dust cloud often hung over the combine working its way around the golden grain field. Dad said, "That dust made it hard to breathe. When I came in from the field every day, the only clean spot on my head was the bald spot that my hat had covered."

He went on to tell how the teamster sitting high up on the combine was proud of his ability to drive so many horses. He reined them to walk in the stubble right at the edge of the standing grain. This would keep the header facing the grain so the reel could sweep the stalks against the sickle. The teamster not only handled several sets of reins to guide the horses, but had to watch how the combine was working. He kept an eye on the sickle gliding back and forth cutting the stalks, noting how they fell on the moving apron, which took them to the inside of the combine. All the machine parts had to move smoothly with no weeds or stalks plugging them up or wrapping around the gears.

Our grain was almost ready to bind by the time Dad got back. First to ripen, the winter wheat had turned golden, but when he broke a head off and shelled the grain into his hand, he said, "It's not quite dry enough. I'll wait until next week before starting to bind."

Compared to what he had been doing on that big wheat ranch, that was a simple job. He only had to harness four horses to pull the binder, much lighter than a combine. It would take him less than a week to bind the grain. The binder cut the grain, gathered it into bundles – tying a binding twine around each bundle – then kicked it out into a carrying basket on the side. When the basket was full, Dad tripped a lever, dumping the five or six bundles in a pile on the ground, and continuing binding until all the grain was cut. We three older kids started shocking the bundles soon after Dad dumped the first load of bundles. We picked up a bundle and forced it to stand upright on the stubble ground. Then we continued adding bundles until each shock held eight or ten bundles. The grain was somewhat protected from rain and would dry out more before threshing began. Once, when Dad finished binding and we still had a lot of shocking to do, he helped us finish. If we'd had enough money to buy a combine, which threshed the grain as it cut it, there wouldn't have been any bundles to shock.

When our second-hand binder broke down, it took longer than Dad's estimated week to bind the grain. He went to Colville to get a new part, put it on the binder, then continued binding. And all the while, he hoped to get done before the binder broke down again and before a hard rain came. Rain and wind could knock the grain down, making it impossible for the binder to pick it all up and cut.

One fall after Dad had worked in the harvest near Kahlotus, two men he had worked with, Ray Maroney and Ray Clark, came up to hunt deer with him. Those big ranches had a lot of acres of wheat, but didn't have deer like we had in our mountains. In giving them directions to find our farm, he told them if they got lost, to just ask anyone where Bill Riley lived. Then added, "Why, I can practically guarantee you'll get a couple of bucks."

Right away we could tell why Dad had invited them. They were always laughing and joking and having a good time. Lester and I immediately took to them because they joked with us, too. Ray Maroney told me he had a girl of eleven, just my age, who had a new swing set and a big shiny slide. But she was lonesome and needed another girl to keep her company. He asked, "Ines, would you like to go live with us so she would have someone to play with?"

Visualizing that lonesome girl swinging all by herself, I felt sorry for her. With a brother and sisters around me all the time, I was never lonesome. Despite all this, I wasn't tempted. All I could think of was having to live in a country without mountains or trees and the terrible loneliness I'd have without Lester, Dora, Leola and Effie – and I'd certainly be lost without Mom and Dad! These thoughts ran through my head while I realized Ray couldn't be serious. After a moment, I said, "I'm sorry, but I can't go with you and keep your little girl company."

On one of Dad's trips to Colville, a man there told him about a rich farm area way up north in Alaska. The U.S. Government was sponsoring a homestead program so pioneers would settle the Matanuska Valley. Its rich soil and long daylight hours made vegetables grow to huge sizes, and that Alaska was called 'Land of the Midnight Sun' because in the summer the sun was still shining at midnight. Dad told Mom everything he'd heard, ending with, "Up there, cabbages grow as big as washtubs! The government wants more farmers to move to Alaska, so will help them get settled."

Mom listened quietly while Dad tried to convince her that moving to Alaska would be a good thing for us to do. We watched her face for some sign of what she thought, afraid it might light up to match Dad's enthusiasm. But she never showed any interest in uprooting her family and moving to an unknown place. At the same time, she never said anything against it. After a few days when we didn't hear any more talk about the Matanuska Valley, Lester and I breathed sighs of relief. We didn't want to move there and had been afraid Dad would persuade Mom to go.

In late summer that area in Alaska made newspaper headlines when Will Rogers and his Pilot, Wiley Post, were killed in a plane crash on August 15, 1935. Just the day before, Will Rogers had talked to a crowd of settlers in Matanuska for over an hour. Before they took off the next day on what was to be their last flight, he sent his daily news dispatch telling about the seven or eight hundred settlers in the Matanuska Valley.

Forty years later, Henry and I were on vacation in Alaska and saw several of those homesteads, now abandoned. It was then I realized how wise Mom had been to want to stay put on our farm in Washington instead of going on a wild-goose chase to Alaska.

Three New Additions

In the fall of 1935, we had a new addition when Dad traded in our old Star as part payment on a second-hand Nash sedan. We'd had the Star since Dora was only a few months old, and I had thought we'd keep it forever. It had brought us from Oregon and taken us over many miles of road since then. But soon I wasn't missing the Star at all. The Nash gave us better protection from the weather with its metal top and glass windows that cranked up and down. The wind couldn't blow in like it had through the gaps of the Star's isinglass side curtains. The part that Dad liked best was the automatic starter button on the floor boards near the gas pedal. He could just push on it with his foot and the engine would start. The only times he had to crank it was on freezing mornings.

It was a good thing we got a better car. Mom would no longer be worried about keeping our next two additions warm in winter. On January 19, 1936 she gave birth to twin girls, naming them Viola and Vida. That morning soon after Lester, Dora and I had ridden off to school on our horses, her labor pains had started. And for the third time, Dad took her to Mrs. Aldredge's Maternity Home in Kettle Falls. They had dropped Leola and Effie off at Abe and Margaret Heidegger's, whose daughter, Ruth, would take care of them until Dad returned. He didn't worry about anyone taking care of us three when we got home from school. We were old enough to get supper and take care of ourselves for awhile.

Upon getting home from school that day, we knew before getting into the house that Mom's time had come. When we had topped the hill where we could see the house down below, there wasn't any smoke curling up out of the chimney, which meant nobody was home. Kicking the horses into a trot, we rode on down to the barn and tied them into the stalls, then ran to the house. It was just like we figured. Mom had left a note telling us Dad was taking her to Mrs. Aldredge's.

The house was cold without a fire going, and was empty without Mom, Dad, Leola and Effie. While Lester started a fire in the heating stove in the living room, Dora and I started one in the kitchen stove. We laid the fire, using the small kindling in the wood box plus the smaller pieces of stove wood. In a few minutes we had hot fires going and the house warmed up quickly. Then Lester went out to the barn to milk the cows and do the other evening chores while I started supper. By this time it had gotten dark, so I lit the kerosene lamp. I'd just warm up the venison steaks left over from last night's supper, boil some potatoes and make gravy and open a jar of vegetables. As soon as I peeled the potatoes, I asked Dora to run out to the cellar and get a jar of green beans or beets. After Lester finished milking, he brought it to the house and ran it though the separator, then we ate supper. Dora and I had washed the supper dishes before we saw the Nash go by the house on its way to the shed. We waited at the door for Dad to come in with Leola and Effie, and tell us about our new baby. Even before Mom told us that she was having another baby, it hadn't been a surprise. We older kids figured it out because her stomach had gotten big. But when Dad, Leola and Effie came in, it WAS a surprise when he announced, "You have twin sisters!"

Because of the snowy roads, Dad didn't take us kids in to see Mom while she was at the maternity home. So when we got back from school at the end of her ten-day confinement, we were glad to see she was home again. Now the house didn't feel empty any more. And when we looked at the twins, we couldn't believe that they looked so much alike.

Soon Mom took the time to write a letter to the Montgomery Ward Company in Portland, Oregon. In the fall she had ordered a layette – complete outfit of baby clothes – from the catalog for the coming baby. She had noticed a statement saying that the company would furnish a layette at no cost to anyone having twins if they had previously ordered one. So Mom notified them that she had twins, and a couple of weeks later we found a bulky package from Montgomery Ward at our mailbox. It included the same number of nightgowns, kimonos, shirts, receiving blankets, safety pins and Birds Eye diapers as the first layette. Mom had enough clothes for both babies without paying for the second set. In telling all her friends about it, she gave Wards a lot of free publicity.

This latest addition made nine people in our family and meant more work for almost everyone. Wash day came more often, requiring even more trips to the well for water, more wood carried to the wood box and more fire in the cook stove to heat the water required for doing the baby clothes. In the freezing cold, everything froze soon after being hung outside on the line. The water buckets and wood box always seemed to be empty.

Mom started out nursing the twins, but soon found she didn't have enough milk. She put them on the bottle and fed them cows' milk. Now Dora and I could help take care of them more while Mom was cooking and doing other tasks. We didn't have to buy baby bottles, as we had several empty medicine bottles just the right size. The rubber nipples fit on them and their flat sides made them easy for us to hold. We helped Mom with every phase of their care, from feeding and bathing to changing diapers. Since winter's cold kept us inside, we weren't unhappy about the extra work. The twins didn't fuss except when they were hungry or wet.

The three additions to our family were really different. The Nash gave us more comfort; Viola and Vida were so lovable that we didn't mind the extra work.

1936 – 1942
Home Place

In the fall of 1935 Sam Curry drove up in his shiny black car. After visiting with Dad for a few minutes, he got down to the purpose of his visit. He and Effie were moving to Asotin, Washington, so were selling the farm that we were renting. He said, "Why don't you and Audrey buy it so you won't have to pay rent any more?"

Dad replied, "You're asking a fair price, Sam, but I don't have that much cash. I'm afraid to borrow from the bank because I've seen too many people lose their farms when they couldn't make payments."

Since we couldn't buy their farm, Sam and Effie sold it to someone else, and Dad went looking for another farm. He'd heard that the Root Place on the other side of Frank Rupert's farm was for rent, so went to look it over. It was sandwiched between Childers Road (years later re-named "Chamberlin" Road) and Rickey Canyon Road near its junction with the Pleasant Valley Road. He found that only about half of its 160 acres was flat enough to farm. The rest was too timbered and hilly to plow. A spring, which fed into a small creek running through the lower portion, supplied the house with running water. And on the acreage near Frank Rupert's, there was another spring where cattle could water when grazing in that area.

The best part about the house was the location -- it was less than a mile or less from the school house. The worst part, was that there was only one bedroom. After wondering how nine people could fit into it, Dad hit upon a solution. The attic, the same size of the house, could be made into one big dormitory bedroom for us kids. But an added problem was that there wasn't a stair going up to it. No matter, he'd figure it out.

On his way home from looking at the Root Place, he stopped at Heidegger's to tell Abe and Margaret that we would be moving. Abe said, "Bill, we hate to see you leave. You and Audrey have been good neighbors."

In isolated areas where neighbors relied on each other for help, a good neighbor could mean the difference between life or death. So when Abe said that Dad and Mom had been good neighbors, it was the highest compliment he could give. They had been good neighbors to us, too.

Moving day came in late February of 1936, when there was still some snow on the ground. That morning Lester stayed home to help with moving, Dora and I went to school on shank's ponies. We couldn't ride Betty, our sorrel mare, as she was needed to help pull the wagon or sled in moving our furniture. There were a few inches of snow left, but Dad hoped the horses could pull the iron-wheeled wagon through it if he kept the load light. Lester would drive a team of two horses pulling the big bobsled with its double set of metal-plated wooden runners. If they could use both the wagon and the bobsled, it wouldn't take as many trips.

When school was out that afternoon, Dora and I felt we were going the wrong way when we walked up hill toward our new place, only about a mile away. That morning we had walked about three miles to school from the Curry Place.   I said, "Come on, Dora, let's see how long it will take us to get home today. I'll bet we can get there in less than half an hour."

83

By the time we got to our new house, only twenty minutes later, Mom was there with Leola, Effie, Viola and Vida. She had driven the Nash over after Dad set up the heating stove to get the long-empty house warmed up. And before going back for another load, he set up their beds so Mom would have a place to put the babies as soon as she got there. In following trips, Dad and Lester had brought the cook stove and set it up, too, so had two fires going, making the house almost warm.

His next job of making the attic into a dormitory caused a lot more work. After climbing a ladder propped against the end of the house, he used his claw hammer and pried a few lateral boards off the overhang above the front porch. He lowered them to Lester, who stacked them out of the way to be put back on later. Then Dad crawled into the attic through the opening, and waited for Lester to tie ropes on everything to hoist them up. He hoisted up three bedsteads, two small dressers, three link springs, bedsteads and mattresses. To get the mattresses up, Lester rolled each one and tied it in the middle and Dad pulled them up one at a time. When they had everything in the attic that belonged there, they nailed the boards back on that Dad removed to make the opening. Next, he made a trapdoor and a ladder for us kids to climb up. Making the ladder leading up to the trapdoor was a simple job. On the outside wall of the porch overhang, he nailed two 2x4 four boards to the wall vertically, then nailed crosspieces on for the rungs. Now we five older kids had a way to get upstairs to our attic bunk room. Since the twins would sleep in Mom and Dad's bedroom in their oversized crib, everyone had a place to sleep in that one-bedroom house. Dad had found a way to fit all nine of us into a one-bedroom house.

He made a trapdoor by sawing a square hole in the attic floor directly above the ladder, which was on the outside wall of the house near the front door. To make a trap door that we would open, he used the boards he sawed out in making the hole. After nailing on three or four boards crossways and attaching two leather hinges, the trapdoor was complete. The attic part overhanging the porch made the space upstairs bigger than downstairs.

With Mom comfortable in a warm house and all the beds put together, Dad and Lester went back for a small supply of hay and grain for the livestock. They could move the rest when they had more time in the next week.

When Dora and I arrived from school, Mom was putting dishes and pots and pans in the cupboard. Since she was there, our new house already felt like home. A fire was going in both stoves and the house was warm. After she put Dora and me to work peeling potatoes for supper, she said. "I'm only going to open a couple quarts of canned venison and make some gravy for the potatoes. For dessert, we can open a half-gallon jar of peaches. That will have to do for supper."

Just then we saw Dad and Lester coming down the hill by the barn herding the cows ahead of the loaded bobsled. It was piled high with farm equipment, hay and the big wooden grain box, full of grain from the fall harvest. Stopping at the barn, they climbed down from the sled. "Mom, can we go out and see them unload?", we asked. She said we could watch for a few minutes, but we'd have to come back and make up the beds in the attic before supper.

Dora and I got there just as they were taking the heavy grain box out of the back end of the bobsled. With a lot of effort, they carried it through the door into the cow barn, on the left side of the barn. A partition separated that side from the horses' stalls on the right. After getting the grain box in place, Dad said, "That was a heavy sonofabitch. I'm glad we don't have to move every day."

At supper, Dad told us about their busy day of moving. They'd made several trips, using the narrow wagon road that came from the Curry Place to Childers Road. A short distance later, they came through a wire gate into our new farm. He said this route was only about two and a half miles. If they'd gone the way cars went, it would have been seven or eight miles. He added that they had made only one trip with the wagon, as the snow was too deep for its iron wheels. Being too much work for the horses, they used the bobsled for the rest of the trips. Its runners slid over the thin layer of snow, making it much easier for the horses to pull the load.

The next Saturday, Dad and Lester took the bobsled back for more hay and grain. From the kitchen window, we watched as they stopped at the barn to unload. With pitchforks they tossed the hay into the hay mow, and carried sacks of oats through the barn door to dump into the grain box. We could see more full sacks of grain standing upright in the sled, but they didn't carry them into the barn. Instead, they started up the team and drove past the house to the "granary." It was the old house that was left standing when the "new" house was built about twenty-five years earlier. The two-story yellowish building sat about twenty feet from the house. Dad had found time to make two grain bins in each of the two big downstairs rooms by nailing board partitions to the floor. This is where he emptied the sacks of wheat, rye, barley and oats from the sled. The bins kept the different kinds of grain separated. A week or so later Dad went back to the Curry Place for the gang plow, side-hill plow, harrow, spring tooth, shovels and hoes. He would have to wait until the snow melted to bring the wheeled equipment such as the mowing machine, large bull rake, binder and manure spreader.

Going to bed that first time in our new home was an adventure. It felt strange to have to go out the front door into the cold, scamper up the ladder on the outside of the house and go through the trap door, with the last person pulling it shut. I tucked the covers around Leola and Effie in their double bed, then crawled in beside Dora. Lester had a double bed all to himself in the space on the other side of the brick chimney.

Our new dining room had a built-in cupboard from floor to ceiling and also held our rough table, two chairs, two benches and a tall dish cupboard with glass doors. We kids sat on benches, but Dad had a "saloon-type" chair, and Mom had a chair. The living room furniture consisted of a reclining couch, a rocking chair, Mom's New Home treadle sewing machine and chair, and our big metal heating stove. It stood in a corner near Mom and Dad's bedroom and had a fire going day and night all winter long. Their bedroom was just large enough for a double bed, dresser and the twins' extra large crib.

After making the short walk to school for a week, we kids realized how much easier it was than the three-mile trail we'd taken by horseback and shank's ponies for the past five years. We had enjoyed riding the trail on horseback, but when Dad was working the horses and we couldn't ride, we had gotten awfully tired of making the six-mile round trip on foot. Now, because of the short distance to school, we knew that we'd be walking to school. But we also knew that we would be riding while exploring our new surroundings here at the foot of Monumental Mountain in the Huckleberry Mountain Range.

Soon the strangeness of being in a different house and location wore off. Dad's farm work didn't change much, but Mom's life was immediately easier. When she saw that cold water was already piped into the kitchen from the creek, she exclaimed, "I'll never have an empty bucket again!"

And Lester, Dora and I were relieved that we no longer had to use those empty buckets to carry water to the house. Everything was easier for us five older kids except going upstairs to bed. At first we liked going outside and climbing the ladder to the attic. But when February's icy wind chilled us before we got through the trapdoor, we stopped thinking of it as fun.

The ladder to the attic wasn't the only one we had. In the floor between the dining room and living room was a trapdoor. Lester opened it to show a ladder leading to the dirt-floored cellar under the house. On one side of this area, Dad had made two big wooden bins to hold potatoes, carrots and big Hubbard squash. The other side had shelves to hold our canned fruit and vegetables. We realized that an inside cellar right underfoot was an improvement from going outside in cold weather when responding to Mom's order of "getting something from the cellar."

After the miracle of having piped-in cold water and not having to carry endless buckets of water, our next help with a back-breaking job came that spring when Dad scraped up enough cash to buy a gasoline-powered washing machine. Mom filled its tub with hot water, then added a batch of white clothes. In showing her how to start the washing machine, Dad said, "It's something like starting that old Harley Davidson motorcycle I used to have. You have to stomp down on this pedal as hard as you can," and as soon as he stomped down, it sounded like a motorcycle, too!

After the machine's agitator washed the clothes for ten minutes, Mom turned on the wringer's rolls and threaded the clean clothes through them and into the first rinse tub, then pressed a lever to swing the wringer around into position between the two rinse tubs and rinsed the clothes again. A few weeks later while feeding the wet clothes through the wringer, a fold of cloth caught my hand, carrying it through the wringer. I yelled, and Mom hit the pressure-release lever on the top. The pressure let up and I pulled my hand out, unhurt, from between the rubber rollers. Happy that the new washing machine was already saving us many hours of back-breaking work from scrubbing the clothes, Mom sighed with relief, saying, "We'll never have to scrub clothes on the washboard again."

The big cook stove, the most important item in the kitchen, burned lots of wood in its firebox while cooking a meal. Its metal back held a double warming oven, which projected part way over the cooking surface. A water reservoir, attached to the right side and level with the cooking top, was big enough to hold two buckets of water, which heated when a fire was going. During the winter the stove heated that end of the house. And its oven was perfect for drying our wet mittens and overshoes placed on sticks of wood which we had put on the lowered oven door.

Another metal item in the kitchen was the cream separator, which we used twice a day right after Dad and Lester milked the cows. After attaching a cloth to the metal separator bowl with clothes pins, we poured the milk through it to strain out any cow hairs that might have fallen into the buckets during milking. Then Dora, Lester or I turned the handle to crank it. Getting to the right speed, we opened the spigot at the bottom of the separator bowl letting the milk flow inside and through the metal discs. Soon skim milk poured out of the larger spout into a bucket on the floor. A smaller stream of cream poured out of the cream spout into another bucket sitting on the round metal shelf attached to the metal frame. When all the milk had gone through, we stopped turning the handle. Washing the separator parts took longer than separating the milk and was a more disagreeable job. At night, we just ran warm water through to rinse its disks and other parts, but every morning Mom took it apart and washed the pieces in hot, soapy water.

Mom's only work surface in the kitchen was a low wooden cabinet that held three shallow drawers near the top and two large pull-out bins below. One bin held six or seven loaves of home-made bread; the other held almost half of a fifty-pound sack of flour. After my twelfth birthday, Mom expected me to help keep this bin filled. When it was almost empty, she called, "Lester or Ines, bring me another sack of flour."

I was glad when Lester happened to be within earshot. He was stronger and could carry a fifty pound sack easier than I could. Since he was usually working outside during the day, it was often up to me to go to the upstairs room of the old house where we kept it.   Dad had built a large, board platform suspended from the ceiling by wires to keep mice from getting at it. It held ten or twelve sacks of flour. It was all I could do to wrestle a filled sack off the platform and onto my shoulder, and to keep it balanced while going downstairs, crossing the yard and climbing the steps to our porch and into the kitchen. After easing it to the floor beside the cabinet, I untied the two interwoven strings at the top, hoisted the sack up again and poured about half the flour into the bin.

Every fall after threshing, Dad took several gunny sacks of wheat to the flour mill in Colville and traded them for our year's supply of flour. When he brought all those sacks of flour home and carried them up to the storage platform, he kept them separate from last year's flour. Once we made a mistake and opened a bag of the "new" flour before the old had been used. Mom, noticing her batch of bread wasn't as good as usual, figured the flour was better after it aged a bit.

A few years later Dad and Mom bought this farm and it became their home place for the rest of their lives. They remodeled the house and installed electricity, an indoor bath room, hot water tank, electric range, automatic washer and dryer and inside stairways to the attic and cellar. Mom finally had an easier life.

Our Attic Bedroom

After a few days in our new home, we felt we were right where we belonged. Even the adventurous bedtime routine of going out the front door to go upstairs seemed natural to us older kids. We climbed the ladder Dad nailed to the end of the house under the porch overhang, and pushed open the trap door as we reached the top. The last one up closed the trap door and pulled the small rug over the cracks to keep the winter wind out.

 The first one up struck a match and lit the small kerosene lamp in the girls' end of the attic. When Lester came up, he lit his own lamp, and as soon as everyone was in bed, we blew the lamps out. Long ago Mom taught us to be careful with matches – and doubly so with lighted kerosene lamps. As Dora, Leola and Effie grew, they heard the same warning, "If you drop a lighted match or knock over a lamp, you could start a fire and burn the house down."

While we were eating supper, our flat irons had been heating on the kitchen stove. We were going to take them to bed with us to put them at the foot of our beds under the covers. Wrapped individually in old pieces of denim, they would warm our feet without catching anything on fire. We four girls slept in two double beds pushed against the wall on the larger end of the attic; Lester's bed was in the smaller space beyond the chimney. We girls shared a small dresser, and Lester had one all to himself. Mom said that later on she would make a partition by nailing boards between the chimney and the wall. A pole nailed between rafters, and a few nails driven into rafters held our dresses, overalls and shirts. Without many clothes, we didn't miss a closet.

 When daylight came and we saw the roofs' shingles, we realized why we saw our breaths in the cold air of morning. The only heat in the attic was a tiny bit coming from the bricks of the chimney. But we had been warm all night, as each bed was covered with warm quilts Mom had made out of colorful scraps of cloth, sewing them together in a crazy-quilt pattern, with cotton batting inside.

Dora and I were lucky to have a large bear skin to use as a rug beside our bed. A few years ago, Dad had killed a big bear, tanned the hide and given it to us. When we stepped out of bed and ran our bare feet across it, the long fur curling around our toes gave instant warmth.

Not much warmth came upstairs from the heating stove, although Dad kept a low fire going in it all night, getting up once or twice to add another chunk of wood. First one up every morning, he added more wood to the embers in the heating stove and started a fire in the cook stove. Even so, the house was still cold when the rest of us got up. On cold mornings when we didn't want to get dressed in the frigid attic, we grabbed our clothes and scurried down the ladder and into the house to dress beside the warm heating stove. During the nights of below-freezing temperatures, its warmth didn't spread into the dining room or kitchen, and we found ice along the edges of the running water in the sink. We had to let the water trickle all night to keep it from freezing.

Years later during remodeling of the house, the ladder going up to the attic was taken out and stairs were built. Using them instead of the ladder was a great convenience to Mom when she changed the beds. But compared to our scramble up a ladder, it was a tame way of getting upstairs.

Just a Hop and Skip

The best thing Lester, Dora and I liked about our new place was that it was only about a half mile to school. And since it was all downhill, we could make it in twenty minutes if we ran part way. For the five years on our long trail to school by horseback and shank's ponies, we had strict orders to stay together. But traveling as a threesome had become such a habit that we stayed together that first morning from our new place.

After going out our gate to the Rickey Canyon Road, we followed it to its junction with the Pleasant Valley Road, less than a quarter of a mile from our house. We passed our mailbox which Dad had set up with others at the junction, as Ike Cranston, the mail man, didn't drive up Rickey Canyon Road. Getting below Harley and Ethel Adkins' house, we saw Barbara Loven coming out of her trail through the woods. She joined us and the four of us went by the newly-built Assembly of God Church and its parsonage on the plot of ground that Ernie Keck had given to the new church. The Kecks had the only telephone in our end of the valley, and let others use it for emergency messages. That's what Abe Heidegger would call "being a good neighbor."

Seeing their house reminded me a story Dad had laughingly recalled many times. Ernie, a gentle, church-going man with beautiful wavy white hair, had worked all morning with Howard Heidegger harvesting his grain. At the dinner table, Howard's wife, Opal, had topped off Ernie's coffee cup without him noticing. When he took a gulp of the scalding hot liquid, it burned his mouth. He spit it on the floor, saying, <u>There</u> now, damn you, blaze!"

Continuing down the road, I laughed thinking about this kind man spewing coffee on Opal's floor - then making the offense worse by swearing. About this time we heard someone yell at us and turned to see Clarence and Bonnie Chinn running to catch up. Soon we saw the white school house on the left. Upon reaching it and climbing its four wooden steps, I couldn't believe we had gotten to school in less than half the time it took to get there from the Curry Place.   Almost twelve, I was old enough to be grateful that Leola, who would start school that fall, would never have to make the long walk. Now the short walk – and all by road – was just a hop and a skip away.

89

Frank Rupert's Landslide

"Bill, I want you to bring all my land back and put it up on the hillside where it belongs," Frank kidded as he and Dad stood looking at the landslide.

Dad stared in disbelief at the five-hoot high mass of earth in our field. It had slid off Frank's hill, carrying trees and bushes and part of the barbed-wire fence with it, crossed the county road and oozed out onto our land, with a high mass still blocking the road. Shocked to see part of his level field had turned into an unusable brushy mound, Dad replied, "By grab, Frank, I'd sure like to; I won't be able to plant any oats there with all those trees!"

Both men knew nothing could be done about the pile of dirt and trees, so they might as well joke about it. The winter snows had been deep, the hard rains for over a week had caused the saturated hill to break loose. When the rain had finally stopped, both of them went out looking over their land to see if any damage had been done, with Lester and me tagging along with Dad. We found Frank Rupert standing beside the landslide piled on the road separating the two farms. The bushes and small quaking aspens that had been rooted to the hillside slid right along with the dirt, coming to rest right side up as if they'd been growing in our field for years.

Frank didn't care that some of his hillside was gone. But the unwanted pile of dirt ruined part of our level farm land. Dad would have to go around it every time he plowed, harrowed, mowed, raked or cut the grain with the binder. I felt sorry for Dad that a piece of easy-to-work ground was taken out of use. Much of the land was on hills where had to be careful how he worked so the machinery wouldn't tip over. The now-useless spot had produced twenty-five or thirty bundles of oats.

The landslide gave Frank a conversational opportunity to get even with Dad for the joke he'd played on him a few years earlier. Remembering the coyote "steaks" Dad has sent him, Frank now felt he had something to kid him about. For years afterward their usual greeting to each other was, "Hey, Frank, how were those coyote steaks I sent over to you?"

Frank's response always being, "I'll let you know, Bill, when you bring my hillside back to me!"

Dora's Birthday Cake

May 27, 1936, was Dora's ninth birthday, and I was trying to find some brown sugar to make her a birthday cake. I had asked her what kind of a cake she'd like, and if she wanted to help me make it. She said she'd like a chocolate cake, so we looked through the cookbook for a recipe. But we hadn't been able to find any baking chocolate. So we decided to make a coconut cake, but hadn't found any coconut, either. I knew we had all the necessary spices for a spice cake, as the "Raleigh" man had recently come through the area, stopping at every farm house, and Mom had stocked up. Since the recipe called for brown sugar, I had begun searching for it.

I rummaged through every shelf in the cupboard and through the pull-out bins of sugar and flour without finding any. Then I remembered Mom often hid it so one of us kids wouldn't eat it when we got a craving for sweets. I would ask her, as she might have a box stashed away. She was bent over her New Home treadle sewing machine in the living room sewing patches on overalls. "Mom, Dora and I want to make a cake, but we can't find any brown sugar. Do you know if we have some?"

She got up from the machine and went to the kitchen cupboard. Standing on her tiptoes, she reached up to the top shelf and fished behind some sacks. She held up her hidden box of brown sugar and said, "Here it is. If it had been a snake, it would have bitten you!"

It was a phrase that Mom said to me on many occasions. All the family knew I had trouble finding things – even if they were staring me right in the face.

Now that we had all the ingredients for our cake, we were in business. Dora asked what she could put into the mixing bowl. I told her not to do anything yet, as I had to get the fire started in the cook stove and heat the oven up. Mom had long ago taught us to lay a fire that would start easily and get going fast. The fire drew better if the fire box wasn't full of ashes, so I put the grate lever in the notch and shook it to make the ashes fall into the ash box. Crumpling up newspaper, I put it all along the bottom of the fire box, then added small pieces of pitchy pine kindling. On top of this, I put larger kindling, then small pieces of firewood. After opening the damper on the stovepipe, I adjusted the slot in the side of fire box so the fire would draw. Opening the drop-down door in the fire box at the front of the stove, I lit the paper with a match from the tin box on the wall behind the stove, and shut the door.

Letting the fire roar for a couple of minutes, I closed the damper in the stovepipe a little. Another few minutes I added a big piece of wood and adjusted the damper until it was straight across the stove pipe. We'd have too hot a fire if we left both the damper and the draft wide open. From now until our cake was baked, we would control the heat by making adjustments only with the draft and by the amount of wood we put into the stove.

With the fire going good, Dora and I started the cake. The big green crock-type mixing bowl was almost too heavy and awkward for my twelve-year old hands to hold, but it was the right size. I measured the lard and sugar into it, and mixed them together. Using her favorite bowl, the glass one with a knob handle, Dora sifted flour, salt, baking powder and spices together. Leaving her to add the eggs and other ingredients and mix them into the lard and sugar, I went to tend the fire, which now needed more wood. I added enough to fill the fire box, then checked the gauge on the oven door. It was just about the right temperature. I closed the draft a bit more so the oven wouldn't get much hotter.

Satisfied with my steady fire, I knew it would maintain the right oven heat with only a big stick of wood added about every ten minutes. I was glad Dad had bought a new cook stove. Our old stove hadn't had a temperature gauge, and Mom had to guess how hot the oven was by how long the fire had burned. I hadn't baked enough to know when the oven got hot enough.

While I tended the fire, Dora stirred the ingredients together. I took over and beat the cake batter until my arm got tired. I wondered why I couldn't keep beating as long as Mom did. After all, I had developed strong arm muscles hoeing weeds and shocking hay. After another session of beating, I poured the batter into two round cake pans that Dora had greased and floured. Then holding the pans level, I put them into the oven, one at a time. The gauge indicated the heat was just right. Now we had to keep a steady fire going until the cakes were done. We didn't know what type of frosting to make, so back to the living room I went to ask Mom. She said, "Look in the cook book and see if you can find one that calls for brown sugar. That would be good on a spice cake."

We found a recipe that didn't look difficult. We could make it after the cakes came out of the oven and were cooling. I opened the oven door and poked a toothpick into one of the cakes, and it came out with batter on it. Waiting ten minutes, I tested it again, and the toothpick came out clean, so I took them out of the oven. While they were cooling, we started making the frosting. It didn't take long to mix, but we had to be careful not to boil the mixture too long. It would get too hard to spread. Asking Mom how to tell when the frosting was done, she came in to watch. Seeing the bubbly dark mix pale to just the right color, she said, "I think that's cooked long enough."

After Dora placed one of the cooled cakes on a plate, I spooned on the hot frosting, spreading it with a table knife all over the top and sides. Then she placed the other cake on top and put toothpicks through both layers to keep them from sliding apart. After I frosted that layer, I used the point of a paring knife to draw a big number nine in the soft frosting. We licked the pan, smacking our lips, knowing we had picked out the best frosting recipe in the whole cookbook. So for dessert that night instead of canned fruit, everyone ate birthday cake. In his usual joking manner, Dad gave it his highest praise, "That's almost fit to eat!"

Since moving to the new farm in early 1936 we had seen many changes. And later that hot summer we saw something else that we'd never seen before. One afternoon we saw a smoky haze blowing in from the west that soon covered the sky. And soon bits of ash started floating around, so we knew there was a fire burning somewhere. The next day Dad learned that another fire was burning in the Tillamook Burn, many miles away near the Pacific coast west of Portland, Oregon. Eventually the fires burned over 350,000 acres of timber, causing millions of dollars of damage.

Sewing Lessons

Mom made sewing seem like magic with her treadle sewing machine when she turned a flat piece of material into something to wear. She didn't regard making new clothes as work; it was more enjoyable than the never-ending job of patching overalls and other clothes. When she had pieces of material left over, she saved them for her "crazy" quilt tops. Instead of using a quilt pattern, she sewed scraps of all shapes and sizes together until it was large enough for a quilt top.   Watching her sew pieces together had made me want to learn how to sew. The first thing she taught me was how to sew a straight seam. I put two edges of material together, lowered the presser foot and pushed the treadle with my right foot. When I finished, I looked at what I had sewn. My stitches were too zig-zaggy, so I kept practicing until my stitching was straight. Mom looked at the result and said, "It looks like you're ready to sew some quilt pieces together, but first you'll have to cut out the pieces."

She cut out a triangular pattern from a piece of cardboard, then asked which scraps I wanted to use for the quilt block. After I picked out a flowered piece and a plain one for contrast, she showed me how to hold the cardboard pattern on the material, positioning the pattern on the straight grain of the material and tracing around it with a pencil. I needed to cut out four pieces of each color for each quilt block. The triangular patter of alternating colors made a block that looked like a paper pinwheel spinning in the wind.   Cutting out pieces for two blocks and sewing them together kept me busy until it was time to help get supper.

Both quilt blocks were pretty, but one was a slight bit bigger than the other. Since I had used the same pattern, I was puzzled as to what caused the size difference. I compared the seams and discovered I'd taken a wider seam on the pieces in the small block. "Your blocks are pretty," Mom said, "and you sewed nice straight seams, but tomorrow you'll have to take one block apart and make its seams the same width as the other one so all your blocks will be the same size."

The next day after making both blocks the same size, I eagerly cut out more triangles so I could see what the two materials looked like when put together in a block. Finding a yellow-flowered scrap, I searched in the scrap box until I found a plain yellow piece. When I had them cut out and sewn together in a block, I had another pretty pinwheel!

Besides piecing together quilt tops, patching overalls, making dresses and blouses, Mom also made cotton bloomers for the four little girls and brassieres for herself out of emptied flour sacks that she had washed and bleached.   As we emptied each fifty-pound sack of flour, she washed the sack so it would be ready to use when she got around to sewing. Having been tightly woven to keep flour from sifting through, the material gave good wear.

Once, Mom deviated from her usual flour-sack material by buying a couple yards of black cotton sateen that was on a special sale at J. C. Penney's. She had started the twin's toilet training and would need several pair of bloomers. The black material would be better than white anyway; it wouldn't show the dirt from their outdoor play.

In my spare time for the next several years, I continued making quilt blocks until I had a stack of them. But I was careless with the seam width and ended up with different sized blocks. Although never learning how to make the same sized seams, I learned how to sew a straight seam with a treadle sewing machine.

These early sewing lessons helped me in later years when I turned pieces of material into shirts for my sons, and dresses for my daughter and myself, just like magic as Mom had done. But despite her patient training, I still had to rip out seams occasionally and start over.

Our New Neighbors

The location of our new home on the Rickey Canyon Road and near the Pleasant Valley Road gave us several neighbor families instead of just one. We had moved from the isolation of our dead-end road to where we could see two roads with traffic. It didn't take us long to get better acquainted with Ernie Keck, down the road about half a mile. In early spring, when weeds started growing in his raspberry patch, he asked Lester and me to get rid of them. We were experienced workers, having hoed weeds out of our garden for years. Two days later, when we finished weeding, Ernie put two heavy silver dollars in our palms. A dollar a day was the going pay for grown men working in the hay fields. We knew we had done a good job of weeding, but when Ernie paid us harvest hands' wages, it showed he knew we had done a good job, too.

Across the creek from the schoolhouse was the log house where Raymond and Ruth Heidegger lived with their big family. Albert, Margaret, Lillian and Raydene could leave home as the school bell began ringing and not be late. We laughed to see them spew out their door, race down the hill, jump the creek and dash through the schoolhouse door just as the bell stopped ringing.

That fall when hot weather was over and Dad could butcher a hog, he asked Jack McCarroll and Paul Holter to come help him. Paul's house was less than half a mile away, and Jack's was just below the school house, both on the Pleasant Valley Road. Jack's wife, Dessie, came to visit Mom, and their neighbor boy, Leonard Higgins, had come with them.

With everyone gathering around, Dad led the big sow out to the orchard near our house where he and Lester had dug a pit long enough for the hog-scalding vat. By now the fire under the vat had heated the water. Dad held the end of his gun barrel behind the sow's ear and pulled the trigger. It slumped dead to the ground. After cutting its throat so it would bleed out, he and Paul looped two ropes around its middle. Paul stood on one side holding both ends of his rope, while Dad did the same on the other side. Jack and Lester helped, and with two men on a side, they eased the heavy hog into the vat of steaming water. Two minutes should be long enough to loosen the hair, so they could scrape it off. Pulling on their rope loops, they rolled the hog from side to side. Then, with much heaving, they pulled it out of the vat and onto the wooden stone-boat beside the vat, and began scraping its hair off.

Built low to the ground with poles for runners, the stone boat was useful for hauling rocks out of our fields. Now it served as a platform to keep the hog off the ground while the men worked on it. After finishing, they were ready to hang it on an apple tree limb. Dad bound a wooden single-tree between its hind legs and tied a strong rope to it. The other end of the rope went through a pulley fastened to a thick limb of the apple tree. To hoist the hog, Paul, Lester and Jack pulled the rope while Dad and Leonard pushed up on its body. When its head cleared the ground a couple of feet, Dad quickly tied the rope to the tree trunk while the others strained to keep the heavy body hoisted. Only then did they let go of the rope.

With the back-breaking part of the job done, they sat down to rest, glad to have the worst over with. By the time Jack rolled a cigarette and finished his smoke, they were rested. Pulling his pocket knife out, Dad cut open the hog's belly and detached the intestines and stomach, letting them fall into a tub to be thrown out later. He cut out the heart and liver and put them in a bucket. They would be ready to eat that night. Paul and Jack had helped with a tough job, and now Dad owed them a like amount of work. And when the three helpers went home that afternoon, they carried with them parts of the liver for their supper.

The next day, Dad cut up the hog. Dessie came again to help Mom make head cheese and render out the lard. To make head cheese, they used scraps of pork along with the gelatin obtained from boiling parts of the head. Finishing with that, they cut the hard, white fat into strips and fried it in skillets to render out the lard. Happy to have had Dessie's company as well as her help, Mom gave her some pork and two small buckets of lard.

Leonard Higgins, Jack and Dessie's neighbor boy, lived just across the road from them with his father, brother and sister in a one-room shack. Leonard's widowed father, Millard, had brought his family from West Virginia two or three years earlier. Speaking with a drawl, they used a few different words than we did. In talking about a sack of candy, Millard called it a "poke" of candy. At school, the three kids surprised us and our new teacher by saying, "Yes, Ma'am" or "No, Ma'am." Mrs. Graham seemed startled, but her smile showed she liked it. We had heard men called "Sir," but no one ever said, "Ma'am."

Mrs. Bovee lived about a half mile below Jack and Dessie's place. Her house was screened from the road by cedar, birch and alder trees that grew along Quillisascut Creek. Her grown son, John, always lived with her. And part of the time, another son, Ernie, lived there with his wife, Jessie, and daughter, Esther, about Dora's age. It was this couple that we kids had visited a few years ago while going back home from school to the Curry Place when they were digging a mine. Mrs. Bovee invited our family to supper and served canned strawberries for dessert. She had a large strawberry patch in front of her house so they canned some for their winter use. As Esther took me through the house, I noticed a white, claw-footed bathtub sitting in Mrs. Bovee's bedroom. I wondered how she emptied it, as there was no drain to pipe the bath water out.

About two hundred yards farther down the road was the house where Howard Heidegger lived. After his wife, Opal, died in 1933, Howard's sisters, Mildred and Ruth, had spent time helping take care of the children. But Howard needed full-time help with baby Kenneth, Jean, Rose Marie and Betty Mae, so he hired Peggy, a nurse from Colville, to take care of them. A few months later Howard and Peggy married.

Carl and Dell Rose didn't have far to walk when they went to grange, as the Quillisascut Grange hall was just across the road from them, about three hundred farther down the road from Howard Heidegger's house. Carl and Dell's daughter, Hazel, was my oldest friend, as I had walked to her house from the Hays Place when I was only five years old. Carl's brother, George Rose, and his wife Leona lived just down the road from the grange hall. George owned a cattle truck, and made a living by hauling farmers' cattle to the stockyard in Spokane. Their daughter, Ethel, was very friendly and I was disappointed a year later when they moved to Colville and we couldn't play together any more.

Lawrence and Ruby Hays and their two children, Mervyn and Helen, moved into the small house that had been built at the top of the Hays' Hill. This was across the road and down from the two-story house we had lived in a few years ago – when we'd had so much fun coasting down the Hays Hill. George and Elizabeth Abernathy lived almost at the foot of the Hays' Hill. Their daughter, Georgia, in her late teens had joined us and shown me older kids liked sleigh riding, too. She swooped down the hill on her sled, having just as much fun as we younger kids did.

In the next house down the road lived Walt and Frances Lickfold and their son, Everett, who had been the "big" boy in the eighth grade who walked Lester and me to school when I was in the first grade. Now he was going to Kettle Falls High School and had acquired the nickname of "Toar." His brothers and sisters, Howard, Hazel, Ruby, Roy, Shirley and Stanley, were married and gone from home. Their main access came in from the Heidegger Road just above Donald Jamieson's log house on the corner.

Standing across the Pleasant Valley Road from Lickfold's was the empty house where Hyatts had lived when we were on the Hays Place. Driving by there now reminded me of how Mrs. Hyatt had once saved Lester's life by giving him beaten egg whites after he had drunk some blackleaf forty poison.

Donald and Elsie Jamieson lived in the log house on the corner of the Heidegger and Pleasant Valley Roads. The fall of 1936, Elsie gave a bridal shower for Ruth Heidegger before her marriage to Walter McNutt. Around fifty women on the area attended, including Mom. She was happy to get out for a social gathering, taking Effie, Viola and Vida with her while the rest of us were in school.

A quarter of a mile below the log house was the house where Walt and Rose Clemons lived with their boys, Russell, Orville, Irving and Ivan. A few years later, when Lester and I went to high school, Walt was our school bus driver. Lou Schenegge, next down the road, had orchards on both sides of the road and sold many boxes of red Delicious apples every fall. His house sat on one side of the road; his red packing shed stood on the other side.

Not far below was the Meriwether Place where we once lived – where Dad had first put me on our work horse and taught me to ride bareback. And practically across the road was the farm which Tom and Letha Peters had bought in1934, moving in with their children, Jim and Betty-Jo.

The last family that could be considered "neighbors" was Donald Jamieson's parents, Gavin and Mary. They had migrated from Scotland several years before. After building his two-story house, Gavin had painted a sign, "New Caledonian Ranch," and hung it over the drive leading to the road.

Other neighbors lived closer to our house up the Pleasant Road's junction with Rickey Canyon Road that led past our new home. Paul and Ethel Holter became close friends over the years as well as good neighbors. They didn't have any children and always seemed happy to visit with us kids. If they came along while we were walking home from school, they'd always stop to give us a ride. We'd hop on the running boards and hang onto the window frames as Paul drove up the curving road, stopping at our mailbox at the junction of Rickey Canyon Road to let us off. Even though their house was less than a mile from ours, we couldn't see it because of the timber between the two farms. But the distance didn't keep us from hearing Paul. As Lester, Dora and I were shocking bundles in our grain field one day, we heard a distant yelling. Stopping work to listen, we recognized Paul's voice yelling at his work horses, "Giddap, dammit, move along, pull, you lazy sunsabitches." We laughed, knowing he didn't realize anyone could hear him. And in bed that night, our voices imitated Paul's "Giddap, dammit, move along," as we laughed again, calling across the attic to each other.

Paul's brother, Albert "Dutch" Holter, visited Paul often enough to become Dad's good friend, too. Although mistrusting most government men, he didn't hold it against Dutch that he was a game warden. But when we ran out of meat and it wasn't hunting season, he had enough respect for the law and his friend's position to hunt far away so Dutch wouldn't hear him shooting.

Ella Loven's house was across the road from Paul and Ethel, where she lived with her mother, Mrs. Carter, and daughter, Barbara. Ella's father had homesteaded the farm years earlier. The canyon above them was called "Carter Canyon." After her husband, Art, had died a few years earlier while hunting, Ella had run the farm without much help. When driving her team of horses, she wore work overalls, but when she finished her outside work for the day, she washed up and changed into a house dress.

Mr. and Mrs. Christian Mathis, and their son William, lived on past Holters and Lovens, up over the top of the very steep Folsom Hill. They had a large dairy herd and sent their milk to Colville on the same creamery truck that picked up Holters' milk. In Mrs. Mathis' spare time, she sewed wool mittens, giving them to Miss Dean at the Pleasant Valley School for children who didn't have mittens. After seeing me come to school one morning with ice-cold hands, Miss Dean gave me a pair. And until my hands grew out of those warm mittens, my fingers were never cold again.

Although we had moved from the Curry Place, we were glad Frank and Julia Rupert were still our neighbors. We had just moved to the other side of their farm. Klaus and Leona Heide, sons Wayne and Wendell and daughter, Dorothea lived on a farm just north of Rupert's in a small two-story log house on Childers Road (later changed to Chamberlin Road). Dorothea, just my age, liked riding horses, too, and we soon became good friends. But after her mother died, they left the farm, moving to Spokane.

The next few summers, Lester and I saw most of the neighbors who lived along Quillisascut Creek, After Dad told us there might be some trout in the creek, we cut small branches off a tree for poles, tied fish hooks and lines to them and fished as far down the creek as the grange hall. Occasionally, we caught enough Rainbows or Dolly Varden for supper. Most were barely over the six-inch minimum size, but we caught enough eight and nine-inchers to keep us going back for more.

Since we were closer to the grange hall as well as to new neighbors, Dad and Mom started going to grange meetings and dances more often, usually taking us kids with them. But once in awhile, when they didn't want Leola, Effie, Viola and Vida to stay up late, Dora and I stayed home and took care of them. While some of our neighbors lived as far as four miles away, Dad and Mom thought of them as neighbors. Being closer to other farmers let Dad get together with them more. He enjoyed their companionship and joking. And arranging to trade work time was easier. Few farmers could afford to hire a hand; they just traded time. He also like the thought of never being snowbound, as we now lived close to a county road that was kept open. He wouldn't have to hitch the team to the vee to plow out half a mile of road like he did on the Curry Place. The best advantage for Mom, who had often been lonely on our hilltop, was having many neighbor women nearby. She felt she could visit when she had some free time.   She never got quite as lonesome just knowing she had friends close by. Abe and Margaret were wonderful neighbors when we lived on the Curry Place, but they had been our only neighbors. Now we enjoyed having wonderful neighbors in every direction.

(I've called our new farm, the "Home Place" because after a few years of renting it, Mom and Dad were finally able to buy it, living there the rest of their lives. And after Lester came home from the Philippines and World War II, he bought Gavin and Mary Jamieson's farm, with the New Caledonian Ranch sign over the gate. In 1967 Kettle Falls School District annexed the Pleasant Valley School District 32. Lawrence Hays bought the school house and had it torn down. The community bought the school bell and tower, giving it to Paul and Ethel Holter, who built a bell tower for it near their garage. When Dad died in 1970, Albert "Dutch" Holter, now Sheriff of Stevens County, showed how much he had thought of his long-time friend by leading the funeral procession from Colville to the cemetery in Kettle Falls. It was the last contact between the former game warden and his friend, the out-of-season deer hunter.)

Visiting at Ella Loven's

I was trapped atop the fence post, holding the basket full of eggs I had just taken from Ella's hen house. To steady me on my precarious perch, I hooked the heels of my oxfords over a strand of barbed-wire fence separating the barnyard from Ell's house. The Rhode Island Red rooster that had me treed strutted around, jumping up every minute or two in his attempts to flog me.

It was the summer of 1937. I was thirteen and staying with elderly Mary Carter while her daughter, Ella Loven, and granddaughter, Barbara, went to Spokane on an overnight shopping trip. Ella didn't want her mother to be left alone that long, so had asked me to stay until their return.

I had walked down the Rickey Canyon Road to the junction, turned left onto the Pleasant Valley Road and started a gradual uphill climb. In about a quarter of a mile, I was opposite Paul and Ethel Holter's house. I turned left and went through the little gate into Ella's field, and soon reached the other little gate that opened into the shaded green lawn surrounding her house. A mountain stream kept her grass green and watered a profusion of flowers, reminding me of the oasis pictured in my school book. This coolness was a sharp contrast to the surrounding cheat grass-covered hills.

I opened the back door, walked through the kitchen to the dining room. Ella and Barbara were sitting at the round table and Grandma Carter was in her rocking chair. We visited for a few minutes, then Ella said it was time for them to go. After awhile Grandma Carter, wanting me to feel useful, handed me the egg basket and asked me to gather the eggs from the hen house, out through the back gate near the barn. I had rummaged in all the straw-filled nests, finding enough eggs to fill the basket, and was headed back to the house. Suddenly a big rooster came flying around the corner of the shed and jumped up on me, raking me with his sharp talons. If I hadn't been wearing my sturdy denim overalls, he would have bloodied my legs.

Not wanting to spill my full bucket of eggs, I couldn't run, and didn't have anything to hit him with to chase him off. Being next to the fence, I climbed up on a post so he couldn't flog me any more, thinking he'd soon go away. But he just kept strutting around my fence post, occasionally flying up to try to claw my legs. Standing guard, he had treed me on the fence post. And then I heard the gate behind me squeak open. There was Mrs. Carter, white hair piled atop her head, hobbling along with her cane. She said, "I forgot to warn you about that mean old rooster," and whacked him over the head with her cane.

Relieved to have been rescued, I climbed down, my eggs still unbroken. Until my meeting with Ella's rooster, I had been sure I could tackle almost anything. Before I was ten, I had found my way through the woods by myself, battled yellow-jackets, and helped kill deadly rattlesnakes. At thirteen, I was very embarrassed to have let a mere rooster chase me up a fence post.

On arriving at Ella's, I had found the cookie jar full of peanut butter cookies, their tops showing crisscross fork tracks. Grandma Carter said, "Go ahead and help yourself; eat all you want." Knowing Mom wouldn't want me to act like I didn't have any manners at all, I only took two. But the cookies were so good, I helped myself many times. By the time I left the next day, there weren't many cookies left. While realizing I'd eaten too many to be polite, I was proud of my self-control for leaving at least a few in the jar.

The next afternoon, after we had finished the housework and I had gathered the eggs, we went into the dining room to rest. Grandma Carter picked up some hand sewing, saying she liked to keep busy even when resting. I sat on the window seat opposite her and looked around the room. My eyes latched onto a very curious object hanging on the wall behind the heating stove. Made up of Chinese coins, it hung by its braided cord from a nail. Red cord strung through the square holes in the coins' centers laced them together in the shape of a sword. The sword made me think of Chinaman Tai who sent to China for the firecrackers he sold at our Fourth-of-July celebrations. And later Barbara told me that her mother had bought it at the small store that the Chinese had near Daisy at the edge of the Columbia River.

There weren't many chores or housework to do like there were at home. It had taken only a few minutes to throw some grain out to the chickens; the cows were dry so I didn't have to milk. I had already filled the wood box and helped Grandma Carter cook, wash dishes, sweep the floors and every thing else she asked me to do. After breakfast I had swung on the long swing hanging from a limb of a towering maple tree, squished through the wet lawn around the sprinkler, and looked at all the pretty flowers. I hadn't found anything interesting to read, and there was no one to play with. I learned how Barbara must feel not having any brothers or sisters to play with. Mom and Dad weren't telling me what to do, and Lester and my sisters weren't here to argue or play with. We were a rowdy bunch of kids, always doing things together, and I missed the hubbub and laughter of our house. It was lovely here at Ella's, but too quiet and genteel for my tomboy ways.

Finally, in late afternoon, Ella and Barbara drove up the lane and parked outside the gate. They got out of the car loaded down with packages and sacks, came into the dining room and upended their paper sacks onto the table. Bright floral colors spilled out, turning into pieces of cotton dress material. Before they left, Ella said she would bring back material for a new dress for me. Now, with one sweep of her hand, she spread the pieces out and said, "Ines, you can pick out the one you like best."

I looked at all the pretty pieces, then my eyes locked on one with bold stripes of brown and yellow. It looked dashing – and that's the one I picked. As I got ready to head for home, Ella said, "Remember now, if your mother doesn't have time to sew up that dress, come back and I'll make it for you."

My return walk home didn't take as long as the walk to Ella's the day before. It was mostly downhill and I was eager to be with my noisy family again and to show them my gift from Ella. I spilled the material out on the table. Mom admired it, then put me to work peeling potatoes for supper. Glad to be in the bustle of our home life again, I didn't mind not having time to finish the story in Western Story Magazine that I had begun two days earlier. The long hours with no one to play with had shown me how much my large family meant to me.

A couple of weeks later Mom said, "I have a stack of things to do, so it might me quite awhile before I can get around to making your dress. Go over and ask Ella if she still has some spare time."

So back I went carrying my dress material. Ella didn't seem surprised to see me. When I asked her if she'd have any extra time, she quickly replied, "Yes, in fact, I have a little spare time right now, " and brought out some of her dress patterns. She said, "Maybe you can find one here that you like. We're about the same height, but you're thinner than I am, so I'll have to alter the pattern."

The one that appealed to me was a princess style without a belt. The four buttons in two rows gave it a double-breasted look. I thought the yellow and brown striped material would look good with the stripes running up and down. After Ella took my measurements, she said, "Come back in a few days and we'll see how your dress fits."

Going back the next week, I found Ella had the dress pieces sewn together. Eagerly, I pulled it on over my head, expecting to look dashing, just like the material. But the dress was too big. Ella gathered the looseness with both hand and said, "It's too full, but I'll fix that by taking up the side seams."

After pinning it in at the sides, she pinned the hem up to the right length. I got into my other clothes and Barbara and I went outside to play. When we went inside a little later, I found Ella had the dress finished except for the hem. She said, "Try it on again; it might fit better now. It's all done except the hem and you can sew that just as well as I could."

Trying the dress on once again, I found it fit perfectly, and felt better, too. And I thought perhaps it did make me look a bit dashing. In anticipation of showing my new dress to Mom, I ran part of the way home. She was as pleased with it as I was, and grateful to Ella for finding the time to make it. Eager to wear it, I sat right down and hemmed it by hand, taking tiny stitches, too small to be seen on the right side. Now I had a new dress to wear when I went into the eighth grade at school that fall. The dress was doubly special because Ella made it for me and because it was so bright and bold.

Staying at Ella's hadn't been the first time I had spent the night there. Earlier in the summer, Barbara had asked me to stay over so she would have someone to play with for parts of two days. When I asked Mom if I could stay, she said, "There's nothing special for you to do here now, so you can go, but watch your manners. And I want you to come back right after breakfast."

Barbara and I had taken turns on the swing tied to a high limb of a maple tree and had long swooping rides. Barefooted, we watered the lawn, enjoying the water squishing up through our toes as we moved the sprinkler from place to place. Visiting at Ella's also gave me an experience with inside plumbing. Before going to bed that night, I got to do something I'd never done before: take a bath in a real tub. Ella had one of the few inside bathrooms in the valley, complete with a tub long enough for my long legs to stretch out. It was roomier than our round galvanized metal wash tub where I had to draw my knees up almost to my chin. My long legs made up most of my five feet, six-inch height.

Ella had a water tank behind the cook stove that heated water whenever a fire was going. All I had to do to fill the tub was turn on the faucets and out poured hot and cold water. When the tub was half full, I turned the faucets off and stretched out to soak. I enjoyed sitting full length instead of having my knees bent as I had to do in our round galvanized wash tub. Then, remembering Ella saying, "You can use that small brush to scrub your heels," I picked it up, ran it over a bar of soap, and attacked my grimy heels, thinking that if I wore socks in the summer, my heels wouldn't get so dirty. When my bath water cooled, I just pulled the plug and the water ran out by itself. I didn't have to lug the tub to the door and pour the water out like we did at home. The only work was scrubbing out the tub with cleanser.

It hadn't been long after this that Ella and Barbara had gone to Spokane and I stayed with Grandma Carter to help her. As it turned out, she was the one that helped by rescuing me from that feisty rooster after he chased me to the top of the fence post.

102

(In the summer of 1989, my husband, Henry, and I returned to Ella's, staying in the farmhouse which Barbara and her husband, Harvey Scott, had turned into a Bed and Breakfast lodging. That was also the year the farm was declared a Washington State Centennial Farm, having been homesteaded in 1889 by Barbara's grandparents, William and Mary Carter. On this visit over fifty years after having eaten so many peanut butter cookies, my eyes wandered to the kitchen counter as if expecting the cookie jar to still be there. Barbara gave me Ella's recipe and I treasure it because of the memories. A letter from Barbara in 1993 told more about the wall hanging made of Chinese coins: "It came from Ah Tai's little store down near the Columbia River at Daisy, probably purchased sometime in the 1920's.)

The Outdoor Toilet

Just as I'd reached an exciting part in my story in <u>Ranch Romances Magazine,</u> Vida tugged at my arm. Visions of the "cowboy racing his horse to rescue his sweetheart from outlaws" faded as I looked into the anxious face of my little sister. Tugging my arm a second time, she said, "wanna go pee pee."

Dropping the magazine, I grabbed her hand, and we ran through the open kitchen door, hotfooting it for the toilet, partially hidden behind some lilac bushes in our back yard. Not yet two, Vida and Viola were afraid to sit alone over the big round holes of the toilet's bench seat. Since it was possible for them to fall through the hole, someone always had to go with them.

Dora and I had helped take care of them since Mom had brought them home from Mrs. Aldredge's Maternity Home. If they had wet pants, we changed them; if they were hungry, we gave them their milk bottles, using the flat sided, small necked medicine bottles saved after cough syrup was used up. Later on when they were old enough to take solid foods, I held Viola in my lap at mealtimes and fed her while Mom fed Vida. So when Mom started their toilet training, Dora and I naturally helped with that, too.

Now, while holding the twin on the toilet seat, I saw for the umpteenth time how the single layer of rough boards, nailed on vertically, formed the building, leaving a few spaces between. A fly was buzzing around and lit on Vida's head, so I swatted it away with a rolled up piece of catalog paper.

The carpenter had chosen a wide board for the seat, long enough to stretch from wall to wall, and had sawed the three big holes at an angle, then sanded the edges. Years of use had made them smooth. Overhead, a single layer of thick cedar shingles covered the pitched roof. In nice weather, we might dawdle while looking through last year's copy of the Montgomery Ward catalog, kept on the seat for use as toilet paper. But while free, the pages weren't soft. The colored pages were too stiff for use; even the black and white pages had to be crinkled to make them usable. That exasperating fly came back and had lit on Vida's head again, but this time I was ready for him with some rolled-up pages and smacked it. It fell to the floor dead and I shoved it through a crack with my shoe.

The summer's heat made the toilet even more unpleasant than in the winter because of the odor. To help cut the smell, Mom dumped lime and wood ashes into the pit all through the summer. But despite her efforts, she could not get rid of the smell. While the hottest place on the farm in summer, it was also the coldest place in winter. The combination of ice-cold seat and frigid wind blowing through the building's cracks made the toilet too cold to stay longer than necessary. It was such an unpleasant place that we girls didn't want any men to see us go there. In the fall when the threshing crew came down from the field at noon to eat, we waited until they returned to work before going there.

Every six or seven years the pit filled up, and Dad and Lester had to dig a new pit nearby. They moved the light building into position over the newly-dug pit and shoveled the loose dirt into the old one to fill it. Most farmers with outhouses made sure to get this job done before Halloween. If news of a full toilet pit got around, that toilet was likely to get tipped over, perhaps as a hint it was time to move it. When Vida and I returned to the house a few minutes later, I was glad to get back to my exciting story and found that the cowboy had caught up with the outlaws, rescuing his sweetheart.

A few months later Mom got a bright idea of how the twins could go out all by themselves. In one corner of the toilet, she sawed a hole in the floor and nailed the wooden potty chair (which had been made from an apple box) over it. Sitting over a smaller hole and with their feet touching the floor, the twins couldn't fall in and felt safe. They also felt very "big" to be able to go to the toilet alone.

(Since those long-ago days on the farm, I've found outdoor toilets in other parts of the world. In search of a rest room at a roadside cafe in rural Spain, I followed a sign pointing to the "servicio." It led me outside and around the corner. While in that old-fashioned outhouse, this scene from my past played itself from memory, blotting out my surroundings. I no longer saw the servicio's white-painted interior, but the unpainted, weathered-brown boards of the outdoor toilet back on the farm.)

City Relatives

As the unfamiliar car drove in through our big swinging gate, we kids wondered who could be coming to see us. It came to a stop near the house and a red-headed lady got out. When none of us greeted her, she asked, "You don't know who we are, do you?"

She was right. We didn't know her, the three children or two other grown-ups who had piled out of the car. We were sure that Mom and Dad would have known them, but they had gone to town that morning. The red-headed lady looked somewhat familiar, so I had a hunch they could be relatives. "Well, Ines, it's been a long time since you've seen me, so you don't remember your Aunt Lizzie. But I know you and Lester, and Dora. Leola was only one year old the last time I saw her. I guess this little girl is Effie -- and these toddlers must be the twins!"

We knew Lizzie was married to Mom's brother, Lester, and they lived in Lewiston, Idaho, but we hadn't seen them for about six years. Aunt Lizzie then told us the names of the others. "These boys are your cousins, Guy and Virgil, and my niece, Tacky, is your cousin, too. This is my mother, Pearl, and our friend, Vance, who drove us here. Your Uncle Lester couldn't leave his job in Lewiston to come."

After Grandma and Charley had moved back to Idaho a few years ago, we didn't have any relatives nearby. Dad's brothers and sisters lived in Oregon, still farther away. Not many could afford to visit us. And tied to our farm by lack of money and having cows to milk twice a day, we couldn't go far from home. So that summer afternoon when our relatives came, they seemed like strangers. After Lizzie introduced everyone, she asked, "Where are Bill and Sis?"

Lester told them that they had gone to Colville to shop for groceries and probably wouldn't get back for a couple of hours. After the brief greetings, we kids didn't know what to say. As the oldest, Lester and I felt responsible for making them feel welcome, but hadn't had much practice in talking to strangers. Dad had drilled into us that we had to keep still when grown-ups were talking. Aunt Lizzie had been looking at the steep hill out beyond our creek and the timbered mountain in the other direction. In Lewiston, she had houses all around her, but here there wasn't another house in sight. Turning to me, she asked, "Don't you get lonely here so far away from any place?"

Puzzling about how I could be "far away" when I was in the center of my whole world, I replied, "No, I never get lonely. Everything I know and like is right here."

Waiting for Dad and Mom to return, we sat on the worn boards of the front porch. I was still worrying about what to talk about that would interest these city people. Seeing the alert faces of my cousins, I wondered what games they liked. But thinking it wouldn't be polite to leave the grown-ups while we played games, we sat anchored to the porch. At long last our car came into sight on the Pleasant Valley Road below its junction with the Rickey Canyon Road, and a few minutes later drove through our gate and into the back yard. After opening her car door, Mom recognized our visitors and ran to Aunt Lizzie, throwing her arms around her neck saying, "Oh, I'm so glad to see you!"

Mom's happiness broke the long silence. Suddenly everyone was talking at once. Disappointed at not seeing Uncle Lester, Dad's first question was to ask where he was. He had been the one who had introduced Dad to Mom years ago. After the grown-ups followed Mom and Dad into the house, we heard their bursts of laughter. And at last, released from our self-imposed responsibility to the adults, we kids launched into our usual country games. In seeing who could run the fastest, we raced around the house, feeling good to be using our stored-up energy, then slowed down to play ante over, catching the ball as it got thrown back and forth over the roof.

Tiring of these games, we asked our cousins if they'd like to see the barn and blacksmith shop. Curious, they followed us to the barn and through the horse stalls to the cows' stanchions. Lester said, "This is where we put the cows to milk them. These bars are stanchions. They keep the cows from pulling their heads out and walking away. When we're through milking, we open the bars and the cows go out to the corral. But the stanchions don't keep the cows from kicking if Dad or I happen to pull a sore teat."

I pointed at the ladder leading up to the square hole in the ceiling and told them, "That leads to the hay mow. From there, we fork hay down into the manger so the cows can eat while they're being milked."

About this time, Tacky wanted to go to the house, so Dora went with her. From the barn, Lester and I took Guy and Virgil to the small blacksmith shop, about a hundred feet from the barn. "What's that thing?" one of them asked, pointing at the small forge.

Lester and I told them how Dad used the forge for heating pieces of iron. "He uses coal to make a fire hot enough to heat the iron until it's red. Then it's soft and he can bend it by laying it on this big anvil and pounding it with a hammer. We get the fire in the forge hot by puffing air into the coals with these bellows."

The boys took turns picking up the bellows and compressing it to force air out of its pointed end, and hefting the big hammer to feel its weight. Leaving the blacksmith shop, we took them to the creek behind the barn where the cows and horses drank, then stood by the pig pen watching the pigs root around. Heading back to the house, we took a quick peek in the door of the chicken house. We liked showing Guy and Virgil around, who seemed interested in everything. Two days later when our city relatives left, we hated to see the "red-haired lady" and others leave.

The next year Elmo and Bob Dryden, Mom's brothers, drove up from Lewiston in their Model A Ford. Mom had filled our heads full of stories about taking care of her four little brothers. Now that two of them were here, she seemed happier than we'd ever seen her. Usually our men visitors pitched in to help Dad with the chores. But that first night when Dad and Lester went out to milk, Elmo and Bob stayed inside "to talk to Sis." It wasn't that they didn't like Dad, they just <u>had</u> to be near Mom after not having seen her for a long time. Bob later said, "Sis was more of a mother to than Mother was."

Early the next morning, both men went out to the barn with Dad to help with the chores. After breakfast, Dad said he had fence to fix. Elmo said, "I'll go with you, Bill, I'm good at digging post holes."

They set off with Elmo carrying the post hole diggers over his shoulder and Dad carrying a hammer and a bucket of nails. Mom said, "Well, I have work to do today, too, and began sifting flour into the big aluminum dish pan, the one she kept for mixing yeast bread.

Bob had stayed inside again with Mom. It surprised me to see a man helping in the kitchen – and obviously enjoying it. Although we girls and Mom did many outside chores and field work, Dad and Lester never helped with the cooking. After Mom and Bob had filled several loaf pans with the bread dough, Bob said, "I'd sure love to have some maple bars; let's make some."

Mom said they could, as she had just bought some maple flavoring from the Raleigh man, and started shaping the remaining bread dough into bars. Bob joined in. As they happily worked together, they talked about their childhood days, laughing at funny incidents. When they had shaped the rest of the dough into bars and placed them on a greased baking sheet, Mom set them aside to rise. Later, while they were baking, she made a powdered sugar icing, adding the maple flavoring. It was ready to be spread on the bars when they had cooled after baking. Mom usually made cinnamon rolls with the leftover dough from bread loaves, but we weren't disappointed at the substitution.

That night at the supper table, Elmo started a story with, "Do you remember . . ." and off the four gown-ups went telling about events that had happened before any of us kids were born. Then one of them mentioned the cheat grass fire that Uncle Frank's car had accidentally started when we went to pick chokecherries. It had been several years ago when we were living on the Hays Place. Uncle Frank had come in late July, after a month of hot weather that had dried out the cheat grass. The day after his arrival, he said he had a craving for chokecherry jam. "Sis," he asked, "do you know where we can find some chokecherry bushes?"

Mom knew there were a lot of bushes growing high on the hillside above the grange hall. "The only way to get there by car," she told Frank, "is to go up the road and turn off on that narrow dirt track just beyond the grange hall."

Grabbing our gallon berry-picking buckets, Frank, Mom, Lester, Dora and I (that was before Leola, Effie and the twins were born) piled into Frank's car and up the road we went. Getting even with the grange hall, Mom said, "Slow down. There's our turn up ahead."

Frank turned sharp left onto the narrow wagon track leading up the brush-covered hill. Driving slowly, we came out onto a flat stretch of land, then chugged up a steep grade in low gear, following traces of old wagon tracks running alongside a barbed wire fence. We stopped at a gate in another fence and Frank got out of the car, pushed the wire loop off the post of the flexible pole-and-wire gate and pulled it aside so Mom could drive the car through. Then Frank shut the gate behind us and climbed back into the car. Mom pointed up toward the rocky bluff and said, "There's your choke-cherry bushes way up there on the hill."

We climbed slowly up the rocky, cheat grass-covered hill. Rocks clanked against the framework of the car, and low bushes scraped its bottom. We climbed slowly until the engine sputtered and died. The hill had become too steep for the Model A Ford, and the jagged rocks had gotten worse. "Guess that's as far as we can ride," said Frank, turning the switch off and pulling on the emergency brake. Carrying our buckets, we got out and headed uphill toward the choke-cherry bushes. Lester happened to turn to look back at the car and yelled, "Hey, the cheat grass is on fire!"

We all looked back and saw a wavering line of low flames in the dry grass around the car, leaving behind curls of smoke over a burned and blackened area. Wind fanned the reddish orange flames and made them race up the slope west of us. Frank spun around and ran back downhill, jumping over burning grass on the way, sprang into the car and released the brake. The car rolled backward, out of the flames. Re-joining us, Frank said, "The hot exhaust pipe must have set that dry cheat grass on fire. I'm glad the car didn't catch fire, too!"

We all stared in disbelief at the blaze eating its way uphill. There was no way we could put it out; all we could do was stay out of its way. Fortunately, it ran only a short distance before coming to a rock slide. With no more grass to feed on, the fire died out. We climbed on up to the choke-cherry bushes and started picking. Most were taller than grown ups, but we just bent the branches down and picked the small, purplish-black cherries that were mouth-puckering bitter. When I found one that was dead black, I bit into it, thinking it might not be so bitter. But it made my mouth pucker up and my tongue dry up, so I spit it out. Now I knew how they got their name -- they'd choke you if you ate them!

Mom had made jam out of them the year before, but it never tasted good. No matter how much sugar she added, the result was more like syrup than jam – and never tasted sweet. I couldn't imagine why Uncle Frank wanted to go to all that trouble to get choke-cherries that only made bitter syrup.

A few years later after we had moved to the farm on Rickey Canyon Road, one of Dad's brothers from Ashland, Oregon brought his wife and three daughters up to visit. When Dad saw the unfamiliar car drive in, he went out to see if someone was lost and needed directions. But the man who got out car wasn't lost, he was a younger brother, Elmer, whom he hadn't seen for many years. When Dad saw who it was, a big grin spread across his face. He grabbed Elmer's hand and pumped it, saying, "By grab, it's sure as hell good to see you!"

By this time Mom and the rest of us had gathered around, excited to see Dad's meeting with his brother. After a woman and three girls got out of the car, Elmer said, "This is my wife, Ruth, and our daughters, Betty, Maxine and Barbara."

Mom welcomed Ruth and led her to the house. But Dad didn't follow. He stood with his hand on top of Elmer's shiny gray Chevrolet, feeling the smoothness of its unblemished body. After admiring every inch, he opened the door and looked inside. He saw the clean upholstery and smelled the new-car small, then exclaimed in wonder, "I've never had a new car, but this looks brand new to me. You must have just bought it!"

With a shy smile, Elmer replied, "Yes, I did. And I wanted to try it out on a trip. We drove over seven hundred and fifty miles from Ashland, Oregon and it didn't give us a lick of trouble."

Lester, Dora and I were glad to meet more cousins, to have someone else who belonged to us. To entertain them, we offered to show them our favorite view of the Columbia River from the top of the hill. They were wearing pretty dresses, so we didn't think they'd want to go through the barn and blacksmith shop and see the pig pen that we'd shown our other cousins. Pointing to the hill behind the barn, Lester said, "From the top of that hill, you can see the mountains clear across the Columbia River, and if you look the other way, you can see the top of Monumental Mountain. Come on, you'll see!"

The six of us set out walking up the wagon road behind the barn, telling them that the wild Mariposa lilies might be in bloom and that we might see a deer in our grain field. Chattering away in our excitement to show them what we liked best, we hadn't noticed the girls hadn't shown any interest. We had gone only about a hundred yards up the road when we realized they were lagging behind. Then we knew that they weren't dressed to explore the countryside, and didn't <u>want</u> to explore it. The next day, we figured out they were content as long as we didn't stray far from the house and yard. They just weren't natural-born explorers like we were.

Yet, a couple of days later, I regretfully watched as Uncle Elmer drove out of the yard taking his family away. My eyes followed the car until it went out of sight below the mailboxes at the junction. I couldn't help but wonder what games these town girls liked. Now it was too late to ask.

All the relatives who visited seemed to enjoy being there. Once while standing outside and gazing at the mountains, Uncle Frank remarked, "Oh, how good it is to breathe clean mountain air again!"

Uncle Bob had kept going back to the kitchen spigot for another drink, saying, "I just can't get enough of this cold spring water." And as much as they liked "Bill and Sis" and certain things about our valley, they knew they couldn't make a living here. For Aunt Lizzie, it was "lonely so far away," and a shock to not have electricity or indoor plumbing, which all of them had in town. Somehow, we sensed that none us would trade places.

Target Practice

"Okay, you girls, I'm ready for that target now," Dad said as he sat down in the chair outside the kitchen door, holding his rifle. Leola and Effie had made a target from an end flap of a cardboard box, using a black crayon to draw the solid round bull's eye and the four or five circles around it. Dora picked up the target and handed it to me. We both ran through the barnyard toward the steep hill, waded through the creek and climbed about twenty-five feet up the hill. This was about a hundred yards from where Dad was sitting near the house, a good test distance for sighting-in the rifle. Shooting into the hillside was a safety measure which prevented the bullets from hitting any people or livestock.

Dad was the only one in our family who did any target practicing. When one of his shots missed a deer, he knew that the rifle's sight had gotten moved accidentally, so needed to adjust its sights. If one of the rifles started shooting too high or too low, he sighted it in, adjusting the back sight until the rifle shot straight. With a shell in the firing chamber and six more in the magazine, he was ready to use them all until it shot straight. The last time he'd shot at a deer, he missed it completely and guessed he must have banged the sight while going through the brush.

Dora and I found the right spot on the hill and set up the target by propping rocks in front and behind the lower corners. We didn't want it falling over before Dad had a chance to shoot. To make sure it would stand by itself, Dora poked it with her finger. It didn't fall, so we raced back across the creek to join Dad and Mom and the four little girls near the kitchen door.

Now Dad was ready to take his first shot at the target. Sitting in his sturdy chair, he rested the long barrel of the rifle on the back of another chair in front of him. To see how the rifle was shooting, he needed to keep it right on target without wavering. With his left hand on the stock and right hand extended on the barrel, he pulled the butt firmly up to his left shoulder, hunching down until his jaw pressed against the stock. Pulling the hammer back with his thumb and holding the front sight deep in the notch of the rear sight, he aimed at the middle of the bull's eye. Slowly he squeezed the trigger.

The sudden loud boom made me jump, even though I was expecting it. No matter how often I watched him shoot a rifle from close by, I always jumped at the noise. And I was somehow always surprised to see him shooting left-handed, as he did everything else right-handed. "Go get the target, kids, I want to see how far off this gun is shooting," he directed.

Eager to help again, Leola and Effie ran up the hill to get it. Bringing it back, they proudly held it up for him to see. Noting the bullet hole in one of the circles five inches above the crayoned bull's eye, he said, "Well, it's no wonder I missed that deer. I shot right over its head!"

Dad continued making test shots and adjusting the sight until he put a bullet hole right in the middle of the bull's eye. Grinning in satisfaction, he said, "Now this gun is shooting like it ought to!"

He put a shell in the barrel and refilled the magazine, took it into the kitchen and stood the fully loaded rifle behind the kitchen door. It was ready for his next hunting trip. Dad knew that the rifles were safe where they stood behind the kitchen door, as he and Mom had taught us to never to touch the rifles unless we were going to use them.

In the summer of 1936, when Lester was fourteen and I was twelve, we got plenty of target practice. But we shot at ground squirrels instead of a cardboard target, and used twenty-two caliber rifles instead of the thirty-thirty rifles. Lester used the repeating rifle, which had a clip that held six bullets and one in the chamber, which gave him seven shots before he had to re-load. I used the single-shot rifle, and I had to reload after each shot. We killed these grayish-brown squirrels because they dug holes in the grain fields and grazing land, piling the loose dirt up in high mounds around their holes. When Dad was cutting the hay and grain, the sickles of the mowing machine and binder could dig into the dirt piles, which would dull the sickles' teeth, or at worst, break them. The squirrel holes were an even greater hazard, as a horse stepping into one could break a leg. Not wanting to lose a work horse, Dad encouraged our target practice by keeping us supplied with twenty-two caliber shells.

Despite how many squirrels we killed, we never ran out of targets. They seemed to multiply faster than we could kill them. But shooting them was good practice. While thinning them out, we became comfortable handling rifles and learned to be careful so we wouldn't shoot anyone. And by learning to shoot straight, we made a few nickels and dimes. We cut off the tails of every squirrel we killed, as the Stevens County Extension Agent paid a bounty of two cents a tail. Dad took the tails into Colville and turned them in as proof, and collected the bounty for us. We were happy with the money he brought home, even though it was usually less than a dollar. We never ate ground squirrels as we did the few pine squirrels Lester shot. We called them "flying" squirrels, because in jumping from tree to tree where their nests were, they seemed to be flying.

When I was fourteen, these two rifles brought me a prize of $10.00 when the Washington Farmer, a monthly magazine, sponsored a photography contest. Leola and Effie posed for me sitting in the front yard, holding the rifles crossed in front of them in the shape of an "X." Buster, our German shepherd, sat on his haunches beside them with his ears perked up like he was posing, too. When Mom got the roll of film developed, we liked the picture, so I sent it in to the contest. Two months later I received a letter and a check for $10 from the magazine. Their next issue listed my name as one of the contest winners. I was thrilled that I'd won a prize and that my name was printed in the magazine!

Our target practice never succeeded in killing many squirrels, so Dad had to resort to something drastic: poison. He added strychnine to some oats and told Lester, Dora and me to help him carry the poisoned oats in buckets up to the field. He said, "This strychnine is deadly poison. Keep your fingers out of your mouths while we're dropping the oats into the squirrel holes. And as soon as we get back to the house, wash your hands and faces with soapy water."

We poured two tablespoons of oats down each hole. In an hour, we dropped the oats into all the holes we found and were looking around for more holes. Dad said, "I think we got 'em all except these two here. If you have any oats left in your buckets, pour them into the holes. We won't take any back down to the granary, as someone might accidentally feed them to the chickens."

This method killed off the squirrels faster than our bullets had, but it wasn't as much fun as the "target practice" had been. Our early shooting taught us gun safety along with making us feel at ease using the rifles. From the time we had helped Dad clean the rifles a few years back, he taught us never to point a gun at anyone and always act as if a gun was fully loaded, even if we had just ejected its shells. And shooting straight gave the added bonus of spending money, which didn't hurt our feelings, either!

To Rice by Horseback

Part of the money Lester earned from shooting ground squirrels went for his first watch. After hearing me tell Mom I'd ride a horse to the Rice store to buy some things she needed, he asked me to buy a watch for him. Giving me a silver dollar, he said "Bring me one of those Ingersoll pocket watches."

Rice was about seven miles from our house, but since I was always looking for an excuse to get on a horse, it didn't seem far. Mom had started mixing up a cake without realizing we were out of brown sugar. She thought of a couple more items she needed, so added them to her list. Her cake mixing could wait until I returned, as she hadn't added any liquids to her mixture. Catching Betty, my favorite horse, I bridled her and headed out, riding bareback, as we still didn't have a saddle. Hanging around my neck was the old denim lunch bag I'd used when riding three miles to school from the Curry Place. It would be handy for carrying things home from the store.

Almost an hour later I topped a rise and saw the few buildings making up the village of Rice in the distance. There were five or six houses, post office, a two-story Odd Fellows Hall (which sometimes held dances), and the tall, false-fronted Rice Mercantile Store. Arriving at the store, I slid off Betty's back and tied her to the white picket fence beside the store. My overall legs, damp with Betty's sweat, had horsehair stuck to them. Brushing off, I walked past the gas pumps and up a couple steps, opened the screen door and stepped into the crowded inside. Horse collars hung from long nails, while the rest of the harnesses draped from nail to nail on one white-painted wall. On the oil-stained wood floor, golden spools of binding twine sat in neat stacks, their pungent smell mingling with that of coiled new ropes nearby.

These things were all for sale, but for me, the most fascinating item was not for sale. The large cash register with shiny buttons sat on top of a large glass case just inside the door. A magic part inside it rang a bell every time someone opened the cash drawer. I told Mr. Clinton what Mom needed, and he went through the store finding them.

When he set the items on the glass counter, I dug her money out of my pocket. He pushed some buttons on the cash register and gave the crank a couple of turns. A bell dinged and the drawer flew open. Again fishing in my overall pocket, I brought out Lester's silver dollar. Pointing to the watches inside the glass case, I said, "And Lester wants one of those Ingersoll pocket watches."

Mr. Clinton smiled as he slid open the big glass door on his side of the counter, reached inside and brought out a square, white cardboard box. Taking the lid off, he lifted out a round watch with a big stem on top. He said, "I'll set it to the right time and wind it for him. See, this is how you do it."

Outside the store again, I paused to open the box. After admiring Lester's new watch, I put it under the other things in my denim bag, and slung it over my shoulder. Ready to go, I untied Betty's rope, climbed up on her back and headed home.

With Betty plodding along on our uphill route, we got home about an hour later. I turned Betty loose in the barnyard, then handed Lester's box to him. As he opened it and looked at his first watch, a pleased grin lit up his face.

Smoky, The Buckskin

Smoky's nearly-white mane contrasted with her dark golden body, making her almost light enough to be called a palomino. When Dad brought her home, he called to us, "Come out and look at our new buckskin."

I took one look at her and said, "I love that yellow color. Let's call her "Smoky." She was smaller than our other horses, so I hoped Dad would find that she wasn't strong enough to help pull the heavy farm machinery. With her white blaze face and long, sweeping tail, she would make a pretty riding horse. I could just picture riding her around to show her off to my friends.

Smoky was about two years old and hadn't been broken to ride or work. As Dad put a harness on her, she laid her ears back, jumped around and tried to bite him. When he finally got the collar, hames and rest of the harness on, he hitched her and Star to the wagon. Eventually he got her broken to harness, but used her only for light work. She wasn't strong enough to help pull something as heavy as the binder, and was too flighty to ever be a dependable work horse.

One morning, Mom looked out the kitchen window and got the scare of her life. Four-year old Effie was standing behind Smoky, holding her long tail! Mom was sure Smoky was going to let loose a kick any second. She went outside and walked slowly up to the horse's head, talking soothingly to her, while Dora took Effie's hand and led her away from those dangerous heels. Since Smoky hadn't kicked Effie, Mom thought she might stand for a small load on her back. While holding the neck rope, she slowly boosted Effie up to Smoky's back. As soon as Effie grabbed a handful of mane, I took their picture. The muscles of the skittish horse quivered and her ears laid back, so Mom eased Effie off of her back. Later she told us that if an older person had held Smoky's tail, she might have kicked their heads off, saying "Sometimes an animal senses that small children don't mean any harm, so won't kick them."

Smoky was never any good for working – or for riding. With that one exception for Effie, she bucked off everyone who got on her. After seeing her pile Lester and one of his friends, I knew I'd never have the courage to get on her. When Uncle Elmo Dryden came to visit, he said he'd ridden a lot of bucking horses and just knew he could stay on her. Dad said, "Go ahead and try it."

Elmo had won prizes riding wild broncs in rodeos, but those horses had been saddled. After putting a bridle on her, he swung up on her back and gripped the reins. Smoky lit out across the barnyard running and bucking, head down and back arched. After two jumps, Elmo flew off. He got up, brushed dirt off his pants and grinned sheepishly, saying "I guess that's one horse I'm not going to ride."

The five minutes Effie sat on Smoky was the longest anyone ever stayed on her back. On my fourteenth birthday in 1938, Mom took a picture of me feeding her an apple. She still seemed skittish even while getting a treat. I was disappointed no one could break her to ride, as I'd never be able to ride any place and show her off.

The Garner Place

Mom got our work day started by saying, "It's going to be hot today. Let's get up to the Garner Place early and get the weeds hoed out of the garden while it's still cool."

This farm was government land on which the Garner family had a long-term lease. No one had lived on it for many years. Since its edge was just across the Rickey Canyon Road from our place, Dad rented it to have extra pasture for the cows and sheep, paying less than a hundred dollars a year. But we soon started using a piece of ground near the old house for our garden spot, too. In addition to the grazing land and garden, there was an old orchard and two small fields of about twenty acres that Dad planted in oats. We were familiar with it, as Grandma and Charley Adams had once lived there.

Now with Mom leading all six of us girls, we headed on foot for the garden, more than a half-mile away and all uphill, carrying our newly sharpened hoes. Dad had sharpened them all on his grind stone in the blacksmith shop the day before. Sparks flew as he held each hoe's blade to the grind stone while sitting on its framework and pumping the foot board that made the stone go round. When he finished sharpening the hoes, he said, "They should stay sharp for awhile unless you hit too many rocks."

Behind the Garner house, the top of Monumental Mountain rose 5,500 feet. We appreciated it in the summer, as its cool night air swept the hot air out of the valley. And it was beautiful in all seasons with its tamarack and aspen trees that turned gold in the fall, making bright splashes against the dark green of the pine and firs. The winter's snow made it seem even taller than it was, rising up into the blue sky.

Irrigation water for the garden came down a ditch from a spring on the mountain into a small v-shaped wooden flume, splashing into a ditch running past the house. From there it ran down to the garden area. The spring ran continuously, and the run-off water from the garden seeped out into the pasture, watering about a quarter of an acre of grass. In late summer it stayed green, making a cool contrast to the bleached white grass around it. Nearby a few neglected apple, cherry and prune trees still bore fruit. Beyond this orchard a brushy slope fell abruptly to another fairly flat grain field. Below this field a steep bank plunged down to the dirt road near our house. Since the garden area was so far from our house, getting there on foot was as much work as the planting and hoeing. Long before any vegetables were ready to eat, we walked back and forth many times.

Tomato plants needed protection from frosts, so we planted them near our house, in the shelter of our woodshed where they weren't so apt to get nipped. We also had separate areas to plant our dry beans, potatoes and sweet corn, which took much more ground. They could do without irrigation, so Dad plowed up an acre or so for them near our grain fields.

A little excitement one day took the drudgery out of our work day when Dora, Leola and I went up to hoe weeds in the garden near the Garner house. After climbing the last hill, we looked up at the house and saw a steer sticking his head out of the upstairs window. Most of the doors and windows were missing, as no one had lived in the house for some time. We knew from the manure piles on the floors that cattle wandered in, but we hadn't known they climbed stairs! Not knowing how we could get the steer back downstairs, we finally decided to climb up, sneak through the doorway and get around behind him to chase him back down.

It didn't work that way. The steer saw us when we got to the top and didn't wait for our next move. Before we could get around him, he plunged out the window. We raced back down the stairs expecting to see him lying on the ground with a broken leg or two. But when we got there, he was walking away on four good legs as if he jumped out of windows every day.

My earliest memories of the Garner Place were of events that happened long before we rented it. I was about four, and we had gone to see Grandma and her husband, Charley, who had recently moved there from the Aldredge Place. Just starting to cook supper, Grandma had a hot fire going in the cook stove when a car drove into the yard and four men, all strangers, piled out. Dad and Charley went out to see who they were and what they wanted. Showing their badges, they said they were game wardens. One of them said to Charley, "Someone reported you've been killing deer out of season. We want to look through your barn and other buildings."

So Charley and Dad went with them and watched while they searched the barn, bunkhouse, chicken house, shop and woodshed. While they were looking in all the possible hiding places where Charley could have hung a deer, Grandma was busy frying up the last of the venison steaks.

Fifteen or twenty minutes later they came back from the barn empty-handed. Grandma said, "Supper is ready," and invited the game wardens to join us. They sat down at the table and ate, obviously enjoying the steaks. When they finished, they thanked Grandma for the good meal, got back into their car and drove away. Since there was no evidence of Charley killing deer out of season, the game wardens couldn't very well haul him off to jail.

As they drove out of the yard, Dad said, "By grab, Charley, they knew all along they were eating deer meat. They just didn't want to arrest you for killing a deer to feed your family."

That night Mom let me stay overnight with Grandma, the first time I'd ever stayed away from home. As Grandma put me to bed, I noticed the bright red colors in the small braided rug on the bare boards beside the cot. Landing on that rug during the night woke me up; I had dreamed I was flapping my arms and flying.

We pastured a couple of dozen sheep along with our cows on the Garner Place. One spring Dad found a bear had killed a lamb, so set about to trap the bear. He took his largest trap – the one with big teeth in its jaws – up to the orchard, opened the jaws as far as they'd go, and set it. Using the strong chain attached to the trap, he anchored it to a prune tree.

A couple of evenings later, he set out to check the trap, taking his rifle with him. Getting to the orchard, he saw he had a bear all right, but it wasn't caught exactly the way he had in mind. It was sitting in the middle of the open trap, eating prunes that had fallen off the tree. Dad raised his rifle, took aim, and shot it sitting there in the trap. So we had bear meat for a few weeks instead of venison, and Dad had another bearskin to tan.

After making a garden at the Garner Place for three years, Dad decided to give it up and make a garden spot by our house, despite the irrigation problem and poorer soil. We were relieved we wouldn't have to make that long walk uphill every time vegetables needed picking or when we had to hoe weeds.

Logging Camp Activities

The screen door of the Garner house slammed behind me as I arrived to begin my day's work for Jo Naff, whose husband's logging crew was cutting timber in that area. She said, "I have to go into Colville to stock up on supplies today. You can cook the noon meal for the logging crew by yourself."

She said there was already a beef roast in the oven. All I had to do was peel and boil some potatoes, make gravy with drippings from the roast, open and cook two cans of green beans and wash the strawberries for dessert. Jo then got into her car and drove away and I was on my own. I'd been helping cook for about a week, so wasn't upset about being left alone. After all, I was fourteen and had been Mom's right-hand helper for years. I set to work immediately and put more wood in the kitchen stove to keep a steady fire going. The roast would be done too soon if the fire got too hot. But it wouldn't get done by noon if there wasn't enough fire going. Then I peeled the potatoes and put them on the stove and got the beans ready to heat.

By the time the four loggers came into the yard and started washing up outside, I had the table set and the meal was ready. I hurriedly dished up all the food and set it on the table. But suddenly I thought of the strawberries that I'd forgotten to wash, then felt like a failure. Starting to wash them, I soon had help from Fred Wooley, the logging-truck driver, who had seen how flustered I was. This big, friendly man about Dad's age got up from the table and stood at the cabinet beside me, washing and stemming each berry with his big fingers just as carefully as I did. The three other men continued eating, glancing sideways at us from time to time. Not many men helped in the kitchen, and I wondered if they'd razz Fred later about doing woman's work. I was glad Dad had been working that day close to our house and had gone there to eat his noon meal. Always wanting him to be proud of me, I would have been embarrassed if he'd seen dinner wasn't completely ready when they came in.

Roy and Jo Naff were the last people to stay in the Garner house before it became rundown. Roy was logging off the big pine and fir trees in the section next to that place and had brought Jo along to cook. While we rented that farm, we never had any use for the house, so Dad let Roy use it as headquarters for his logging operations. Two men bunked in an outbuilding near the barn and one man lived close enough to drive home at night.

Dad had to leave earlier than I did, as the logging crew had to be out in the woods ready to start work shortly after daylight. Since Jo didn't need me that early, I didn't go with Dad so had to get there on my own. After walking a short way up the Rickey Canyon Road, I ducked through a barbed-wire fence, taking a short cut up over the hill through the pasture and up over another brushy hillside. For the month I helped Jo, I walked up every morning and stayed until after we had washed the supper dishes.

Although Dad had left the logging business after leaving Oregon to live in Washington, he still had his sturdy leather boots with spikes in the soles. Loggers called these caulked boots "cork" boots. When the men had to walk on top of felled trees to lop their limbs off, the spikes kept them from slipping off. Roy had hired Dad to run the log jammer, a large noisy machine with a winch on it that skidded logs from where the sawyers felled them to a loading area, then loaded them onto Fred Wooley's dual-carriage logging truck. At the beginning of the operation one of the crew driving a bulldozer had gouged out a rough road so the jammer, logging truck and pickup trucks could get up into the woods.

Occasionally after the moon meal, Mom and my five sisters walked up to watch the activities. After Jo and I had finished washing the dinner dishes, I was free to go with Mom and the girls and track down the crew and watch them work. Walking up a skid road in the shade of tall trees, we breathed in the smells of crushed pine and fir needles and piles of yellowish-white sawdust beside newly cut stumps. The last time we had been in the woods, we'd seen a bulldozer butt its way through brush, push over small trees and gouge out a new track for Fred's Wooley's truck. Now we heard the loggers before we saw them, heard the sound of a cross-cut saw, the warning shouts and the solid thump of a tree falling heavily to the ground. Soon we heard the bucker chopping limbs off the tree with his double-bitted axe. From farther away came the low rumble of an engine and I could imagine Dad operating the controls to make the log jammer's thick cable snake a log up the hill.

As we came around some brush, we saw two sawyers and waved at them. They waved back, motioning for us to stay where we were. We watched as one of the men headed toward the next tree to be cut down, balancing his cross-cut saw on one shoulder with its teeth facing outward away from his neck. The handled ends of the saw hung down, springing gently as he walked. When he reached the tree, a big fir about seven feet around at its base, his partner joined him. To make the tree fall in a certain direction, they had to make a notch on that side of the trunk. Each of them then took hold of one of the wooden handles on the saw and placing the teeth next to the bark, make a short slanting cut. They used their axe to finish chopping out the notch. Going around to the opposite side, they started sawing toward the notch. Their saw cut in deeper and deeper. After sawing for about ten minutes, they stopped to rest and take a swig of water from their jug. It took a lot of muscle to pull that six-foot crosscut saw back and forth through the tree trunk. Then they started up again. Just before their saw reached the notch, we saw the tip of the tree start waving. It was almost ready to fall. The sawyers glanced up, too, and took another pull. When the tree tip began to sway, they quickly drew the saw out of the cut and yelled "T I M B E R" to alert anyone close by, then jumped off to one side. The big tree came crashing down, breaking limbs off other trees on its fall, and slammed into the ground with a thundering crunch.

After resting again from their strenuous sawing, the two men picked up their axes and headed for the fallen tree. One of them said, "Guess we'll have to <u>buck</u> these limbs off; we sure can't <u>wish</u> them off." And with that, they climbed onto the tree trunk, and began cutting the limbs off flush with the trunk. Upon finishing, they marked with chalk the length for each log where they would saw.

One day the men had a little excitement while chopping limbs off. One of the sawyers carried kerosene in a flat pint whiskey bottle to pour on his saw when it got sticky with pitch. The bottle just fit into his hind pocket. As he walked on top of a downed tree lopping off its limbs, his caulked boots caught on the stub of a limb and he fell on the tree trunk. He landed on his backside, breaking the bottle, with pieces of glass lodged in his rear end.

Two other loggers helped him down to the barn and laid him face down on a blanket. They picked out the pieces of broken glass, and found that the cut was so big it needed to be sewn up. One of the men came into the house and told Jo what had happened and that someone had gone down to Ernie Keck's to telephone a doctor in Colville. They asked if Jo might have a clean cloth to cover the wound. She found a white cloth and gave it to him. Having heard only bits of the whispered conversation, I wanted to know the whole story, so told Jo I was going out to the barn to see what was going on. I hadn't heard enough to know a man was lying in the barn with no pants on because of a gash in his butt. She stopped me by saying, "That's no place for a girl right now."

Almost an hour later the doctor arrived and sewed up the sawyer's cut. The gash didn't stop the logger, but for a few days he sawed and chopped at a slower pace.

The two loggers who bunked at the Garner place spent their free time playing cards or with other amusements. One of them had brought a toy from his southern homeland – a jointed, wooden doll. A connection on its back made it hang suspended over a wooden slat. During one noon hour while Mom and the four little girls were visiting, he showed us how he could make the doll dance by hitting the slat with his hand. The doll swung its arms and clacked its feet against the board, clogging while the logger sang in a high-pitched twangy voice. Leola and Effie were enthralled, and asked him to make the doll dance again and again. They were disappointed when the noon hour ended and the logger had to head back to the woods.

Toward the end of logging operations, when there weren't many big firs left to cut down, the hooker quit, leaving Roy Naff short handed. The hooker's job was to set the choke, attaching the cable's tongs to each log so the log jammer could skid it up to the landing and load it on the truck. Since Roy knew he couldn't find another logger on short notice, he asked Dad if he could take on that job, on top of his regular job of running the jammer. That meant Dad would have to get off the jammer, pick up the heavy tongs attached to the woven wire cable, pull it to the log, hook the tongs, then climb back to the jammer -- fighting his way through brush and over rocks – to operate the controls and snake the log up and load it on the waiting truck. He would have to do this for each log. Because Dad wanted to make extra money, he took on this extra work. But strong as he was, he couldn't do the work of two men without wearing himself out. Every night he came home dog tired -- and every night he went to bed immediately after supper so he could rest up for the next day's work. Mom scolded him, saying, "That extra money isn't worth killing yourself for."

When the logging operations ended two weeks later, Mom was relieved. She had constantly worried about Dad after seeing him come home tired and dragging his footsteps. He had become so exhausted that he was still tired after a full night's sleep. He knew he wouldn't have been able to keep doing the work of two men much longer. We were all glad to see the end of the logging operations.

Helping cook for a logging crew taught me a few things and gave me new adventures, as well as giving me some extra money. Jo Naff was easy to work for, the work hadn't been hard, and I had enjoyed being a part of the logging operations.

Grandma Adams

In late fall Mom got to worrying about how her mother in Lewiston would be able to buy a turkey for Thanksgiving. Grandma's husband, Charley, had recently deserted her and their two sons, and they had no means of support except from county welfare checks and what little money her married sons could spare. Their jobs didn't pay much, so they were having a hard time supporting their own families. As Mom was getting supper, she glanced out the window and saw our hens pecking at the grain thrown out for them. That gave her and idea – she would send Grandma a couple of chickens.

A few days before Thanksgiving, Mom killed and dressed out two good-sized chickens and hung them outside in the freezing night temperature. In the morning they were frozen stiff, so she wrapped them in several newspapers and put them in a cardboard box. Dad made a special trip to the Kettle Falls post office to mail them, as by then the Rice post office had already sent out its day's mail. The chickens reached Grandma a couple of days later, in time for her to roast them for their Thanksgiving dinner.

After Grandma had moved from Pleasant Valley to Idaho, we didn't get to see her except when she rode the bus to visit us during summer, staying about a month. Dora and I liked hearing her home remedies for preventing wrinkles and gray hair. She said, "To keep wrinkles away, splash your face with cold water first thing in the morning."

We thought that advice must be pretty good, because Grandma was fifty-seven and didn't have many wrinkles. But we didn't think much of her remedy of using sagebrush tea on her hair to keep it from going gray. It was already gray, and the tea just made it stink. She made the tea by boiling silver-leaved sage brush branches in a pot of water for several minutes, turning the water brown. Then she tossed the branches out, but saved the water in a jar. After Grandma combed the water through her hair, it smelled just about as bad as the tea had when it was simmering. We tried to steer clear of her until after most of the stink evaporated. She had brought chittam bark tea, another of her remedies she made from cascara stems. Every two weeks or so, she made us take some of the bitter-tasting liquid whether we needed it or not.

In addition to telling us of her home remedies, Grandma gave her opinion on other things. When we picked up fresh-cut wood chips and bark for starting fires, she thought we should pick up all the old wood chips littering the ground near the woodshed. In Lewiston, she had to buy all her stove wood, and never had enough kindling for starting fires. But we couldn't see any sense in picking up old stuff that had lain on the ground all winter. After realizing her scolding wasn't going to change our minds, Grandma walked all around the woodshed, her thin frame stooping to pick up each piece. When she collected an armful, she took it into the kitchen's wood box.

The day I got my first permanent wave, I was glad to have her with me. It was the fall of 1938 before Lester and I started our freshman year at Kettle Falls High School. Mom knew how I'd always wished my horsetail-straight hair was curly, so said I could get a permanent. Dad needed something from the hardware store, so he would take me to the beauty parlor. Grandma needed some sewing supplies, and would go, too. When Dad let us out of the car, he said, "I'm going to go back home as soon as I find what I need, but I'll find you a ride home or come back and get you."

The beauty parlor had a lot of surprises. After cutting my hair, the operator rolled it on long skinny rods, pulling very tight. When all the hair was wound up, she took me to a chair that had an odd-looking contraption standing over it. Its long, dangling electrical cords with clamps at the end of each one reminded me of a picture of an octopus. As the operator attached a clamp over each rod, my head felt heavier and heavier. When all the rods had clamps covering them, they were so heavy it felt like a ten-pound sack of sugar was sitting on top of my head. The operator then turned on the electricity so the rods would get hot. She said, "I'll leave it on for about twenty minutes to make a good wave."

My neck got tired and stiff and I thought the twenty minutes would never end. Finally, the time was up and the operator took off the clamps and rods. She rinsed my hair, put another solution on it, and took the rods off. With all the weight gone, I felt light headed. The operator rinsed out the strong-smelling solutions, rolled my hair up in curlers and put me under a cone-shaped machine that blew hot air and dried my hair in no time at all. After she removed the rollers and combed my hair, I saw my hair was curly, like I'd always wanted.

Sitting in the back of a neighbor's pick-up truck on the way home, Grandma kept touching my hair in admiration, saying, "My, don't you look nice with curly hair", which made me feel so good, I silently forgave her for all the chittam bark tea she'd made me drink.

Grandma belonged to the Seventh Day Adventist Church and was thankful to the Lord for her daily existence. One of her ways of showing it was saying a lengthy blessing before supper. We had never said grace, and we weren't happy with Grandma changing our routine. Finding Mom alone, Dora and I complained. She shushed us saying, "It won't hurt you to wait a few minutes."

It was plain to see Dad didn't think much of Grandma's long-winded blessings. At first he endured them, fidgeting while Grandma went through her five-minute list of "thank-you's." But one day he got tired of waiting, picked up his fork and began eating before she said "Amen." Grandma noticed and from then on, she just bowed her head and asked a silent blessing. Even though we kids had grumbled about waiting, it now seemed impolite to start eating, but Mom was the only one who waited.

Dad's unwillingness to wait puzzled me. In other ways he lived by the Golden Rule. Although his every-day speech had plenty of swear words sprinkled in, he thought it unforgivable if someone stole, lied, cheated, or went back on his word. He didn't like or trust anyone who was guilty of that. He was what people called, "a square shooter." He and other farmers never used written contracts, but made agreements that ended with a handshake instead of a signed paper. Many times he told us, "A man's word is his bond."

At the end of Grandma's month's visit, Dad and Mom took her to Colville to catch the bus back to Lewiston, taking her remaining chittam bark tea with her. In some ways, we weren't sorry to see her go. We settled into our usual routine minus the silent blessing, sagebrush and chittam bark teas and scoldings about gathering firewood. After all, we kids took our orders from Mom and Dad and they hadn't told us we had to mind her.

When I told Grandma during her next visit that I had learned to type during my sophomore year in high school, she was happy to hear it. She said, "Oh, good, you can set down my life story on paper as I tell it to you and write down the history of my parents and grandparents! I've seen many changes in the settling of the country, moving from one farm to another in a covered wagon and now almost everyone drives a car."

I would like to have done it for Grandma, but we didn't have a typewriter and couldn't afford to buy one. So we never got her life story "set down" on paper. After pondering Grandma's hard life, Mom added, "I think her hardest job was scrubbing clothes on the washboard. She was always too poor to buy a washing machine or to hire someone to wash for her."

In the fall of 1941 Grandma got sick and Dad took Mom to Colville to catch the bus to Lewiston to visit her. The house felt empty all that time. Dora and I wrote a letter saying we missed her, and told her what everyone was doing since she left. When she finally returned three weeks later, we were mighty glad; and the house no longer seemed empty.

Grandma got lonely, too, and often wrote two-page letters to us. Despite this and her many misspelled words, we figured out what she meant. One of her letters went: "My dearest children, one and all, Why in the Devil don't some of you take time to write to an old guy like me look and look for a letter an none comes this makes three letters I have written an I guess you did answer one of them I do hope this finds you all well an at work but haying over isn't it but soon will be time to can corn an are you going to dry some an how I like to have some . . . Love to all. XXX OOO Mary M. Adams"
Glad to get her letter, we counted the "hugs" and "kisses" at the end. When we replied, we sent some back to her. Grandma died August 8, 1946, at the age of 65. Death let her escape her life of pain, poverty and hardship. An autopsy showed a broken rib penetrating her lung, the result of a beating many years ago by her mean husband.

Grandma Adams was the only grandparent we ever knew. Hard times, with its shortage of money, had kept Dad from visiting his parents after he left home. His mother, Dora Wheeler Riley, died in Idaho in 1925, the year after I was born. His father, Peter Riley, died in 1921 in Redmond, Oregon while working on his rented farm. He is buried in the Madras cemetery.

The envelope to Grandma's letter is dated August 8, 1945, and bears a three-cent Iwo Jima stamp. When I read her letter, I can again smell the pungent sagebrush tea in her hair, hear her querulous, yet caring voice, and see her gaunt frame stooping to pick up wood chips. And I think of the Sunbonnet Girl quilt she gave me, and marvel at how hard she worked to applique those flowered dresses and sunbonnets. I've handed down this heirloom to my daughter, Janet Eileen, to put her in touch with her Great-Grandmother Mary Margaret Denney Adams.

In later years Uncle Lester told about all of Grandma's husbands, and said, "My father, George Steeley treated Mother better than any of her other husband did, but he went to the store one day and just didn't come back."

Grain Binding

Sitting at the edge of the wheat field, our new John Deere binder was a beauty. Its green and yellow paint shone in the sunshine. The varnished wood arms would soon be going round and round, pushing the standing grain against the binder's sickle. In its shining newness, it looked bigger than our old, rusted binder held together with baling wire that Dad had struggled to keep running for the past five years. The smile on his face showed he was glad he'd been able to save up enough money to buy a brand new one. He had checked the wheat for ripeness the day before, and said, "When I broke a head and rubbed it in my palms, it shelled out easily; the chaff practically jumped off the grains of wheat! I'll start binding tomorrow morning."

So the next morning, he and Lester harnessed Maude, Star, Pepper and Pet, our strongest horses, and hitched them to the shiny, new binder. Sitting on its contoured and perforated metal seat, Dad held the long leather reins and drove the horses as they pulled the binder up the steep grade and into the first grain field. Lester, Dora and I followed on foot. We had to go along and shock the grain bundles. When we arrived at the wheat field, Dad told us that before he put the binder into gear and start cutting, we had to oil all its working parts. Picking up an oil can, he said, "I'm going to put oil in all the holes. I want you kids to watch so you can oil it from now on before we start binding."

With all three of us peering over his shoulder, Dad pointed out where the oil holes were, lifting up their little hinged lids and squirting oil into each one. When he'd found them all, he climbed up to the metal seat, slapped the reins lightly against the horses' rumps, called "Giddap," and reined the big team onto the swath around the standing grain.

About three weeks earlier he had cut a couple of swaths around the edges of the field with the mowing machine. This made room for the binder to work without knocking down any grain. He and Lester had already gathered the still-green grain up in the wagon, taking it to the barn to use as hay for the cows and horses. Now as soon as the binder got next to the grain, he put it into gear. The revolving arms hit about half-way down on the stalks, pushing them against the sickle. The sickle, on the edge of the binder bed, glided back and forth under the guards, cutting the stalks. The cut grain fell onto the moving canvas bed which took it up into the binder. There the hidden machinery gathered up the stalks into a tight bundle, wrapping it with binder twine. The curved needle darted out so fast to tie it that all we saw was a blur. A knife cut the twine, and a lever automatically kicked the bundle out to a carrying basket. When it had four or five bundles in it, Dad tripped another lever and the bundles dropped to the ground.

We had watched Dad bind grain before, but it was still a marvel to see standing grain turned into neatly tied bundles that we could stack into shocks. To make them stand, we jabbed the first two bundles hard into the stubble, propping them upright against each other. We put six to eight bundles in each shock, then lay two bundles across the top to help keep out any rain.

While pulling the binder on level ground, the horses could walk at a steady pace, but on the hilly parts, Dad had to stop them often to let them rest. When they got to the steepest pitches, all four leaned into their collars, straining forward with all their might to pull the heavy machine. When Dad pulled on the reins and stopped after a steep pull, the horses stood heaving, their necks and haunches wet with sweat and their muscles trembling from exhaustion. Looking at them, Dad said, "They need a rest more than we do."

The next morning when we got to the grain field, it was Dad's turn to watch as Lester and I oiled the binder. With a small oil can apiece, we squirted oil in all the holes we could remember, and thought we had found them all. Dad stood silently, just watching. When we finished and started putting the oils cans in their places on the binder, he said, "You missed a couple of holes. I'll show you where they are again and you'll remember them the next time."

He was right. The next day we found every hole and were proud of ourselves for being able to oil that big, expensive piece of machinery all by ourselves. After Dad cut all the grain and we had shocked it, he didn't worry quite so much about bad weather damaging the year's crop. But he never completely relaxed until threshing was done and the grain safely stored in the granary.

124

The Threshing Crew

Whooping with delight and dripping from water that we Dora, Leola, Effie and I had thrown on him, Paul Holter stopped his team, wrapped the reins around a post at the front of the grain wagon and jumped down. Red faced with laughter, he grabbed a bucket and drenched all of us in one throw.

Our annual water fight had begun! It continued until our wash tubs were empty. Then Paul reluctantly climbed back up on the wagon, his bib overalls and blue work shirt completely saturated. Water-soaked but refreshed on a hot day, he drove back up to the thresher for the sacks of grain that would be waiting. By the time that Dora, Leola, Effie and I had re-filled the galvanized wash tubs from the spigot in the yard, our clothes had dried off enough so we could go back into the house to help Mom cook dinner for the crew without getting the kitchen floor all wet.

At fourteen I was more interested in outdoor fun than in looking for extra jobs to do in the kitchen. And my sisters, delighted with the idea of throwing water on Paul, had eagerly helped me fill the tubs for his next trip down. He was one of our closest neighbors and traded work with Dad. His job was to haul the gunny sacks full of threshed grain down the hill to the granary, next to our house. As soon as he emptied all the wheat into the grain bin and turned the team around to head back for his next load, we had thrown water on him.

Our water fights went on all afternoon, but they were no longer a surprise to Paul. Mom stood at the window laughing, enjoying them almost as much as we did. We thought he was lucky, being the only one in the threshing crew who got cooled off on a hot day. The men working and sweating around the threshing machine with chaff sticking to their bodies and blowing down their necks would have been glad to change places with him!

Each year, Dad's announcement, "The threshers are coming!" was a sure way to get all of us excited. But that summer of 1938, we heard them long before they arrived. With the throbbing of the tractor's engine reverberating up the valley, Dad hadn't needed to tell us they were coming. Looking beyond our mailbox down at the junction of the Pleasant Valley Road, we glimpsed the tall threshing machine looming above the big tractor pulling it. In a few minutes we saw two pick-up trucks following the thresher and we knew they held the rest of the threshing crew. As the tractor turned onto the Rickey Canyon Road and headed toward our place, Dad said, "Lester, run out and open the gate for them."

Creeping along, its engine roaring, the tractor soon drove through the gate and into our yard. Lester swung the big gate shut, and pulled the wire loop over the top of the gate post. The tractor driver stopped at the house and cut the engine back to idle. Still, he and Dad had to shout over the racket as they greeted each other. Besides being big and noisy, the tractor vibrated, making me think of a giant gray frog squatting there, huffing and puffing, breathing hard with its sides heaving. Its racket almost drowned out Dad's words as he told the driver to follow him uphill to the grain field.

With Lester riding with him on our hay wagon, Dad led the threshing machine and the three other wagons the quarter of a mile uphill to a level spot in the middle of the shocked grain. By that time most of the threshing crew had arrived, bringing their own teams and hay wagons. Paul could come later, as he wouldn't have any grain to haul until after the thresher had been set up and a wagon load of bundles hauled to it.

Having the threshing crew at our farm meant a change in our everyday routine. For us kids, it promised excitement, as there were new people and actions to watch. For Mom, it guaranteed hard work with all the extra cooking. Dad was always relieved when they came to our place, as his grain crop would soon be stored in the granary, safe from the weather. Before it was cut, hail or a hard rain with wind could almost ruin a crop by knocking down a lot of standing grain. But aside from having his crop safe, Dad also looked forward to the crew's company and to hearing the local news some of them were sure to bring.

The man who owned the thresher traveled from one farm to another with two or three of his own crew. Dad could make a good guess when they'd arrive by finding out where they were working, then counting how many farms they had to finish before getting to our place. The crew with the thresher might arrive any time during the day, depending on when it had finished at the previous farm. Getting the rest of the workers who drove the two horses for each hay wagon hauling grain bundles from the field to the threshing machine was up to Dad. And Paul Holter, who owned a sturdy, narrow bodied "grain" wagon, just right for hauling full sacks of grain from the thresher to the granary, always came with his two horses and wagon to help with our harvest. The thresher and its tractor were the only machines used. The rest of the hauling work was done by a two-horse team pulling each wagon.

The big tractor that pulled the thresher from farm to farm provided the power to run it. After arriving in the field where it would be set up, the tractor unhooked from the thresher and moved the right distance away to match the length of the long drive belt that ran between it and the thresher. It had to be lined up straight so the belt would stay on the pulley and to make the thresher's gears run frontwards instead of backwards. The twist in the long belt also helped the belt stay on the pulley. The thresher, a large gray metal contraption, looked short and incomplete with its blower pipe and grain pipe swing back against itself for traveling. After the tractor pulled it up to the field of shocked grain, the men set it up to make it ready to receive grain bundles by putting the pipes and other movable parts into their working positions. The long spout would blow straw out; the shorter pipe funneled the threshed grain into burlap bags attached to it.

After the men got the thresher started up, it took three wagons hauling bundles to keep it supplied, as the thresher's operator didn't want to shut it down while waiting for another load of bundles. Dad and Lester worked on our hay wagon, and four neighbor men manned two other wagons. The hay wagons had a flat bed and a front and back rack. That left the sides open so the pitchers could pitch the bundles into it easily. Hauling grain bundles took two men for each wagon: a loader and a pitcher. The loader drove the team between two rows of shocks so they could pick up both sides with only one stop. Some teams were so well trained, they moved ahead to the next shock without the driver having to pick up the reins. He just tied them to the rack, leaving a little slack. When he was ready to move the wagon forward, he yelled, "giddap." When they reached the next shocks, he yelled, "Whoa," and the horses stopped.

The pitcher stuck his pitchfork into a bundle from the shock and threw it up onto the wagon. The loader stayed on the wagon, positioning each bundle with his pitchfork. He threw them butt ends out along the edges of the wagon bed with the heads facing toward the inside of the load. All we could see when the wagon was loaded were the butt ends. The only way anyone could climb on a loaded wagon was up the front or back racks. The loaders took pride in being able to place the bundles in such a way they made a load that wouldn't slip. If any bundles fell off on the way to the thresher, they would have been the butt of many jokes.

The driver moved his team up and stopped close to the thresher where the two men took turns pitching bundles onto the conveyer that carried them inside. And there, with much clanking and rattling, the gears and other metal parts that made up the threshing machine performed their magic. They beat the grain heads off the stalks and loosened the dry chaff from around each grain kernel. They shook them over a shaking screen where a fan blew away the chaff and straw. The kernels of grain fell through the screen into the pipe which funneled them down a two-ended grain spout to the waiting gunny sack. The straw and chaff blew out of a bigger pipe, making a straw stack. When the stack was so high that the spout almost touched it, the pipe swung over to one side and started making a new straw stack.

The grain pipe had a lever that could direct the flow of grain down either of the double spouts and into a gunny sack that hung from each one and reached to the ground. When one sack was full, the bagger turned the lever to direct the grain into the other spout and its empty sack. He then gathered up the looseness at the top of the filled sack with one hand and whipped a length of binding twine around in a miller's knot to keep the grain from spilling. One of the men at the thresher helped Paul hoist the almost-hundred pound sacks into his grain wagon. It was smaller than the hay wagons and had a narrower bed. When the wagon was full, Paul drove it down the hill to the granary beside our house and emptied the sacks into the grain bins. The granary was the old house that stood next to the one we lived in. Dad had partitioned off its downstairs rooms into separate bins, a different one for wheat, oats, barley and rye.

Temperatures were usually in the nineties during threshing season – and that was in the shade. Workers brought their own canteens or water jugs. Dad had made his own water jug by covering the main part of a gallon vinegar jug with denim strips, hand-stitching them together so they overlapped, making a tight covering. After filling it, he let the cold water run over it to saturate the denim cover. When he got up to the field to go to work, he set the jug in a shade spot, which kept it fairly cool for a few hours.

Dora and I did our part in helping Mom cook the large meals. There was a lot of work needed in getting dinner ready for our family of nine plus a threshing crew that could number nine or ten men. We cooked dinner and supper for them during the two or three days they were with us, and in pitching bundles and hefting heavy sacks of grain, the men worked up good appetites.

Our meals were simple but big: meat, potatoes and gravy, vegetables, beet and cucumber pickles, tomatoes, jello salad, honey, bread and butter and pitchers of Kool-aid to drink, with pie for dessert. Since we didn't have a refrigerator, we set the jello in the creek to make it set up, surrounding the bowl with rocks so it wouldn't tip over. We started our day's baking right after breakfast by making four or five pies. The crew's favorites seemed to be apple, but we also made huckleberry, coconut, lemon and pumpkin pies.

Because of the mountain's closeness to us, bringing early frosts, we weren't able to grow pumpkins, but Mom thought of a good substitute by using carrots instead of pumpkins, and adding the usual spices. With whipped cream on top, no one knew they weren't eating real pumpkin pies! Many years later when my husband and I were spending the winter in Mexico and I couldn't find any canned pumpkin, I used Mom's ingenious idea of using carrots to make "pumpkin" pies for a potluck dinner.

The threshers always raved about Mom's fried chicken, so we usually included that in our menu at least twice during their time with us in addition to ham and venison. Getting chickens ready for the frying pans took more time than all the rest. We started by catching and killing five or six good-sized fryers, followed by scalding and picking feathers off before cutting them up to fry.

The crew came down for dinner promptly at noon. After working around the threshing machine and pitching rain bundles all morning, they had dust and chaff all over them. Some of them asked Dora or me to sweep them off with a broom. They washed up outside by the kitchen door where we had placed two granite wash bowls, a bucket of water and a bar of soap on a bench. The towels hung from nails on the side of the house above the bench.

At mealtime the men joshed and told funny things that had happened that morning. Mom, Dora and I were kept busy re-filling bowls and platters, but were still able to enjoy the bantering. After handing a jar of honey to Clarence Carson, an unmarried young man, I asked, "Do you want some honey, Clarence?" Ernie McKinney, a long-time family friend, laughingly revised my question to, "Do you want some, HONEY Clarence?"

Being a trifle bashful I was embarrassed that Ernie had made it sound like I was calling a man "Honey." Toar Lickfold, Paul, Dad and the rest joined Ernie in light-hearted laughter. Not wanting anyone to see my red face, I whirled around, took the shortest way out of the room, flew through Mom's bedroom and her open window. I stayed outside until the men went back up to the field. By the time they came down again for supper, my embarrassment was gone and I was ready to do a little kidding myself. Remembering how much fun it was for everyone– including me– it didn't take long for me to forgive Ernie for his teasing.

Our kitchen duties didn't keep Dora and me tied down all day. When Mom didn't need us, we took Leola, Effie and the twins up to watch the exciting activities at the threshing machine. We liked seeing the long belt twisting and flapping as it ran from the tractor to the thresher. The whole outfit – tractor chugging, long belt flapping, and thresher vibrating, rattling and shaking while gobbling up grain bundles and spitting out straw and grain – made a fascinating sight. We enjoyed seeing everything else, too: the grain bundles flying from pitchforks up to the top of wagons, men laughing as they worked and horses straining, their reins slapping and harnesses creaking with the effort the horses made in pulling loaded hay wagons uphill. All of this made up the excitement of threshing.

Despite the news, fun and good spirits the crew brought with them, it was a good thing for the cooks that threshing didn't take any longer than it did. Cooking in large quantities was a hard job. With no ice or electricity to provide refrigeration, our supply of meat wouldn't stay fresh very long. I saw Mom's sigh of relief when the threshers finished and drove their rigs and noisy machinery out the gate and headed for the next farm.

128

By next year's threshing time, all of us would have forgotten the hard work. At the expected time for the tractor to come chugging up the road pulling the thresher, we four girls would again feel an inner excitement as we gazed down the road, watching for it. And remembering how much fun we had in our water fights with Paul last year, we were all ready for him again with full wash tubs.

Years later Lester, Ernie McKinney and Everett (Toar) Lickfold served in the American Army in the Philippines. Ernie and Toar weren't our brothers, but they'd been with us so much that they seemed like part of our family. Ernie was captured by the Japanese and survived the brutal Bataan Death March and three years of imprisonment, which included slaving in Japan's coal mines. His wife later told me that for the rest of his life he had nightmares about those captive years. Lester came back from his service in the Army with "jungle rot" boils on the back of his neck from the hot, humid climate. He had been in the Philippine jungles bulldozing airstrips for our fighter planes. Toar, the 'big' eighth grader who had walked Lester and me to school in my first grade, couldn't forget his years in the jungle. The first time I saw him after his return, he was sitting in the shade near the Rice store with others who had helped dig Carl Rose's grave in the nearby IOOF cemetery. When I asked if he were going to the funeral, he shook his head somberly and replied, "I helped dig his grave, but can't go to his funeral; I saw too many of my buddies killed in the jungle. I just can't go."

129

1938
Starting Kettle Falls High School

In September, the first day of high school, Lester and I hurried down Rickey Canyon Road to its junction with Pleasant Valley Road. Carrying notebooks and sack lunches, and with enrollment money in our pockets, we hurried to make sure we'd get to the junction before the "stub" van got there. It would pick us up and take us to Rice where we would board a larger bus that would go the seventeen miles to Kettle Falls, picking up more kids along the highway. For the first time in our lives, we felt the luxury of riding to school instead of getting there by horseback or shank's ponies.

Lester, edgy about going to a town school, couldn't stand still. He walked back and forth and looked up the road to see if he could spot the stub van. Just as he said, "It should be getting here soon," we saw it round the bend and barrel down the gravel road toward us, dust swirling behind it. The driver, Walt Clemons, pulled to a stop beside us. We ducked through its low doorway, squeezed past the folded-down passenger seat next to Walt and sat on the bench seats along the sides of the van. I found room beside Arlene Conner, who gave me a big smile of greeting. I guessed she was as excited about starting high school as I was. Ralph Byrd, another freshman, sat across from us.

A few hundred yards on, we stopped for Ellen McNutt, my newest friend. She and her parents had recently moved into Adkins' house, just below our mailbox at the junction. In a few minutes we stopped at Childer's Road junction where Dorothea and Wayne Heide were waiting. They were on time, too, after having walked about a mile from their home. Our next stop was opposite the grange hall to pick up Hazel Rose, and a mile or so later we made a last stop for Betty Jo Peters. Driving on down past the little church, we reached the state highway and turned left, heading south for our transfer point at the Rice store.

We boarded the large bus, which had a partition down the middle for separate seating. Obeying the driver's rules, we girls sat on benches closest to the door and the boys went past the partition and sat on the far side. The driver of this bus had started his route south of Rice, making stops in Daisy and along the road to pick up Marian Sites, Fred Esvelt, Bob Cranston and Richard McReynolds, who lived along the Columbia River. Along with Effie Ball and Vivian Rice, who lived in Rice, they were already seated. When we were all settled, the driver headed north along the highway. Soon, he stopped to pick up Donna Kalinouswki, who had recently come to live with her grandparents, Mr. and Mrs. Abris.

Six or seven miles north of Rice, the highway went down a steep grade to the sandy flats along the Columbia River where truck farms and orchards used to be. Workers had almost finished cutting down all the trees in the orchards and removing houses and other buildings below a certain elevation level. When Coulee Dam was completed, the backwaters would soon cover this low-lying area. Llewelyn Gardens, with a white painted wooden sign over its gate, had been one of the largest truck farms along this area of the Columbia River.

We drove across the Colville River on the iron-trussed bridge. Looking left, we saw where it flowed into the Columbia less than a half-mile away. Soon the shade trees and buildings of the small town of Kettle Falls came into sight, and in no time at all we were going down the main street and turning right to go up a slope to the high school. The driver wheeled past the locust trees edging the wide sidewalk leading up to the main entrance and stopped beside the one-story brick school building. We had finally arrived at the Kettle Falls High School.

Other buses brought high school students in from the outlying areas of Kelly Hill, Highland, Greenwood and Meyers Falls. For the first time in our lives, we Pleasant Valley kids would have a lot of strangers for classmates.

Compared to our country schoolhouse, the high school with its many classrooms seemed immense. Sitting in Study Hall, I felt lost when we had to go to different rooms for each class. That first day, I didn't know where to go when the bell rang. Rose Aubertin, a pretty Kettle Falls girl with shining black hair and a dazzling smile said, "Come with me. I'll show you where we have to go."

And all that day when the bell rang, I followed Rose from the study hall to different classrooms. The first time I relaxed was a few days later when several of us country girls ate lunch together outside on the lawn. Arlene Conner, Ellen McNutt, Effie Ball, Dorothea Heide, Hazel Rose and I found the cool shaded lawn under the locust trees was a good spot to eat our sack lunches.

Being thrown in with strangers in new surroundings left me feeling timid and shy. My new feeling of timidity puzzled me. I was still the same girl who had killed rattlesnakes and coyotes, fearlessly ridden the quaking aspen trees to the ground, and stuck like fly paper on the back of a horse while galloping and jumping ditches. I wondered how many of these town kids could find their way around the mountain like I could, or could drive a team of horses or shoot ground squirrels. But knowing how to do these things no longer seemed to count. The following winter, the freshman class hosted the sophomores at a sleigh-riding party on the Hays Hill. And there where I had coasted as a small girl, I no longer felt out of place among my "town" classmates.

I knew starting high school would be exciting. But hadn't realized it would be such fun to see all the historic changes that would take place along our bus route. And during that school year, I became accustomed to the luxury of riding a bus. Guilt no longer rode with me for enjoying its ease or for depending on someone else to get me to school.

131

The Rising Waters

The backwater from Grand Coulee Dam would make the Columbia River rise over hundreds of acres in our area. It would cover all the highway from the bottom of the grade below Engleson's farm to Kettle Falls and beyond, the Colville River bridge, an Indian burial ground and church and much of the town of Kettle Falls. It would also cover and silence that thundering roar of raging cascades named Kettle Falls. Remembering how its rushing torrents had held me spellbound as a seven-year old standing high above the falls and watching the Indians fish, I didn't want those falls to disappear.

Surveyors had already gone all along the Columbia River above the dam site, peering through their transits, measuring distances and leaving yellow-ribboned stakes behind. They pounded the stakes in the ground at 1,310 feet above sea level, the expected water line of the lake behind the dam. As we rode the bus to school and saw their yellow ribbons fluttering a mile or more from the river, we couldn't believe that the Columbia would rise that much.

Workmen had almost completed construction of the dam they had begun in 1933 to generate electricity and irrigate the desert land in the Columbia Basin. When the floodgates closed, the Columbia River would rise and flood all the land being cleared: farms, homes, towns and much of State Highway 22. The lake behind the dam would be 151 miles long, backing up to just south of Northport, Washington, a few miles from the Canadian border.

From the school bus windows all that year, we watched as drastic changes took place all along the Columbia River. We saw a highway crew make a new road at a higher grade level and saw house movers jack up buildings and haul them to higher ground. Loggers cut down the timber and fruit trees in the Llewelyn Gardens and other orchards below the surveyors' stakes. They sawed the pine and fir trees into lengths, loaded them onto logging trucks and hauled them off to a sawmill. On hastily-made logging roads, the heavy trucks trailed dirty dust clouds behind as they plowed through the powdery soil. Smoke clouds hung in the sky from the burning fruit trees and pine and fir branches.

Later, after the new highway was finished, which included a concrete bridge built upstream across the Colville River, workers tore down the old iron and steel bridge. That site would soon be under water, as the Columbia would back up more than two miles into the mouth of the Colville River.

Since the rising water would cover the old Indian burial ground near the Colville River's mouth, the graves had to be found and the bones dug up and moved to higher ground. As always, Dad was eager to earn extra money, so got a job working on that crew. He had dug many graves in the Mountain View Cemetery (at one time called "I.O.O.F. Cemetery") above Rice for friends who had died, but had never dug up human bones. After his first day on the job, he came home sick to his stomach. Mom took one look at his gray face and asked what was wrong. He replied, "Digging up those bones just about made me pass out. We had to sort them, and put a complete skeleton into each wooden box. Handling those bones made me just as dizzy as seeing human blood."

The work wasn't as hard as many jobs Dad had done, but as far as he was concerned, it was the worst one ever had. Despite getting sick to his stomach every day, he stuck it out until the work crew had dug up all the bones and re-buried them farther upstream on the bank of the Colville River.

Soon the State highway crews came in with their dump trucks, bulldozers, and other big machines to build a new highway. The biggest changes started at the grade below the Engleson farm, about four miles north of Rice, and went as far as Meyers Falls, by-passing the town of Kettle Falls.

We heard the racket of the road crew's machines through the open windows of the school bus. Big dump trucks hauled in ton after ton of large boulders to fill in the low spot at the bottom of that first grade leading up from the river. Rocks clanged against the dump truck's metal sides and beds when they were loaded, and again when they were dumped. With their heavy loads, drivers had to shift down to low gear, still their engines labored under the strain. Bulldozers made more noise than the dump trucks. With their powerful engines roaring, gears screeched and blades clanged against boulders, the drivers gouged out a new road going up the high bank. As they advanced and backed up while digging and scraping, the ponderous machines clanked and belched smoke. And like the logging trucks, they sent up clouds of dust.

Of all the changes brought on by the rising water, the one that affected us the most was moving the whole town of Kettle Falls. All the buildings below the high-water line would be torn down or moved to Meyers Falls, uphill and about four miles away. In the spring of 1939, workers started pouring in. They came to move the town, bringing their special equipment. They also brought their own houses to live in -- little houses on wheels that they towed behind cars or pickups.

There were plenty of men living in the area who could log off timber and dig up bones, and the State Highway Department had its own crews to build roads, but none of the local men had the experience or equipment to move buildings. That took special skills and equipment. The men who came had both. They set to work jacking up houses off their foundations and putting them on huge flatbed trailers. Powerful trucks pulled them up Main Street, stopping at each intersection so the men riding on the roofs could prop overhead wires out of the way. At times we could see a row of big trucks carrying four or five houses, creeping up the road and rolling haltingly out of town. Turning a right-hand corner, the trucks slowed to a crawl to climb the winding grade leading toward the town of Meyers Falls where the houses would be placed in new surroundings. The trucks and houses took up all the roadway. A few wide spots on the sides of the road allowed cars to pass.

After school was out in May of 1939, the workers took the high school apart and moved it, too, a section at a time. So that fall, we went to the same red brick high school building we had attended the previous year, but in a different location. My classmate, Dorothy Covington, lived along the river on our route a few miles before we reached the Rickey Canyon Junction. She and her family were among the 3,000 whose houses had to be moved because they were either below the 1,310- foot level or too close to new highways. When the loggers, WPA workers and highway crew finished, they took their noisy machines and left, leaving behind a cleared area below the engineers' yellow-ribboned stakes plus a new highway on higher ground that the rising river wouldn't reach.

The people in the towns of Kettle Falls and Meyers Falls had a lengthy argument over the name of the combined town. Since the site had been named "Meyers Falls" for many years, its residents wanted to retain its name. But the Kettle Falls people whose businesses, telephone office and post office had moved there wanted the town to be called "Kettle Falls." Finally, federal officials settle the argument; the government would pay for a new city water system if the town were named "Kettle Falls." For many years to differentiate between the two, everyone called the combined town "New Kettle," and the previous site "Old Kettle."

Coulee Dam's floodgates were closed in late 1940 and the Columbia River started backing up. It overflowed its banks and kept climbing. The next summer when the backwater neared the tribes' long-time fishing area called "Kettle Falls," Indians began arriving. Some came from miles away as they had when they fished for salmon. Others living nearby on the Colville Indian Reservation also came. They gathered to hold a Ceremony of Tears and watched as the water inched up the falls, finally covering them. Centuries of salmon fishing at the falls had ended forever.

A partial statement from the June 22, 1940 issue of "The Statesman Examiner" in Colville, Washington said this about that event: "Kettle Farewell Ceremony is Great – Chiefs of Nations Mourn Loss of One-Time Food Producing Falls – Indians and whites from every western state joined in the huge farewell celebration at the mission grounds above Kettle Falls last week Friday, Saturday and Sunday and participated in the ceremony of "tears" dedicated to the ultimate passing of the falls on the Columbia river which have been for centuries a source of livelihood to the Indians and beauty for all who viewed them. . . . "

After Coulee Dam was built, salmon had no way of getting past it to swim farther upriver to their spawning grounds around the Kettle Falls, as there wasn't money budgeted to build fish ladders around the dam. The prohibitive cost of building fish ladders around the 550-foot dam kept engineers from including them in their plans.

By the end of our first year in high school, Lester and I and others riding the school bus had seen the uprooting of a whole town. Cement foundations littering the site were all that was left of Old Kettle. All houses were moved except a few located safely above the high-water line. The next fall when we went to high school at "New" Kettle, our bus traveled on the highway we had watched being built. During the next few months, we saw the water rise higher and higher. It crept up over the flats and finally covered the old highway. By the summer of 1941, it reached the surveyors' yellow-ribboned stakes.

Traveling on the new highway gave us different scenery. We followed the wide expanse of the Columbia's shining lake to the mouth of the Colville River. On our left, the rising waters of the Columbia had pushed into the Colville River, forming a beautiful cove. The river narrowed at the new concrete bridge, which had no high railings to obstruct our view. Past the bridge, the highway took us up a long sandy grade studded with pine trees. In the canyon to the right, we caught a glimpse of the Colville River tumbling off the hill in the cascade called "Meyers Falls." And soon we were on the edge of the new town of Kettle Falls where our high school building and many houses from the old site had been relocated.

After the river climbed its banks, it changed from a fierce river with a strong current to a quiet stretch of water, gliding smoothly along with no apparent current. It had no rapids and no falls. It spread out to almost three miles wide along the flats near where Rickey Canyon Road junctioned with the highway. And upriver from the bridge, it had spread out to four miles at the Marcus Flats.

On a sunny day the lake stretching northward looks almost bluer than the sky itself. Before Coulee Dam was built — when the Columbia was dangerous with its strong current and whirlpools, I was afraid while crossing it on the cable ferry to Inchelium. But now, the river is a quiet elongated lake of 151 miles.

The December 1971 issue of the "Reader's Digest" describes the dam: "Seventy miles west of Spokane is an awesome sight: Grand Coulee Dam, which stands athwart the Columbia River like a fortress, the water foaming over its spillway forming a rainbow waterfall twice as high as Niagara Falls. The dam is more than 12 city blocks across; the water it backs up forms Franklin D. Roosevelt Lake, which stretches to Canada – 151 miles . . ."

The town of Inchelium on the west bank of the Columbia River also had to be moved to higher ground. A national recreation site now encompasses the part of Old Kettle not covered by water, some of it where the high school once stood. In 1967, my classmates, Rose Aubertin Geer, Bernice Lewis Bailey and Ralph Byrd arranged to have our 25th class reunion picnic there. Later reunions turned into an "Old Kettle Reunion." My former teachers, Gladys Graupner Fritz and Cecile Fahey Chesley attended. We had become friends, and I was happy to talk to them as an adult instead of as a student.

After all these years – after the town moved and the river rose, we still ate our lunches in the shade of the tall locust trees where the high school once stood. In August 1989, area people celebrated the fiftieth year since the town of Kettle Falls moved. Louis and Jo Nullett put together a large pictorial display showing the "old days." There were pictures of buildings being hauled away, of Indians fishing, of the falls that gave the town its name and pictures of area pioneers. This display is now in the Kettle Falls Public Library. And now there is a swimming area called Bradbury Beach, not far from where classmate Dorothy Covington's house once stood.

My Christmas Card Route

Head down, my sorrel mare plodded up the steep Folsom Hill, her nostrils blowing twin columns of steam into the cold November air. Riding bareback, I felt Betty's body heat through my overalls, keeping me warm. On this cold and blustery day, I was glad we didn't own a saddle.

It was Saturday, and I was off to see if any of our neighbors wanted to buy some Christmas cards. I had ordered them after seeing a magazine offer saying kids could earn money by selling a box of fifty for a dime apiece. I carried the cards in my old denim shoulder bag Mom had made when I rode horseback to school from the Curry place. Ready to go after that promised money, I bridled Betty and set off to try my luck. As I rode past the house, I waved goodbye to Mom standing at the kitchen window. Selling Christmas cards was the only way I knew that a fourteen-year old girl living in the country could earn money in the winter of 1938. With seven children, Dad couldn't give us spending money. He barely had enough cash for necessities. I'd heard a lot of talk about the "Depression" and guessed it meant everyone else was strapped for money, too.

Although we hadn't had snow yet, it covered the trees on top of the mountain above us. Mom laid down the law for us to start wearing our long wool underwear. They were scratchy, but kept us from freezing. I was also wearing a long-sleeved flannel shirt, bib overalls, sweater, heavy jacket, stocking cap and cotton-jersey gloves.

My first stop had been at Paul and Ethel Holter's. After asking Ethel if she needed any Christmas cards, I spread them out on the kitchen table to show they weren't all the same. Looking at the colorful assortment, she picked out four and gave me forty cents. I put her coins in my pocket, thanked her and left, happy with my first sale.

Mounting Betty again, I crossed the road and headed up the lane to Ella Loven's house. Tying Betty's neck rope to a fence post, I followed the long boards that led to the kitchen door. Surprised to see me, Ella said, "Well, Ines, come in, come in. What are you doing out on a cold day like this?"

Getting inside, I handed her my box and said I was earning money by selling Christmas cards, then greeted Ella's mother and daughter, glad to see them, too. Ella poured the cards out on her table and asked Grandma Carter and Barbara which ones she should buy. They picked out a few they liked, and Ella said, "Yes, those are pretty. They're the ones we'll take," and soon I was on my way again.

As Betty continued plodded up the steep Folsom Hill toward the Mathis place, I hoped they would need a couple of cards, too. I had found out the Mathises were good neighbors when I was in first grade. Mrs. Mathis had sewn several pairs of mittens from wool material and sent them to school with her son, William, asking Miss Dean to give them to children who didn't have any. When Miss Dean had called me in from recess and handed mittens to me, I was surprised – and grateful. That day on my way to school, my bare hands had felt like ice. After pulling those wool mittens on, I knew my hands would never get cold again. Eight years later, Mrs. Mathis again showed her good neighborliness by buying some cards.

The road leveled off, but would tip downhill before getting to the next farm house where John and Dessie Byrd lived. Their son, Ralph, was in my class, but I'd never visited them or anyone past the Folsom Hill before, so Dessie was surprised to see me. With help from Edna and Goldie, her older daughters, Dessie picked out some cards. Thanking them, I pulled my jacket on again and headed out of their warm house. Climbing on Betty, I rode down the steep pitch of road about a quarter of a mile to Ebbie and Gladys Conner's house. Gladys urged me inside to their warm living room and asked me what I was doing outside on such a cold day. After shedding my jacket, I gave her the box of cards and explained my mission. Ten minutes later I felt warm again and had mounted Betty and was on my way again with more coins. When I left, I had no idea that six years later I would be visiting Gladys and Ebbie's house as their son's bride.

I hated to leave the warm house, but went out and climbed on Betty again. The wind gusted in my face, making my nose numb. My fingers in thin gloves felt like brittle sticks and I was wishing I hadn't outgrown the wool mittens that Mrs. Mathis had given me. Because of the blustery cold, I decided to make only one more stop, at Lonnie and Nina Conner's. I turned right onto the narrow dirt track of Day Road which was shielded from the wind by tree-covered hills and soon was inside their house. I was glad to see their daughter, Arlene, one of my best friends and their son, Alvin. While Nina looked at my dwindling supply of cards and made her selection, I enjoyed visiting with Arlene and Alvin.

Because of the bitter cold, I planned to head straight home instead of making more stops. But while riding through the cleft in the hills, the wind was no longer biting my face, so made one more quick stop. Reaching the Pleasant Valley Road, I turned left a short distance and came to Jack and Dessie McCarrolls's house. They were surprised to see me, but happily selected two cards.

I then headed back up the Pleasant Valley Road, rode past the schoolhouse, with Betty holding her head higher and picking up speed. Somehow, she knew she was heading for the barn. Fifteen minutes later I rode through the gate into our yard and soon was in the barn. I took off her bridle and threw some hay into the feed box. Now I could go to the house and get warm. Having seen me ride by the house, Mom met me at the door and asked, "How did you do?"

Smiling happily, I said, "I'll show you!" and poured all the coins out onto the table. They clinked as they made a loose pile of silver. "Just look at all the money, Mom, I sold all but five cards!"

Mom looked at the money – and the few cards that were left and said, "That's good! I'll buy those cards and send them to Grandma and your uncles and aunts."

She sent a check to the greeting card company for the necessary amount and I got to keep what was left. In these hard times a dollar a day was the usual pay for a man's work, so I felt lucky to have earned a little over a dollar – big money – on my six or seven mile Christmas card route.

Visit to Idaho

Uncle Bob Dryden drove into our yard one summer morning, surprising us with his visit. He pulled his car to a stop in our front yard, opened the door and swung his white-shod feet to the ground. White shoes on a man! Farm men always wore brown or black ones, so it was astonishing to see a man wearing white shoes. We were glad to see him, as not many relatives had enough extra money during these hard times to make a 200-mile trip as he had done. Recalling his last visit when he helped Mom make maple bars, I asked, "Can you help make maple bars again?"

"No, I have to go back to Lewiston tomorrow," he replied. The next morning Bob wore an old pair of Dad's boots and went out to the barn to help milk. While the men were outside, Mom got out her oval griddle that held eight big pancakes at a time. When Dad, Bob and Lester finished milking and came in, she poured batter onto the griddle and made pancakes to go with our usual breakfast of fried potatoes and eggs.

Mom often told us she had started taking care of her younger brothers when she was only five years old. Now Bob told us kids in awed tones, "Sis practically raised me. She was more of a mother to me than Mother was," and for the for the rest of the day, he stuck close to her. It was apparent that her brother got as lonesome for his "little mother" as Mom did for him.

That day Bob asked Mom if I could go back to Lewiston with him for a couple of weeks. "She'd be good company for me on the drive, and I want her to meet Agnes and the boys. I'd see that she got to visit Lester and Lizzie and her cousins."

I was surprised when Mom said, "I guess I could do without her right now, and it would be good for her to see the others again" She asked me if I'd like to go.

My answer was out almost before she finished. "Yes, I sure would. I'd like to meet Aunt Agnes and see Lester and Lizzie again."

"Well, hop to it and get a few clothes to take. Bob will be ready to leave in about an hour, so don't keep him waiting," Mom said.

I got out her black suitcase and hurriedly put in a couple pair of overalls and shirts, a dress and some underclothes. I thought I was ready to go, but Mom reminded me to take a comb and a toothbrush. Bob was already in the car, so I hugged Mom, told everyone "goodbye" and got in the car.

Bob drove through Rice and on down the Columbia River on Highway 22 past Daisy, Gifford and Hunters. He said, "After we get to Davenport, we'll take another highway into Spokane, and then head straight south."

After driving almost an hour we hadn't seen but a few cars on the road. When we came to a long stretch of straight road, Bob asked, "How would you like to take the wheel?"

Although I was fifteen, I'd never learned to drive – and Bob was offering to let me drive! He stopped the car on the edge of the road, and we changed seats. I was so excited my hands were shaking as I gripped the big steering wheel. Then I asked, "What do I do first?"

"You see that left-hand pedal down there on the floor? That's the clutch," he said. "When you step on it, it throws the car out of gear. So push the clutch in, turn the key on, and step on the starter."

As soon as I did all that, the engine started, and Bob continued his directions. "This lever sticking up from the floor is the gear shift. I'll shift gears for you until you learn how. It's in low now and when you get the car moving, you'll have to shove in the clutch again so I can shift into second gear, and then into high."

That didn't sound too complicated, and I soon found it wasn't. It seemed to be mostly a matter of timing and easing the clutch out so the car didn't jerk each time we changed gears. It was easy to keep the car going straight and on the right side of the road. It felt like we were going pretty fast, but I couldn't take my eyes off the road to look for the speedometer. Bob was watching it, though, and said, "Say, you better ease off on the gas. You're going fifty miles an hour."

In Bob's old 1935 Chevrolet coupe, we <u>had</u> seemed to be whizzing past the trees lining the road. I was glad he told me how fast I was going, and slowed to a more reasonable speed for a first-time driver. As we rounded a curve, we saw below us the Spokane River flowing into the Columbia. It was a breathtaking view, but my eyes turned back to the road and I spotted the bridge crossing the Spokane River. When we got closer, the bridge seemed pretty narrow. Thankfully, no other cars were coming, so I drove in the middle of the road across the bridge. I'd begun to feel a little nervous and decided I'd had enough driving for one day. I asked Bob how I went about stopping and he said, "Take your foot off the gas, push in the clutch and tap the brake lightly."

Following his directions, I got the car stopped. I'd hadn't run off the road nor hit another car – or the bridge -- so I felt my first attempt at driving was a success. We were now opposite the neglected buildings of old Fort Spokane, the site of the abandoned old army post.

Bob got behind the wheel, and I was relieved to sit on the passenger side again. He drove through Davenport, Spokane, Rosalia, Colfax and Pullman. When we still had about twelve miles to get to Lewiston, the highway took a sudden plunge down into nine and a half miles of hair-pin turns. Bob pulled over to the side of the road to show me the famed "Lewiston Hill." Seeing all those switch backs below us, I was thankful I wasn't driving. I wasn't even sure I wanted to ride down the hill! But Bob drove slowly and carefully around all the loops and turns, pointing out wrecks of cars that had gone off the road. Safe at the bottom, I looked back up at those multiple curves, which no longer looked quite so scary.

As we drove past the businesses of Lewiston and entered the residential section, I was all eyes wondering which house might be Bob's. After driving about a mile farther, he pointed at a woman walking toward us on the sidewalk and said, "There's someone I know," and stopped the car in front of the house. The woman was wearing a bright green blouse and a welcoming smile when she saw us. It turned out to be Aunt Agnes! Although surprised at the unexpected company, she made me feel welcome. Only seven years older than I, she seemed more like an older sister than an aunt.

Agnes' father, "Grandpa" Nelson, soon came home from a walk with his two small grandsons, Bobby and Arden. Later in the evening another cousin, Lorene "Tacky" Hunt, came to spend the night. As Tacky's mother was dead and her father worked in various locations, she lived with Uncle Lester and Aunt Lizzie most of the time. Tacky was younger than I by a couple of years, but knew a lot more about living in a city. At bedtime, I went into the bedroom and started peeling off my clothes. Tacky gasped when she came in and saw me half undressed with the window shades still up. She said, "You're supposed to pull the shades before you undress!" and ran to pull them down.

The next day I went with Bob when he drove Tacky over to Uncle Lester's and we stayed to visit awhile. Before we left, my relatives made me feel part of a big family. On the way back to Bob's house, he gave me my second driving lesson by letting me drive. I felt more confident this time and managed to shift gears all by myself. I only killed the engine once when I forgot to push in the clutch when coming to a stop.

A few days later I wanted to visit cousins Guy, Virgil and Tacky and asked Bob if he'd take me. He pulled the car keys out of his pocket and handed them to me. "Take the car and go see them."
Not having had much practice, I wasn't sure I could drive clear across town on my own, but Bob assured me the second lesson had been all I needed. "You know the way, so you should be able to get there by yourself."

I got into the car, shoved in the clutch, turned the key, stepped on the starter, put the gear shift into low and started off. I was going through town feeling pretty good until I remembered - with dread - the narrow, Eighteenth Street Bridge across the Clearwater River. When I reached it, there were a lot of cars on it, most of them coming toward me. The bridge hadn't seemed narrow when Bob was driving, but I knew I could get across by being careful. From my seat behind the wheel, I couldn't see how close the bridge girders were to the right side of the car. But I could see cars coming at me, so tried to leave a couple feet of space on my left. Despite my worries, I made it across safely.

Getting to Uncle Lester's house, I found all three cousins sitting inside with nothing to do while Lester and Lizzie were at work. They didn't have any work to do – and it was too hot to play outside – so we sat inside and talked. I noticed Aunt Lizzie's ironing basket was full of clothes, so I told Guy I'd iron them. He found the ironing board, and plugged the electric iron in. It worked faster on shirts and dresses than our old flat irons at home that we had to heat on top of the cook stove. I went through that whole basket of clothes while we were having a good time talking and arguing.

When Aunt Lizzie came home from her job of plucking chickens at the Lewiston Poultry Packing Plant, she started right in getting supper. Tacky and I tried to help, but there wasn't much to do. Aunt Lizzie fixed Spanish rice. I liked it and hoped I'd remember how she made it so I could tell Mom. It was mostly rice, but had hamburger, onions, tomato and some green things in with it. It was just spicy enough to make it zesty. We ate as soon as Uncle Lester came home from his plumbing job.

While it was still daylight, I set out for the return trip, looking forward to another session behind the wheel. Crossing the bridge over the Clearwater River didn't make me nervous this time. That feeling came later. While climbing out of the car after reaching Agnes and Bob's house, I realized I was supposed to have a driver's license when driving alone. Then the shakes hit me. I was doubly thankful I hadn't ran into anything.

I'd been homesick a time or two, but my two-week visit passed in no time because it had been very enjoyable being with Bob and Agnes and seeing Lester, Lizzie and my cousins. Now it was time to return to Pleasant Valley. I packed my few things and was ready to go. Bob and Agnes drove me to the bus depot and I almost cried when I told them goodbye.

When my bus pulled into the Greyhound Depot in Colville, I was glad to see Mom, Dad and my sisters standing outside waiting. I hadn't realized I'd missed them so much. The next day as I was hoeing weeds in the garden at the Garner Place with Mom, Dora, Leola and Effie, I looked at the timbered hills and mountains around us and realized how much nicer this was than the city area I'd left yesterday. While I enjoyed being with loving relatives, I was glad to be back home where I belonged.

Thirty years later I again visited Idaho and discovered a new highway had bypassed the crooked road down the Lewiston Hill. And my Uncle Bob gave me a copy of his poem, "The Lewiston Hill," that had just been published.

141

Deer Hunting

Bill Preston straddled the limp form of the buck lying on the ground. Holding his opened jack knife, he bent down and grabbed an antler, ready to cut the deer's throat. He was hunting with Dad and Pearl Entwistle when Dad's bullet had downed the buck. Having been the closest one when it fell, Bill was going to cut its throat to let it bleed out. But before he could make his slash, the deer sprang to its feet, flinging him up on to its back. He was too startled to do anything but hang on.

Dad and Pearl came out into the clearing just in time to see the deer running down hill with Bill clinging to its back. Hanging onto an antler, he had his long legs clenched around its belly. After crashing through brush and jumping across deadfalls, it went out of sight into the trees. Bill was finally able to reach forward and cut its throat

When Dad and Pearl finally caught up with him, they asked why he had stayed on the deer. He said, "We were all out of meat, so I couldn't let it get away," then added, "It was about time I killed it; I couldn't have hung on much longer!"

The two men razzed Bill Preston for years about his wild ride, but he enjoyed the telling of it as much as anyone. It remained one of their best deer-hunting stories. Dad was the best hunter in Pleasant Valley. Bill Preston and Pearl were the best in the Arzina area, about ten miles away. Having spent a lot of time hunting to keep meat on the table, their experience had taught them where the deer were most likely to be, where they laid up while resting and when they might be moving about.

One of Dad's hunting rifles was a .25-.35 caliber lever-action Savage with half-buckhorn sights on an extra long hexagonal barrel. He killed a lot of deer with it, and Mom used it often, too, with success. Still, he decided to sell it so he could buy a higher powered rifle that shot greater distances. Pearl told him he'd buy it. In handing the .25-.35 to him, Dad said, "Pearl, you won't need to take sight with this gun, it's already trained!"

There were other men he hunted with, but his favorites were Bill Preston and Pearl, in Arzina. To differentiate between Bill Preston and Bill Riley, our friends usually added Bill Preston's last name when talking about him, and just called Dad, "Bill."

Bill Preston lived by himself in a small cabin on land that didn't produce much income. Most of his property was timbered, but he didn't have it logged off because the sawmill's price for logs had fallen. His main source of income came from a small herd of sheep. His only helper was his big black and white dog, Bouncie. Bill had come from the hills of Tennessee, and still spoke in a Southern drawl, which all of us kids loved to hear. He didn't own a car, and often walked the mile or so over to Pearl's place to ride with him to their hunting areas. Other times Pearl and Dad picked him up.

Pearl and Goldie had three children, Gerry, Billie and Janice, and a few years later, they had two more, Jeep and Vicky. Pearl's farm was much like ours and didn't yield much income. Getting meat from the woods was almost as necessary to him as it was to Dad and Bill Preston. The three men hunted in several different areas, their territory stretching over many miles. Favorite spots were Monumental Mountain, within walking distance from our house, and Carter Canyon, which we could see from our house above Ella Loven's farm. Other areas were the North and South Basin, closer to Bill Preston's and Pearl's farms. And during hunting season, they sometimes drove across the Columbia River to hunt in the Sherman Creek area.

By the time Lester and I were teenagers, we hunted with the men as did Mom and Goldie. Dora, only twelve, and I were still only helping on the drives by scaring deer out of the brush. But Lester carried a rifle and often took a stand when Dad didn't need him to make a drive. Mom left Leola to take charge of the house and care for Effie, Viola and Vida. At eight, Leola was very responsible and Mom could depend on her to feed Effie and the twins, and keep them out of trouble.

When we hunted nearby on Monumental Mountain, we walked up the ridges from our house. This climb, which took almost two hours, forced us to get up early, as Dad wanted to be on a stand by daylight, before the deer started moving about. He woke us up at four o'clock by coming to the foot of our ladder and yelling his old logging-camp wake-up call, "Daylight in the swamp!"

While Mom got breakfast by the light of a kerosene lamp, I made sandwiches to take with us. We never expected to get back before dark. Putting our waxed-paper wrapped sandwiches inside our shirts, we slid them around to the back. If we kept our shirt tails tucked inside our pants, the sandwiches wouldn't fall out. We needed both hands free for carrying rifles and grabbing branches to pull ourselves up the steepest slopes.

If we hunted close to the top of the mountain, Dad or Pearl drove us up Carter Canyon or up another road in a different area so we didn't have to walk so far. More importantly, if the truck were part way up the mountain, we didn't have so far to carry our game out. Two men together had all they could handle to pack out a deer without carrying anything else. After they'd gutted the deer, they gave the hearts and livers to us girls to carry – along with their rifles.

Late one afternoon, Dad and Pearl had killed two bucks at the bottom of a gully and we had to pack out uphill. Pearl had left the truck beside the mountain road at least half a mile away. In the falling darkness, we clawed and scrambled our way up the steep hill through the brush. Dad and Pearl, Bill Preston and Lester were loaded down with both deer. Dora had her hands full carrying the hearts and livers on forked sticks, and Mom was carrying Dad's rifle along with her own. The three rifles in my arms didn't balance well and became heavier and heavier as I tried to keep them from banging against each other and ruining their sights. Goldie wasn't with us that day, and we sure missed her!

Although there weren't any sign posts on the mountain, we kids knew which section Dad was describing when he told us where we were going to hunt. Unless an area was already named – like Carter Canyon, Maggie Folsom's Cabin and John Marty's Mine, the hunters picked names for different areas. Goldie had a favorite spot for a stand, so we got to calling it "Goldie's Stand." Likewise, everyone knew Dad's favorite place and called it "Bill's Stand." Then there was Tamarack Thicket, Flat Rock, Salt Lick and Rock Canyon. Dad's instructions often went like this: "We'll be on our stands by daylight. You kids start your drive about a half hour after that below the thicket at the bottom of the canyon. When you finish your drive, meet us up the hill from Flat Rock."

Dad had started our hunting lessons on the Curry Place, so we were accustomed to noting the terrain, tree growth, rock bluffs, game trails and other distinctive features when going through the woods. There were lots of familiar landmarks and no one ever got lost on one of Dad's hunts.

During almost every hunting season, friends or relatives – and sometimes total strangers from Spokane – appeared hoping they could hunt with Dad. He agreed they could go with us under one condition, and that was "no liquor while hunting." He felt that anyone carrying a gun shouldn't be carrying a bottle. He didn't want to get shot again or have anyone else in his party get shot.

Most city hunters carried high-powered rifles with telescope sights and sported big hunting knives strapped to their belts; one had field glasses strung around his neck. Their special equipment and hunting clothes – visored red caps and red plaid jackets – were quite a contrast to the way the rest of us were dressed. We didn't have any red clothes. Dad's usual outfit was his everyday clothes: a cotton-flannel shirt, denim jacket, bib overalls and beat-up gray felt hat. His total equipment consisted of a rifle with open sights, a jack knife, a thin round whetstone and a short length of rope. Bill Preston and Pearl were similarly dressed and equipped.

When a deer was killed, the hunter slipped a metal hunting tag, issued by the State Game Department, around an antler. If the local hunters got their deer, they shared portions of it with the others who hadn't been so lucky; no one went home empty-handed. Some of the city hunters were after the biggest buck they could find. We knew that a buck having many points on a big rack of horns was sure to be an old one and its meat would be tough. And in the rutting season in late fall, the bucks' necks swelled, getting them ready for the fights they'd have over the does during mating season. If a hunter killed this "trophy" buck at that time, some of its meat would be so strong it was hardly fit to eat. Its no wonder their wives refused to eat the meat they brought home, saying it tasted "gamey."

If Dad had a choice, he killed a younger buck. He was more interested in getting a deer that was good eating than in getting one with a big rack. He usually just tossed the antlers over the top of the barbed wire fence around your yard. Later on, he started nailing them up on the end of the granary.

The most memorable hunt Dad ever organized resulted in seven bucks being killed on the same day. I missed all the excitement, as this happened after I graduated from high school and left home, but hearing about it for years afterward helped me piece together their hunt.

Louie Koerner, Ralph Lawson and his daughter, Darlene, joined Mom, Dad, Lester and Dora in the hills near Lawson's farm. In the early morning, several does and bucks ran past Dad and Louie on their stands. Each had a clear shot and brought down a buck. As the remaining deer topped the rise, Mom fired away, getting another one. When the shooting stopped, the four "drivers" arrived to see Dad, Mom and Louie tagging their bucks. After the men gutted the deer, Dad said, "We'll stay here for an hour before moving over this ridge. All that shootin' is sure to have spooked any deer that were here."

By the time they climbed the ridge and looked into the next canyon, Dad had his strategy all worked out. Squatting on the ground to rest, he said, "Since Louie, Sis and I got our bucks, we'll make the next drive. Ralph, you and Lester, Dora and Darlene take stands. Maybe you can hit some of those bucks we're gonna chase past you!" Then pointing in different directions off in the distance where they should take their stands, he continued, "We'll give you plenty of time to get on your stands before starting our drive."

So as not to spook the deer to soon, Dad, Mom and Louie waited for a good hour before quietly working their way down toward the bottom of the next canyon. As they turned and headed uphill, they began making a lot of noise, hoping to scare deer toward the four hunters on stands. About fifteen minutes later, they heard the boom of two rifles almost at the same time. Then more shots thundered, the sounds bouncing back and forth between the ridges. Mom, within sight of Dad, said, "It sounds like we jumped some deer, enough for everyone."

When the firing stopped and the mountain was quiet again, Louie, Mom and Dad continued uphill to find the others. Reaching Lester first, Dad asked, "Did you have any luck?"

"I'll say I did," Lester said grinning proudly. He turned around and pointed to his buck lying behind a bush, and continued, "I'm pretty sure Ralph got one, too. There was a lot of shooting coming from his stand." Then Dad asked Lester how many deer he saw. He answered, "Must have been five bucks and eight does, it was just like a herd of cattle running by!"

Just then Ralph and Darlene Lawson and Dora stepped out of the trees at the top of the ridge above them. Dora yelled down at them, "Hey, you oughta see what we've got up here!"

Dad told the others that they might as well go up there to see what she was yelling about, and headed up toward them, with Louie, Mom and Lester following. They couldn't believe it when they found three more bucks within three hundred yards. Ralph Lawson said, "That was the easiest buck I ever got. It was just like a shooting gallery. You guys really scared up some deer for us!"

The shots echoing through the canyon probably made that the noisiest deer hunt anybody ever heard. Getting seven deer, one for each hunter, made that Dad's most successful hunt. A picture of the hunters and their bucks eventually appeared in the Statesman-Index, Colville's weekly paper. For years we heard Dad's stories about other hunting trips with Lester, Bill Preston, Pearl Entwistle, Toar Lickfold, Ernie McKinney, Louie Koerner and Ralph Lawson.

When Dad killed a deer during the first part of the hunting season when the weather was still warm, the meat wouldn't keep very long without electricity for refrigeration. Mom canned some of the venison, then set aside enough meat to last a few days. She cut the rest into thin strips, sealed them in half-gallon fruit jars and set them in the creek. The water was cold enough to keep the meat for over two weeks. When she got ready to fry it, she dredged it in flour and slapped it into a hot cast-iron skillet.

Mom didn't make jerky until after cold weather set in, as she needed the steady heat coming from the heating stove to dry the meat. After soaking thin strips of uncooked venison in her special recipe, she threaded them on wires strung above the stove, between the wall and stove pipe. The heat dried the meat, making it almost rock-hard. It broke easily when dried, as Mom cut the strips of meat across the grain. We carried the dried pieces of jerky in our overall pockets when we went out to roam the hills.

In cool weather, Dad could let a deer hang in the woodshed for over a week before cutting it up, which made it tender. Then he cut it in quarters and wrapped each one in a white cloth to keep the flies off before returning them to the woodshed. By the time Mom needed to fry it, the steaks almost melted in our mouths. For our suppers, Dad cut off roasts, but for breakfast, we enjoyed thin steak. Every morning Mom lugged a white-wrapped quarter into the kitchen and sliced off thin pieces to fry.

We heard Dad's hunting stories later on in the evenings every time it was his turn to host the penny-ante
poker games. When the men played at our house, their games continued long after we girls went to bed. As Dora and I lay upstairs in bed directly above their table, we could make out most of the words and knew when the story teller got to the exciting parts from the sounds booming up through the ceiling. We identified the men by their laughter. Dad's familiar deep laugh gave him away, Louie's tended to be dry and choppy, and Ernie McKinney's lasted longer and came more often. Toar had a rich, vibrant chuckle that turned into a rolling laugh.

Lying there in our bed, we couldn't help laughing, too. It never surprised us to hear Dad say, "You should . . . Bill Preston ride . . . buck . . . through . . . brush," ending with an imitation of Bill's voice, "I couldn't have hung on . . . longer," followed by bursts of their laughter. We didn't need to hear all his
words. We knew that story by heart.

Many people of that area have told me that Mom could fry the best venison steak in Pleasant Valley. The only steak that's come close to it in flavor and tenderness was the succulent Kobe beef I ate forty years later in a Japanese restaurant, renowned in all Tokyo for its choice beef. Henry and I were visiting his son, Dick, and wife, Jeaninne, who lived there. When Irikin-san, the owner and a personal friend of Dick's, came to our table carrying a white-wrapped, aged quarter of beef to show us, I thought of something else. My mind flew back over the years and I again saw Mom carrying a white-wrapped hind quarter of venison into our kitchen to cut slices for breakfast.

Lester Leaves Home

During our sophomore year in 1939, Lester quit school to go job hunting. Rhodie, a new friend of his had stopped to tell him that he was on his way to northern Idaho, as he'd heard that the Potlach Lumber Company was hiring a crew. He asked Lester if he'd like to go with him. It didn't take long for Lester to make up his mind. He wanted a job so he could make some spending money, and at seventeen, he was two years older than the others in our class. He hadn't started to school until he was seven, then had fallen behind in the fourth grade. He liked high school sports, but didn't like studying or turning in assignments. He was ready for a change.

Dad had always been strict with Lester, Dora and me, but was hardest on Lester. He expected him to do a man's work, yet never praised him for anything. He demanded instant obedience. We knew better than to ask "why", we just did what he told us to do. There was always work to do. In addition to hoeing weeds out of the general garden, we had to keep the weeds out of separate quarter-acre patches of potatoes, corn and dry beans. Lester's daily chores were to help Dad milk and feed the cows and pigs, clean out the barn and harness the horses for the day's work. While Dad drove a team of two horses doing one job, Lester was likely to be driving another team pulling a harrow or springtooth in another field.

One spring after Dad plowed a field he was going to plant to grain, he surprised Lester, Dora and me. Instead of just telling us to go haul rocks out of that field, he said, "I'll pay you kids a dollar apiece to haul rocks out of that field. Use the stone boat, that will be easier than the big wagon."

Dad had built the stone boat by nailing a few sturdy boards to two poles, which he tapered in front so the stone boat could slide along the ground. After making a raised edge on all sides, he attached a single-tree to the poles so a horse could be hitched to it. While Dora and I were washing the breakfast dishes, Lester harnessed a horse and led it to the stone boat. Dora and I got outside just in time to see him hooking the links in the tugs to the harness's single-tree. Lester said "giddy-up," slapped the horse's rump with the long driving reins, and headed up past the barn toward the field, walking behind the stone boat. Dora and I following him up the wagon road, across the creek and up a steep hill, reaching the field in about twenty minutes. While tossing rocks on the stone boat all day, we wondered what had brought about Dad's unexpected offer to pay us. We had worked a lot harder at many other jobs without being paid.

When we later complained to Mom about never getting any praise from Dad, she replied, "Dad doesn't brag on you because he doesn't want to give you a big head. He's proud of you, even though he doesn't tell you so."

That didn't satisfy us, as Dad bragged about what other kids did. After visiting Pearl Entwistle one day, he'd gone on and on about how Janice had worked all day shocking hay, just as if he'd never seen us shock hay all day. Lester was disappointed that Dad never praised him for his hard work, yet commented on jobs that other kids did. So when Rhodie said he was going to look for a job in Idaho, he was ready to make a change. When he told Dad he was going with him to Idaho, Dad told him he should stay home until he got out of school. Lester said, "No, I want to get a job and earn some money."

This was the first time any of us had disobeyed Dad. Grouped around Rhodie's car, we girls and Mom watched in shocked silence as Lester threw some belongings onto the back seat and climbed into the front seat. They drove out the gate and down the Rickey Canyon Road. Our eyes watched the car until it went out of sight below the junction with Pleasant Valley Road, not believing that Lester was really leaving home.

That was the beginning of change in our family. Mom worried about Lester every day. Her face had a closed-up look, and her eyes wouldn't focus at any of us. She wouldn't talk to Dad, silently blaming him for making it so tough on Lester that he left home. Dora and I weren't happy about our leader leaving us, either, and hoped he'd come back. He'd led us in wild adventures, as well as in our work. Now the adventures would stop, but the work would increase.

When Lester's job ended a few months later, he came back for a short time. Mom's face lit up with smiles again. Her worried look never returned, even after Lester went on to his next job. After that, he came to see us as often as his work allowed, especially in the fall during hunting season. But Lester couldn't come home to stay; he was making his own way.

In 1989 Janice and her husband, Joe Harlick, visited Henry and me in Tennessee. We laughed together when I told Janice how Dad had made us kids mad by bragging about her shocking hay, but had never praised us for doing the same thing.

Basil the Hungry Hobo

Eating breakfast with us, Basil put away three eggs, a mound of crispy fried potatoes and two or three thick slices of home-made bread. He said, "Everything sure tastes good!"

This wandering man had walked into our yard the day before asking if he could chop wood in exchange for a meal. During the Depression we were having a hard time until hobos appeared on foot, looking for a meal. The state highway was six miles away, so they had to have been desperately hungry to have walked that far, hoping to get something to eat, and perhaps a place to spend the night. Their first words were always the same, "Can I chop wood for a meal?"

These men weren't beggars. They were merely hungry men on the move looking for work. If they were lucky, they found a farmer who could give them room and board for their work. Their offer to chop wood showed they were willing to work. If they appeared on our door step while Dad was out in the field working, Mom would tell them that they would have to wait and ask him. In the meantime, she offered them a glass of water and invited them to sit outside in the shade and rest. When they told their sad tales, we realized we weren't in such bad shape after all. Unlike them, we never went hungry.

One of these wandering men was Basil, who turned out to be quite a cook. Arriving in late afternoon, he carried only a paper bag holding his belongings. He had a scared look on his face when he asked Dad if he could chop wood for a meal, or work for board and room. Dad gave him the same answer he'd given all the others, "I need some help, but can't afford to hire anyone. But you can eat with us, and chop some wood if you like."

So at supper that night, nine people were again squeezed around the table, the same number as before Lester had left home. Basil took three big helpings, apologizing to Mom for being so hungry. She smiled and said, "That's all right. You can eat all you want."

When bedtime came, Dad gave him a blanket, saying, "You can sleep in the barn's hay mow, but don't smoke or light any matches. I don't want my barn burned down."

The next morning while Basil was helping Dad milk the cows, he asked if he could spend another night with us before moving on. Replying that it would be alright, Dad added, "Resting up an extra day would probably do you some good."

Before helping Dad with his work that day, Basil ate breakfast as if he didn't know where his next meal would come from. He said he hadn't had many square meals in the past year. We believed him by his gaunt face. He must have gone hungry many times. He probably hadn't had money for food or clothing for a long time, as his overalls and jacket looked old and ragged.

They came into the kitchen with their buckets of milk as Mom mixed flour and potato water to start a batch of light bread. Saying he used to help his mother bake bread, Basil asked if he could help her form the rolls and loaves. A startled look came on Mom's face, but she smiled and said she'd like that. Her brother, Bob, had been the only man who had ever volunteered before to help.

After breakfast Dad and Basil went outside to do some more chores, When they returned, Mom was kneading bread after it had risen. Basil said, "I'm just in time." rolled up his sleeves and went to the sink to wash his hands and arms. And soon the two of them were happily pinching off dough and rolling it around to make smooth rolls. A beaming smile replaced Basil's worried look of yesterday. It seemed like a different man was standing there in Basil's shabby clothes.

Mom left enough dough to make cinnamon rolls. I smacked my lips when I saw Basil sprinkling sugar and cinnamon over the melted butter on top of the rolled-out circle of dough. Mom sliced it into long strips, her sharp knife cutting through the dough. She and Basil rolled up the strips into rolls, then put them into a baking pan that held more melted butter, cinnamon and brown sugar.

Our plentiful supper of potatoes, gravy, venison roast, vegetables and fresh-baked bread hit the spot. The delicious cinnamon rolls topped off the feast and filled us up. I felt sorry for our latest hobo. He might never get another chance to help make bread, and faced many tomorrows with perhaps no bread at all. After one more night in the hay mow and another big breakfast, Basil got ready to leave. Picking up his bag of possessions, he thanked both Mom and Dad for the good meals and a place to stay. While Dad shook hands warmly, he said, "You're a good worker, Basil. I wish I could see my way clear to take you on at board and room."

As Mom told Basil goodbye, she handed him a wrapped cinnamon roll and two sandwiches. Maybe that would keep him from starving until he found his next meal. We girls stood in the yard sadly watching him walk out through our gate and out of our lives. The last we saw of him, he was striding purposely down around the bend below the mail box, heading toward the state highway. We hoped he would soon find a farmer who could afford a hired hand, so he would never go hungry again.

Chicken for Supper

Mom looked at me one afternoon and said, "Go pick out a good-sized chicken and get it ready to fry; We'll have chicken for supper tonight."

That meant I had to catch one of our chickens running loose in the barn yard, chop its head off, pluck the feathers off, and cut it into pieces. At sixteen, I had enough experience catching chickens to know which one to select. Mom had specified a fryer, so I'd try to find a good sized spring chicken, big enough to feed eight people. Four year old Viola and Vida didn't eat much, so one full-grown Rhode Island Red was all we needed.

Before heading out to the chicken yard, I put a bucket of water on the cook stove so it would get hot enough to scald the chicken. After adding wood to the fire in the stove, I asked Dora to keep the fire going by adding more sticks of wood to the fire, then headed outside. I saw several chickens scratching around near the granary, then crept up close and made a flying leap at one that was just the right size. I missed, but managed to grab it on the next try and headed for the chopping block to cut its head off. Holding it in my left hand, I lay its head on the chopping block and picked up the double-bitted axe. I swung, but the chicken jerked its head aside. All I chopped off was its beak. On the next swing, my axe was faster and I got the job done.

I dropped the headless chicken on the clean wood chips by the chopping block and went into the house for the bucket of hot water. It was almost boiling, just the right temperature for scalding the chicken to loosen its feathers, so carried it outside. I picked up the chicken by its feet and plunged it up and down in the steaming water a few times. When I pulled out a "test" feather, it didn't come out easily, so I plunged the chicken into the hot water a few more times. The next feather I pulled came out easily, and it took only a few minutes to pull all the feathers off.

My next job was burning the fine hairs off. I made a torch by rolling up a newspaper into a tight roll. Taking one of the round stove lids off the cooking surface, I lit the paper from the open fire in the stove and, holding the chicken over the stove, ran the lighted torch across one side and burned all the hairs off. Then I flipped the chicken over, caught it with one hand and singed the hairs off the other side. Then the torch had burned short enough so I could feel its heat, so quickly dropped it into the stove. After washing the black bits of burnt paper off the chicken, I took our sharpest butcher knife and cut off the wings and legs before opening the body cavity to take out the entrails. Tossing them aside, I saved the heart, liver and gizzard. The gizzard took some patience to get emptied and cleaned. I cut it open around the outside rim and peeled out the inner sac containing the grit before washing it under the faucet. Mom had also taught me to cut out the wishbone in one piece and split down the breast bone to make good pieces for frying. It was all cut up, so I washed the pieces in cold water, then left them draining in the colander. I had finished my job of getting a chicken ready to fry.

A couple of weeks later Mom once again asked me to find a young chicken and get it ready to fry. Recalling my first experience of chopping a chicken's head off, I picked up the loaded .22 rifle from behind the kitchen door and headed outside. I soon located a good sized fryer in the open away from the cattle, so could safely shoot without hitting anything besides the chicken. I lifted the rifle to my shoulder, took aim and fired, luckily shooting it in the head. So this time when I took a chicken to the chopping block, it was motionless as a stick of wood and didn't jerk around and spoil my aim. My first swing with the axe chopped off its head. I was glad to have found a way to get around the hardest part of getting a chicken ready to fry.

Mattress Making at the Grange Hall

We were all quiet during the grange meeting, listening to Dessie McCarroll, Master of Quillisascut Grange, make an announcement. "I've learned of a way that we can have new mattresses at little or no cost, but we'll have to work hard to get them."

In 1941-- a time when no one had extra cash – getting something without spending much money was of interest to everyone. As Dessie talked, everyone paid close attention to the rest of her announcement. She added, "Mr. A. K. Millay, The County Extension Agent told me that President Roosevelt's administration has started a program of furnishing raw materials to groups that will sponsor a mattress-making project."

Dessie explained that this plan would help the families in our area of Pleasant Valley, Rice, Arzina and Daisy, and at the same time use up a lot of the government's surplus cotton. Mr. Millay had said there would be a training period for representatives from each organization. "In addition to receiving training," she continued, "they will receive written instructions to take back so they can teach others how to make mattresses. We can do the work here at the grange hall where there's plenty of room to set up work tables. We can get started as soon as all the materials arrive. Those who have the money to pay some of the cost will work only the basic number of hours required for each mattress. But large families needing several can work extra time beyond the basic hours if they have no money to spare."

I was glad we would be able to get new mattresses without Dad having to fork over any of his hard-earned cash. Our big garden provided vegetables and the mountain provided venison, so we never lacked for food. But since neither place provided warm bedding, mattresses or clothing, Dad had to lay out cash money for them and other necessities like gas and tires for the car and bullets for the guns.

When we got home from the meeting, Mom told us that we were going to put in the necessary time to earn our mattresses. As soon as the project started, she would begin. With Lester away from home and Dad busy plowing the fields and planting the spring crops, Mom was the only one who could work until school was out at the end of May. Then Dora and I would go with her to the grange hall to add our work hours to hers. Ten-year old Leola would stay home to watch over Effie and the five-year old twins, and cook dinner for Dad.

Her statements weren't a surprise to us, as we were accustomed to working hard for everything we had. Leola had been helping Mom cook for quite some time, and with Effie's help, already kept an eye on the twins. I would be seventeen in March, and Dora would be fourteen in May. We were old enough to look on this new venture as just a different type of work. As yet, we didn't realize how much time was involved in earning even one mattress, let alone the four Mom said we needed. We would be working many weeks.

At the next grange meeting, Dessie McCarroll reported the supplies had arrived and work would soon begin. She set a starting date and lots of people signed up to work. The project got underway in early March. Men and women worked as many days a week as they could. The men's hours were limited to the time they could spare from their spring farm work. They had completed several mattresses by the time we kids got out of school at the end of May.

The first day Dora and I went down to the grange hall with Mom, we saw Dessie and the others had a well-run system, with mattresses in various stages of completion. To provide work surfaces, men had moved several long tables out of the kitchen into the main hall, spacing them out so there was plenty of elbow room around each table. A few tables held stacks of supplies. There were bales of cotton, rolls of sturdy blue and white striped sticking, spools of heavy sewing thread, several wooden long-handled flat paddles, and piles of loose cotton batts. There were also two treadle sewing machines which women brought from their homes.

Since Dessie was in charge, she had assigned workers to their jobs and taught them what to do. She now gave work assignments to us new arrivals from high school and to Lawrence Hays, who had just finished another year of teaching at Pleasant Valley Grade School. He had come to help his wife, Ruby, work out the hours they needed. Dessie led Hazel Rose, Dora and me over to some long tables where Hazel's mother and others were standing, pounding firm layers of white cotton that lay on the table in front of them. She said, "Before we can put this into the ticking, it has to be light and fluffy. Just beat the cotton like they are doing. They'll tell you when you've beaten it enough."

Hazel was assigned to the table next to mine and Dora was across from me. We picked up our paddles and started whaling away. At first it seemed easy. But in about twenty minutes, my arm was as tired as if I'd been mixing a cake, beating it by hand. I kept it up, although my arm soon felt like it was about to fall off. Dora was three years younger than I, but hadn't stopped to rest. I wasn't surprised, as she always had been a strong and plucky kid.

Hazel's mother finally told me my cotton was fluffy enough. Thankful to be able to rest my arm, I carried the cotton over to the assembly table, where Mom was working that day. She, Ina McKern and Albert Rose were layering it into the ticking. By the time I brought another batt to my table to beat, I'd had a chance to look around at all the busy workers. Letha Peters and Ruby Hays were measuring ticking material for double-bed size, then cutting it. Dee McKern and Tom Peters were forming and hand sewing the edges of a mattress, making the roll around the top. Dee's mother, "Grandma" McKern, was sewing strips of the ticking together, and Pady Rose was working at another sewing machine. Ethel Holter and Frances Lickfold, at the final step, were hand stitching the big gap through which the last of our fluffy cotton had been stuffed. Dessie was going from one table to another, helping where anyone needed her. Paul Holter, Walt and Rose Clemons, Walt Lickfold, Morse and Blanche McKern found jobs to do, as did "Grampa" McKern, who had only one arm.

When summer's hot weather came, we were still working. By afternoon, the hall became hot and stuffy, which made pounding the cotton a disagreeable task. The stifling, still air – thick with lint around the pounding tables – made it worse. Following our paddles in their steady up-and-down rhythm, tiny wisps of cotton floated around our faces until we were almost afraid to breathe. All the windows were wide open. Still, there wasn't a breeze to blow the lint away or to cool the room.

Even after our arms got used to beating cotton to the fluffy stage, our paddles felt like lead weights. We rested when we felt like it, but it became a matter of pride to keep at it as long as we could. We were glad when lunchtime came, giving us a break from the constant flailing. Escaping the lint-filled area, we stepped to the coolness outdoors and sucked fresh air into our lungs. Sprawled on the ground in the shade, we enjoyed our sandwiches and our free time.

Finally, the project Dessie had started back in March was finished in late summer. Almost every family in the area had worked in the grange's mattress project. Women let their housework go, and men shorted their farming tasks to work their required hours. Everyone had reasons to be thankful: all had new mattresses that we spent little or no money on; we did all the work ourselves; and lastly, the hard work of mattress making was finally over.

In 1988 Ethel Holter wrote to me about this project and said she still had her mattress. She sent me a quote from Paul's journal dated March 26, 1941, ". . .. went down to the grange hall at noon; don't care much for mattress making." Years later, when I returned home on visits, I slept on one of those mattresses and thought about all the work we had done. Our mattresses were still in use forty years later when Mom died.

Leola's Apple Pie

Dad and his small threshing crew finished eating the dinner that ten-year old Leola cooked. Of course, she hadn't done it all by herself; eight-year old Effie had helped. The threshing crew was smaller this year, as the grain bundles were in two big stacks instead of being out in the field, so he didn't need the four extra men it would take to work on two wagons hauling bundles from the field to the thresher. Dad thought he and four others could do the threshing. While he stood on the stack and tossed bundles into the thresher, Jack McNutt would tend the gunny sacks under the grain spout. Verlie Pitts, who owned the threshing machine, was bringing Kenny Clinton to help run it, and Paul Holter would be hauling the grain down to the granary.

On that August day in 1941, Mom, Dora and I were still working at the grange hall making helping make mattresses. Mom worried about getting dinner for the threshers, yet she couldn't stay home and cook. After much pondering, she hit upon a solution: she would put Leola in charge. After all, she had been getting dinner for Dad, as well as taking care of Effie, Viola and Vida since the end of May while Mom, Dora and I had been working at the grange hall. We would be home to cook a big supper for the men to make up for the small dinner.

Mom told Leola that getting dinner would be easy. "All you have to do is peel a big pan of potatoes and put them on to boil, then open three quarts of that canned venison and heat it to boiling. While that's cooking, open quart jars of corn and green beans and put them on the stove to heat. The only thing left to do is to make gravy. For dessert, you can open a half-gallon jar of peaches. While you're busy with all that, Effie and the twins can set the table and keep the wood box filled."

Before it was time to start dinner, Leola and Effie brought all the jars of food they would need out of the cellar. Since the food wouldn't take long to heat up, Leola started thinking how good an apple pie would taste. She could use the jar full of dry pie crust mixture – flour, salt and lard – that Mom had made earlier. She decided she would have time to make a pie. The men deserved something better for dessert than canned peaches.

Leola asked Effie to help her pick some apples. Carrying a milk bucket, she headed out to the apple trees near the driveway. It was early in the season and the apples were still green, but Leola thought she would just add extra sugar to the pie. Effie grabbed a bucket and followed. While picking the largest of the apples, they kept an eye on the five-year old twins playing nearby.

Back inside the house with their apples, Effie set to work peeling them while Leola started in on the pie crust. She emptied the dry pie crust mix into a bowl, added water and mixed it up, then rolled out two crusts. She put one in the pie pan, then measured out the sugar into a bowl, ready to use later. She sliced the apples onto the crust in the pan, sprinkled cinnamon over them, folded the top crust on and put the pie into the oven.

About fifteen minutes later, Leola went into the kitchen to put more wood into the stove. There on the cabinet she spotted her measured bowl of sugar. She had forgotten to pour it over the apple slices in the pie pan. Now she was in a quandary. The sugar needed to be added to the pie, but she didn't know how to get it there without tearing up the top crust. She finally decided to just tell the men they could add their own sugar to the pieces of pie.

The men finished their dinner of canned venison and vegetables, so Leola brought out her nicely browned pie and set it on the table in front of Dad. She set the sugar bowl beside the pie, telling them to help themselves. Dad took a piece of pie and passed it to Paul Holter, who helped himself and handed it on to Jack McNutt. Jack dished out his piece and gave the pie to Verlie. By the time Kenny Clinton took a piece, the others had started on theirs.

After Dad's first bite, he reached for the sugar bowl and poured two or three heaping spoons of sugar on top of his piece. After that, the sugar bowl went around the table just as the pie had. Not one man puckered up his mouth at the tart green apple pie. They all kept a straight face while telling Leola how good it was, bragging about the crust and how the apples were nice and juicy.

True to her early training, Leola still makes delicious apple pies, now with plenty of sugar. Recently she told me, "For years afterward, every time Verlie Pitts saw me, he asked how my pie baking was doing. We would laugh together thinking about that green apple pie without sugar.

Getting Ready for the Dance

The orange colored Tangee Natural lipstick turned pink when Dora put it on her lips. I knew what it looked like on me – and knew its taste. I used it until I was fourteen, then Mom let me use a brighter lipstick.

Getting ready for the dance at the grange hall meant everyone had to take a bath in our round galvanized wash tub. Our "bathroom" was a space in the kitchen near the cook stove. Dad and Joe took their baths and stayed in the living room while the rest of us took turns bathing. When finished, we smoothed Pond's cold cream on our faces and patted a bit of loose powder over it. Mom used a light shade, but for my sun-tanned face, I liked Rachele. The way Mom said "Rashell" made it seem fancy. I found the blue Evening in Paris perfume bottle and dabbed some behind my ears. Last came red lipstick for Mom and me, and the Tangee for Dora, only thirteen. The four little girls only had to bathe and dress to be ready to go.

That was the day a grown-up friend taught Dora and me how to make a substitute mascara. Joe and Alice Richie, using Lester's end of the attic as their bedroom, were staying with us a couple of months while Joe helped Dad with the farming. Dora and I watched as Alice, a pretty woman with blond hair, penciled her light eyebrows to make them darker. Taking the last stroke, she asked if she could borrow my mascara. When I told her we didn't have any, she said, "Well, I guess I'll have to show you how to make some."

We didn't know that anyone could make mascara, so watched with interest as Alice took a small dab of soot off the underside of a cook stove lid and mixed it with a little melted lard. Then using the flat side of a toothpick, she put some of the sooty black mix on her blonde eyelashes. It made them look so long and thick that Dora and I put some on our eyelashes, too. We decided we liked our new mascara that hadn't cost anything. We used our home-made mascara for a couple of years before breaking down and buying some Maybelline.

Dad and Joe didn't take much time getting ready, as they only had to shave, bathe and get dressed. They didn't have to fuss with long hair and get it curly like we girls did. When everyone was ready to go, we went outside and got into the Nash. Alice sat in the front seat with Mom and Dad and we six girls piled in the back with Joe. He and I held the twins on our laps, and Effie perched between Dora and Leola. Thinking of the good time we would have at the dance, we didn't mind being crowded the mile down to the grange hall.

Years later when Henry and I were in Japan visiting his son, Dick, and his wife, Jeaninne, I went to a Japanese bath with their neighbor, Mrs. Numijiri. As I rubbed the bar of soap over her back, I could almost feel my mother's firm shoulders under my hand. And in an antique store recently, I spotted a well-remembered blue perfume bottle. Unscrewing the cap, that familiar scent of Evening in Paris wafted out of it and I had visions of dabbing some behind my ears and heading to the dance!

Dance at Quillisascut Grange

"All join hands and circle to the left; allemande left and grand right and left; meet your partner with an elbow gee and an elbow haw," was the way Tom Peters started calling our square dances at the grange hall. We never knew what he was going to call until he started. Even after recognizing the call, we had to listen carefully, as he liked to throw in a few changes now and then just to keep us on our toes. I liked all the square dances, so it didn't matter which ones he called, just so a guy asked me to dance. If no one did, I had to sit on a bench along the wall, wishing I were dancing, too.

During the monthly grange meetings, the men sat on benches on one side of the hall and the women sat on the other side. This custom carried over to the dances without anyone giving it a thought. About the only women who sat on the men's side were visitors.

Parents took their children with them to grange meetings as well as dances. Mothers put their babies and small children to bed in a large, double decker built-in crib at the front of the hall near the dance band. Attached to the narrow end of the stage, its six-foot length butted against the wall to the right of the stage. A railing around both levels kept the babies from rolling out. The blanket-wrapped babies lay snuggled close together while the music played and the dancers circled the floor. Instead of waking the babies, the music seemed to lull them, keeping them asleep throughout the evening.

Our grange hall was the only one close by. The next closest one was just outside of Kettle Falls. The Odd Fellows (IOOF) also held dances in their hall at Rice, but it never drew as big a crowd. While grange was in session, all children under fourteen had to stay in the kitchen. Until that birthday, when I could join the grange, I looked forward to joining, thinking that sitting in on meetings would make me feel grown up.

When the meeting was about to begin, we kids headed for the kitchen at the back of the hall. The Gatekeeper followed us to close the door, which stayed closed through out the session. Later when we saw that door open, we knew the meeting was over and we could go out into the main hall again. And that's when the fun began!

After meetings, grange members furnished the music so we could dance. Our grade school teacher, Lawrence Hays, played the violin, Ethel Rupert played the piano, and her son Warren, played the drums. Lawrence seemed to get as much fun out of playing "Turkey in the Straw" and other fast pieces as we did dancing to the beat. Unlike the Saturday-night dances that the grange sponsored, there was no charge for the informal dances after the grange meetings.

It was after grange one night when I was ten years old that Mom taught me to dance. Standing at my left, Mom led me out to the dance floor and put her right arm around me. She said, "I'll show you how to do the waltz step first, since it's the easiest. Now step with your right foot, slide with the left and step with the right. That's all there is to it: step, slide, step."

Later Mom showed me how to do the two-step, which was two steps and a slide. I liked it even better, as it was faster and had more turning and twirling. She also showed Lester how to dance, but he didn't seem to like it as much as I did. Soon Dora was wanting to learn, too, so both Mom and I showed her how to slide her feet together for the dance steps. It was wonderful to keep time with the music and to turn and twirl, dancing counter-clockwise around the hall keeping up with the grown-ups. There were always more girls than boys at the dances, so we girls danced together when a boy hadn't asked us.

Dancing after grange meetings wasn't the only fun we had at grange. After each meeting, the lecturer arranged a short program as a bit of entertainment, which varied from question-and-answer games to recitations. One evening Pady Abernathy Rose recited all seventeen verses of "The Highwayman," by Alfred Noyes. Her voice held us spellbound when she got to "When the road is a ribbon of moonlight over the purple moor, A highwayman comes riding, riding, riding; A highwayman comes riding up to the old inn door."

Listening to Pady's recitation reminded me of her soft laugh I'd heard a few years ago at her shivaree. It was soon after she and Albert Rose were married on June 20, 1934. Our family had joined twenty or more others at dusk outside their square brown house near Rice. People rang cow bells and banged on pots and pans to make a lot of noise. One man shot into the night sky with a shotgun. Albert and Pady let the noise go on for several minutes before opening their door. With the lamplight behind them, they stood in the open doorway greeting everyone. Those ahead of us congratulated them on their marriage. When Dad's turn came, he was laughing his big laugh as he pumped Albert's hand saying, "I hope your first one's a boy!"

At ten years old, I'd heard what caused babies, so I was embarrassed, and I felt Pady was, too. But Albert grinned, and it was then I heard Pady's soft laugh. After we filed into the house, Pady and her sisters served juice and candy to everyone.

A letter from Pady in 1992 recalls that evening: "At the shivaree we served fudge and divinity that my sister, Rose, and I had made."

After I had joined grange at fourteen, I was glad I could attend the meetings with the grownups instead of having to stay in the kitchen with all the little kids. At this time Mom served as Chaplain, saying prayers at the prescribed times. I was proud when I was elected to office, as Ceres, one of the three Graces. It was my duty to carry the flag before we said the Pledge of Allegiance.

During a grange meeting when I was sixteen, Ina McKern, the Lecturer, announced the State Grange was sponsoring a writing contest, the subject being "Safety on the Farm," and anyone under eighteen could enter. We needed to turn our essays in at the next meeting so she could forward them to the State Grange for judging. About a month later Ina announced that in our grange Betty-Jo Peters had won first place and I had won second, and asked us to read our essays to the assembly. It made me feel special and I was sure Betty-Jo felt the same.

About once a month, the grange sponsored dances on Saturday nights, charging a dollar admission per couple. It hired a small band, paying them $5 a person. The music started at nine o'clock and ended at one in the morning. Lydia Cranston played the piano in a band called, "The Columbians." Other members were Jim Cleveland and Luke Countryman. Sometimes Luke's sister, Millie, played the drums. Other bands that played included Lawrence Hays, Ethel Rupert, Warren Rupert and Tikey Cox. At eleven o'clock the band stopped playing and the leader announced an intermission. Everyone went back to the kitchen where the grange ladies had sandwiches, coffee and dessert ready. The musicians got to eat for free, but the rest of us had to pay a quarter apiece. After a half hour, the musicians went back to the stage, began playing and the dancing resumed.

By the time Dora and I were teenagers, we could follow the lead of any boy on the dance floor, matching our steps to his. The only time I made a miss-step and was embarrassed was when Toar Lickfold added an unexpected step to the middle of his two-step. But I always enjoyed dancing with him and was pleased when he asked me. Ever since he'd walked Lester and me to school when I was six, I had looked on him as kind of an older brother.

At a dance in the fall of 1938, after I graduated from the eighth grade, I was surprised when Lawrence Hays asked me to dance. He had been my teacher for the past two years and had never asked me to dance before. His first remark when we got on the dance floor explained the difference. "It isn't proper for me to dance with my pupils, but since you're in high school now, I can dance with you. And you can call me 'Lawrence' instead of "Mr. Hays," and from then on, I could count on him dancing with me at least once during the evening.

His wife, Ruby Lickfold Hays became my first grown-up friend. She listened to my little problems as if they were important. Mom and Dad had to listen to my problems or achievements, but Ruby wasn't related to me and liked me anyway. She was much like her brother, Everett (Toar) Lickfold, in that she laughed and had a good time whatever she was doing.

The Saturday-night dances lasted longer and were more fun than the casual dance sessions after grange meetings. Often as many as a hundred people came, some from as far away as Kettle Falls and Colville. Occasionally a few of my high school classmates from Kettle came together when they found a guy who could borrow his father's car.

Not many boys took dates to the dances. They didn't have their own cars – or even enough money to buy gas or pay the admission charge for anyone else. Most young people went to the dances with their parents and danced with everyone rather than having their own special dates. When the music started, we girls waited on our side of the hall for someone to ask us. The men either sat on benches on the opposite side or stood together at the end of the hall near the door. As they headed our way, I hoped one of them would stop in front of me to say those magic words, "May I have this dance?"

Kids from Kettle Falls seldom came to our dances at Pleasant Valley, but at one dance during my senior year several came together. When the band started playing, "Oh Johnny, Oh Johnny," I jumped up from the bench as classmate John Hardwick said those magic words to me. It was a fast piece and we laughed and had a good time spinning and swooping to the music while singing some of the words, "Oh Johnny, Oh Johnny, how you can love!" Toar danced the next dance with me. A few minutes after it ended, Helen Whalen, another Kettle classmate, exclaimed, "I didn't know you knew Toar Lickfold!"

Helen had just moved to Kettle that year and didn't know that I'd known him most of my life – ever since I was a five-year old waving goodbye to him and Lester as they headed off to school. At some time during Everett Lickfold's high school years, someone had pinned the nickname of "Toar" on him and it had stuck. It fit him so well that most people almost forgot his real name. He'd grown up to be a big, handsome guy with wavy blond hair and a good personality. He had a hearty, rollicking laugh that made everyone happy just to hear it.

At another dance, Betty-Jo Peter's father, Tom, came to my defense when I was in a predicament. A young stranger was insisting that I dance with him even though I'd told him it was promised to someone else. The music had started, but the guy I had promised to dance with was nowhere in sight. After my second attempt to explain, Tom appeared at my side, having overheard our conversation. The young man didn't want to give up, and Tom said, "Listen here, young fellow, she's a Riley girl and Riley girls don't lie. If she says this dance is taken, then it's taken."

Not knowing how to handle the situation, I felt awkward, and was grateful Tom had come to my rescue. Afterward, I realized the stranger was probably thinking I just didn't want to dance with him. I should have thought of that sooner and promised him the next dance.

Many years later when Tom reminded me of this, I had the chance as a grown woman to tell him how much I had appreciated his helping that young and unsure girl.

At most of the dance, the musicians ended their session by playing "Home, Sweet Home." When the men heard that song, they headed for their wives. Since it was such a tradition for Dad to have the last dance with Mom, I was surprised one night when he asked me to dance the last dance. Mom had told him I'd sat out a few times and she wanted me to have "her" dance.

Driving home, Dad sang a few lines from one song or another. Sometimes it was, "Show me the way to go home, I had a little drink about an hour ago and it went right to my head," but it most often was, "Be it ever so humble, there's no place like home."

His singing made us feel secure and safe. Sometimes all six of us girls would fall asleep during the two-mile drive home. While our family enjoyed all the activities at the grange hall, the ones I liked best were the dances. I always felt a thrill of excitement when Tom Peters said, "Grab your partners for a square dance!"

Pleasant Valley Boys Go to War

Riding the bus to school on December 8, 1941, shocking news eddied from seat to seat like a whirlwind. Those who had heard on the radio the night before told everyone that Japanese war planes had bombed Pearl Harbor! Thinking they were joking, I didn't believe them at first. Then at school, seniors Bill Clark, Jack Underwood and Art Baxter talked about going to the Army recruiting station to enlist, even though graduation was six months away.

The next day at home we heard President Franklin D. Roosevelt announce on the radio that the United States had declared war against Japan. In Pleasant Valley, first one young man then another went off to war. Toar Lickfold, Ernie and Ab McKinney were among the first to go. Until after the war, no one at home knew exactly where they were fighting. Toar saw raging battles in several smaller islands in the South Pacific. Ernie McKinney was on the Bataan Peninsula and was captured along with thousands of others when the Japanese took Corregidor. He survived what became known as "The Bataan Death March." Hundreds of men died during this forced march of about a hundred miles from Bataan to San Fernando. They were without food or water, and the Japanese bayoneted prisoners who were too weak to keep up. Ernie lived through near-starvation and torture during his subsequent imprisonment in Capas, Tarlac, Cabanatuan and Santo Tomas in Manila. They took him to Japan in a ship's hold, and subjected him to more inhuman treatment during three years of forced labor in a coal mine.

Mick Johnson, who grew up on a farm near Rice, went to Wake Island as a civilian worker in April of 1941. He worked for a naval contractor with the Contract Pacific Naval Air Bases, building landing strips and turn basins for the U. S. Government. In December 1941, before CPNAB finished, the Japanese attacked Wake Island as they had Pearl Harbor – without warning. They took everyone who was left alive prisoner.

Wounded during the invasion, Mick was among the first Americans captured. He spent the next four years in prison camps in Japan and in parts of Japanese-occupied China. His parents, Emory and Euclaire Johnson, heard of Wake's fall, but heard nothing about Mick. Until 1943, they didn't know whether he was alive or dead. He was released from a prisoner-of-war camp in 1945. His older brother, Charles, was an Army officer and also served in the South Pacific. He saw duty in Saipan, the Philippines, Okinawa and Korea, as well as the Aleutian Islands.

Lester, being younger, didn't follow them to the jungles until 1943. When he learned his draft number would soon be called, he quit his job to spend a few days at home. After his basic training, the Army assigned him to the Combat Engineers Division and sent him to the Philippines. He took part in the initial landing assaults on Ulithi and Pelelieu where savage fighting took many American lives. These islands didn't make headlines like Guadalcanal and Iwo Jima did, but their names earned respect for the men who fought there.

After perilous combat in unfamiliar jungle elements, our boys came home at war's end. Their earlier deer hunting in rugged mountain areas had taught them to shoot and helped them survive the hardships of war. Although glad to be home, Lester, Toar and Ernie acted jittery, not yet believing they were safe. They didn't want to talk about what had happened to them. It was as if their silence could blot out the hell they had seen; talking would make them re-live it. They seemed to be carrying unseen battle scars inside.

For several months Lester was plagued with jungle rot – big boil-like sores on the back of his neck. They were visible reminders of the steaming jungle's heat and humidity. Later on, he was able to open up about his fighting in the Philippines. He had run a bulldozer clearing landing strips for our fighter planes. Japanese snipers, not yet cleared out, shot at him and other soldiers working nearby. In telling us about it, he said, "When I heard bullets whizzing by, I'd grab my rifle and jump off the dozer, duck behind the big blade and shoot back. That was a good place to stay until we got all the snipers."

After fourteen months in a war zone, his outfit was sent to Leyte to help bulldoze roads and landing strips through the jungles. Following up on his earlier comments, he said, "It felt good to be in a safe area where nobody was shooting at us."

He also built ramps for landing boats to unload. He was so good at his job, he became an instructor in the operation of a pile driver, a three-quarter yard shovel and other heavy equipment. When his unit went back to Pelelieu to help finish up the fighting, he got more practice in shooting and dodging bullets. At the end of the war, his unit took a troop ship home.

Toar Lickfold wouldn't say much about his three years fighting in the South Pacific. The only time I heard him mention anything was shortly after the war ended. He and two other men sat under a shade tree at the Rice store, resting after having digging a grave in the Mountain View Cemetery for Carl Rose. When I asked if he were going to the funeral, the once rollicking, laughing Toar looked at me somberly and replied, "I was glad to do what I could for Carl by helping dig his grave, but I can't go to his funeral. I saw too many of my friends killed in the Pacific." Pausing as if seeing their faces before him, he huskily added, "I just can't go to another funeral."

All fighting had stopped. The official proclamation said the war was over. But for these veterans, it seemed to rage on in their minds.

After World War II

And it continued to rage for Ernie. Fifty years after his imprisonment, his wife, Pat, told me he still woke up screaming from nightmares.

Mick Johnson wrote that as a civilian, he received a Bronze Star; also a Purple Heart for having been wounded by enemy fire. In 1981, the U.S. Government declared him to be a Navy veteran. His brother, Charles, made the Army his career, staying in for thirty-three years and retired as a full colonel.

After their army tour, Ernie, Lester and Toar never went back to the Philippines. But in February 1982, my husband, Henry Helmstetter, other Veterans Administration personnel and I accompanied a veterans' group that President Marcos had invited to Manila to observe Philippine Liberation Day.

During our group's private audience with President Ferdinand Marcos in Malacanang Palace, I told him that my brother had fought in Leyte. He said, "Oh that's my wife's province," and called to her across the room. Imelda Marcos, in her long, green satin gown with its butterfly sleeves, glided over to us. President Marcos continued, "Meldy, this lady's brother fought in your province."

Tilting her head up to look at me with dark eyes, Mrs. Marcos graciously asked, "And what was his name?" Her question implied she might have met him.

I replied, "His name is Lester Riley, but you would never have met him. He was dodging Japanese snipers' bullets while bulldozing roads through the jungle."

Henry had been especially interested in our trip, as he had become acquainted with President Marcos a few years earlier while working in the American Embassy in Manila for the U.S. Veterans Administration. He had been fortunate enough to golf with the president, although he confided to me that both of them were only hackers, not "golfers," relying on their caddies for better ball placements.

Our group, which included three survivors of the Bataan Death March, toured the Bataan Peninsula, following the route the prisoners had struggled along on foot. Leaders of our veterans' group placed memorial wreaths at various places along the route, starting at the memorial plaque at Mile Zero on Bataan and ending at the impressive white marble memorial at Capas, Tarlac, the concentration camp site and end of the death march. In between, they placed wreaths at Mt. Samat Memorial and at mileposts along the march, honoring our men who had been captured. I thought of Ernie McKinney, my childhood friend, who had been penned up here. Two of the survivors in our bus tried to tell of their capture and the death march, but with voices breaking, they couldn't continue. The third man could not even begin.

Later on Corregidor, we stood beside the Army's bombed-out concrete barracks. Our tour also included seeing the Malinta Tunnel. We walked inside the dark tunnel that had sheltered the makeshift hospital and the remnants of General Wainwright's forces during the Japanese bombings. Viewing all this and imagining the cannon fire and bombs, the smoke and dust, the wounded and dying deepened my respect for those who had taken the wartime "tour."

Epilogue – 1991

We are returning from our winter's stay in Ajijic, Jalisco, Mexico, and as Henry turns the car into our driveway in Oak Ridge, Tennessee, I'm jolted back to the present. On the long drive my childhood has played itself out, flickering on the screen of my mind like scenes from a frontier movie. The past dissolves and the horse taking me to school disappears. With a pang, I remember that my parents, two players in that "movie," have been gone for many years. Dad died in 1970 and Mom in 1984. Yet, I have the odd feeling I could call them if I knew their telephone number. My country adventures ended in 1942 when I graduated from high school and left Pleasant Valley to find work. Two years later I married Hugh Conner, who had grown up in the nearby rural area of Arzina. That marriage lasted twenty-four years and gave us two sons and a daughter.

In 1970 I married Henry Helmstetter, who dropped my first name of "Ines," and called me "Riley," my maiden name. He has taken me to many faraway places, satisfying my longings to see people in other parts of the world. The trips have invited me into history, shown me different cultures and given fascinating geography lessons. In Cuzco, Peru, we boarded a train at an elevation of 13,000 feet altitude, climbed up higher for a few minutes before heading down the mountain to ride alongside the Urubamba River. We got off the train at Machu Piccu's station and learned that the altitude was only around 9,000 feet. After riding a small bus that took us up the winding steep hillside, we reached the ruins and walked all around, gazing in wonder at the fantastic tiers, made from laid up-rocks, that had provided planting ground for the Incas. Our group's guide plunked us down on the rock tiers and recited the history of the long-ago residents. I wanted to walk higher to the South Gate to take a few steps on the Inca Trail, but when the guide finished his "history lesson," he said it was time to return to the small bus, which would take us back down to the train station for our return to Cuzco.

Two years later on our second visit to Machu Piccu, we had the same guide. When he started his spiel, Henry and I played hooky and climbed up to the South Gate There at the top, we walked a short distance on the ages-old Inca Trail to satisfy my sense of adventure. I looked down at the flat rocks that made the trail and envisioned the thousands of bare feet that had trod on them.

Inside the walled cities of Morocco, I felt plunked down in another century. And at the pyramids of Giza in Egypt, the sight of turbaned, djellaba-clad Arabs astride camels sharply reminded me I was a long way from my horseback trails in Pleasant Valley and our sorrel mare, Betty, that I rode to school.

But however interesting people in faraway places are, they can never take the place in my heart of those in my childhood who became an extended family. The time spent at Quillisascut Grange Hall left many happy memories. When I recall going home from a dance, I still feel a rich contentment and hear Dad singing, "Show me the way to go home," with Mom humming along.

In 1997, five of the Riley kids still lived in Washington state. Dora and I were the only ones who strayed. She lived in Arizona where there were no snow drifts for her to wade through. For over twenty years, I hung my hat in Oak Ridge Tennessee, then moved to Surprise, Arizona. I "studied geography" first hand seeing intriguing foreign countries in Asia, South America, Africa, Europe. Then I traveled by airplane instead of by horseback and shanks ponies.

It's now 2017, and I'm back in Bend, Oregon. Leola, who lives in Kennewick, Washington, and I are the only ones left in the Bill Riley family. I lived on an Army Air Force base in North Carolina during WW II, working as a parachute rigger. We returned to Washington state at war's end, then a few years later moved to Lake Grove, Oregon.   After marrying Henry Helmstetter in 1970, we stayed in the Portland area until his retirement from the U.S. Veterans Administration in 1975.   In 2012 we moved to Bend, Oregon where my memories began in 1926 – of living in a tent in a logging camp with my parents and brother.

The End

Made in the USA
Middletown, DE
12 July 2023